TURN AROUND

AND SEE
THE LORD

BY

JOY VASSAL

John 20:14: "At this, she turned around and saw Jesus standing there, but she did not realize that it was Jesus."

Copyright © 2008, 2009 by Joy Vassal

TURN AROUND AND SEE THE LORD
by Joy Vassal

Printed in the United States of America

ISBN 978-1-60647-892-9

All rights reserved solely by the author. The author guarantees all contents are original and do not infringe upon the legal rights of any other person or work. No part of this book may be reproduced in any form without the permission of the author. The views expressed in this book are not necessarily those of the publisher.

Unless otherwise indicated, Scripture quotations are taken from the *Holy Bible, New International Version*®. *NIV*®. Copyright © 1973, 1978, 1984 by International Bible Society. Used by permission of Zondervan. All rights reserved.

www.xulonpress.com

AKNOWLEDGMENT

It is my pleasure to acknowledge those special people of God whose time, talents, support, suggestions, patience, criticism, hard labor, effort and interest made this book possible.

First of all I must thank the Holy Spirit for the drive, direction and energy that overshadowed me during the formative years of this book. There were times of challenges, but the voice of God was audible, so I mustered faith and courage to listen and persevere.

I would like to thank the prayer team, the most dedicated, loving and loyal prayer group, for unceasing supplications and intercessions for me and this outstanding project.

Thanks to my pastor, Bishop Huel Wilson, for being my spiritual authority. His encouragement and prayers are greatly appreciated.

I thank my first editor, Judy Simpson, for her relentless work. She worked with this manuscript for three years, reading, typing, reviewing and editing.

I wish to express my thanks to Pastor Emmanuel Mills for his steadfastness, unwavering faith and zest to research and edit this manuscript. Your commitment and attitude was indeed outstanding.

Sincere thanks to Hugh Cook, my third editor. It is with joy and confidence that I assert that you are one of the most outstanding editors I have worked with. Your work is impeccable and your criticism very constructive. You have mastered your craft, and it was nothing less than excellence.

Thanks to Jessica Tressler, for the phenomenal job you have

done copyediting my manuscript. You are exceptionally gifted.

I would like to thank Daniel J. Vassell Sr. for writing the Foreword, reviewing my manuscript. His encouragement and support is appreciated.

I would also like to thank Lenworth Isaacs for his tireless efforts in assisting me with proofreading and editing the manuscript. His unparalleled dedication and keen insightful contributions are greatly and deeply appreciated.

Last, but certainly not least, I would like to express thanks to my mom, Beryl Vassell, for her continuous support, encouragement and prayers, and to my lovely girls, Lenesha and Sheree, for their support.

God, by His Spirit, has indeed inspired me to pen Turn Around and See the Lord. I believe He has a plan for every individual to turn to Him and achieve or do exploits for His glory. I purpose in my heart to never cease thanking Him for all things, for it is the will of God in Christ Jesus. My fervent prayer for the body of Christ is that they will turn to God. He has all the answers.

INTRODUCTION

In her timeless book *Turn Around and See the Lord,* Joy Vassal talks about the experience she had when meditating on John 20:14, an episode of Mary Magdalene's encounter with the Lord's angels at Christ's sepulcher, which inspired her to write this book. Ever since I met Joy she has been lamenting the lack of miracles, signs and wonders in the life of believers, the dry, less progressive and unsatisfied desires in the life of most of them, especially those who take leadership from her.

According to her, this spiritual quest placed a huge burden on her to turn to the Lord and to discover His will and provision for His children. As she kept climbing "Mount Carmel," the conviction grew stronger and stronger, but this time it was saddled with a responsibility, which was to take another look at the Gospel of John. She says the urge—better still the unction—was to read the entire book. However, when she arrived at the fourteenth verse of the twentieth chapter, her sentiments were placed on hold. More so, her spirit was touched, challenging her to critically examine the spiritual nuggets embedded in the verse.

While digesting these nuggets, she discovered that Mary Magdalene's experience in this chapter and verse was unique. Joy's perception was that the Lord decided to teach Mary something concerning His sovereignty, the inheritance one could derive from hearing God's voice, and the quickening power in the utterance of the living Word or the *Rhema*, as well as the integrity and power compacted in it and the capacity it has to redeem and transform a person according to its own will and intentions.

I do not know whether you have heard this statement before: "The sweetness of the pudding is not in the talking but in the eating." Pudding is a thick, soft dessert, typically containing flour or some other thickener and creamy mixtures of milk, sugar and flavorings, and it tastes delicious. Joy made me believe that her meditation on the verse was like eating a pudding, which reminded me of how David described the sweetness of God's Word in Psalm 19:9-11 (the judgement of the Lord is sweeter than the honeycomb).

In fact, there was this reassurance within me of what the grace of God could do, how it could assist someone to turn around and see the Lord, the exact thing I perceived the Omnipotent One did for Mary. According to Joy it was through the special interest and the challenge she cultivated for Mary's mission that kindled in her a wonderful zeal for God insomuch that she desired Mary as a mentor. In the book she patterns Mary's experience with how the angelic voice consumed her entire being and transformed her from a grief-stricken and despised woman to a glorified vessel saddled with a mission to introduce to the disciples, to Israel, and to all nations the message of Christ's resurrection.

She became a new woman of God designed to change the course of history and the lives of those who have faith in Christ Jesus her Lord. In fact, while the devil was carefully crafting himself into our society to make us either consciously or unconsciously worship him or ourselves, God in His infinite wisdom entered the city of Allison, Manchester-Jamaica, into the house of Clovis Vassell to choose and anoint a precious vessel for this idolatrous, adulterous and obnoxious generation.

Allison, Manchester, is a farmland. It has some of the cleanest air and water in the nation, and friendly neighbors. The residents here care about their communities and each other, keeping the rate and severity of crime incredibly low. Divinity took advantage of Allison's agricultural heritage, the Eden of Jamaica, to begin a new generation with the life of the Reverend Joy Vassal. Hear what she has to say when she was one day asked to testify about her approach to delivering the oracles of God: "I can't explain this kind of feeling; anytime before mounting the podium to preach God's Word, I experience cold feet."

According to Joy, "The atmosphere is not about me but something else. It must be the Lord! Something overpowers the people; they are baptized with the Holy Ghost and you hear people calling on Jesus and God." The radiance of God's glory brightens her outward adorning of her usual white apparel, which gives her a special beauty and glamorous look, creating a pleasant environment for the people to receive God's Word.

The book is fundamentally a scriptural exegesis of biblical quotes and eschatological teachings, in other words a belief or a doctrine concerning the ultimate or final things, such as death, the destiny of humanity, the Second Coming, or the Last Judgment. It is designed for spiritual instead of theological purposes, and is simple so that all can read and understand. Nevertheless, there are definite rudiments or principles and theological connections suitable for research and other religious works such as prayers and meditations.

The author has put together over twenty renowned biblical characters, end-time teachings, and her personal-life testimony to address some of the challenges our generation is facing with idol worship and adulterous and obnoxious practices. In addition, she has carefully tailored the weaknesses and strengths of these biblical characters and how they turned to the Lord and became extraordinary people with exemplary works and successes, so that we may not be swayed by the devil's delicious, sensuous and fascinating postmodern adventure, which makes us see unchaste, profane and blasphemous actions everywhere we turn.

According to Joy, the saints in her book are inspirational examples for us since they shared our fallen nature and struggled with their own lust. She details how they, however, achieved heaven through the desire for salvation and through the supplication of God's grace so that we may find hope for our own salvation. She is aware of the struggles of humanity from the days of slavery to modern-day political intrigue and murder; however, she believes this generation can be saved if it turns and sees the Lord.

The word *turn* in everyone's life is of paramount importance. Its relevance has nothing to do with one's educational background or ethnicity. The reasons to turn may vary and affect our lives in one way or another. Maybe there is a blockage in your way and the opposite direction is the only way out. Maybe you are held captive because of your rebellion and disobedience and you need to repent and turn from your wicked ways. In these dark experiences, it takes the voice of Jesus to call us to turn.

Notwithstanding, a turn could be inevitable in everyone's life, but what is so disheartening is the fact that many a time we are so fixated in a situation that Jesus is right there beckoning to us and we do not recognize Him. We are so far drawn away from who He is that we at times lay blame on Him. Earlier I mentioned that the author has woven together the temperaments of the characters in her book, having related them with certain attitudes prevalent in our society which, according to her, are destroying us. She describes how our society seems to promote the "can-do-it-yourself attitude," which encourages egoism. According to her, little have we considered that egoism, if unnoticed, blocks our connection with the spiritual depths.

Furthermore, she perfectly exposes the fallacy associated with egoism, in that it betrays our deeply cultivated self-seeking ideologies. This is linked to our well-placed and appreciable attitude that makes us believe that life revolves around the self. She therefore shows how that attitude nearly destroyed Jonah's life and how he turned from that attitude to see the Lord to better serve Him.

She paints the stories of Moses, Mary, Elizabeth, and Hannah as instruments of glory, prayerful vessels of destiny who kept faith with their God until the divine promise upon their lives was fulfilled. There are occasions in which she describes the troubles and personal struggles they experienced in their lives, but provide many descriptions that show how these mortals found refuge in the temple of God so that our faith in the Lord would be amplified. In order to make her readers discern her eschatological belief and encourage them to be truth seekers, she makes a bold attempt to treat certain topical and doctrinal issues such as fear, hell, and heaven to allay the fears of readers as to where they may spend eternity should they turn around and see the Lord. This is a book that keeps readers guessing what is going to happen next. Although its inspiration was drawn from the experience that Mary Magdalene had with Jesus and is basically woven around a few biblical characters, this book remains valid and meaningful for Christians of all time.

The Reverend Joy Vassal believes the Spirit of the Lord is leading her to call upon us all to combat the carnal traits within us and wrestle with the principalities, powers of darkness, and the spiritual wickedness in high places by making a concerted effort to follow the saints who fought the same battles against temptation and sin, and succeeded. Moreover, she believes that if we would sincerely heed the voice of the Lord and pursue the letter and spirit of her book, we will find the grace to turn around and see the Lord.

Pastor Emmanuel Mills
Trinity Church of God

FOREWORD

I am very honoured and blessed to be asked for a second time to partner with the international ministries of evangelist Joy Vassal. It was a great delight of mine to read the manuscript, Turn Around and See the Lord, and write the Foreword.

This is not going to be just another book you will read. It will be a transformative journey. The conviction and passion of the writer will move you to action. Joy was impacted by the biblical story of Mary Magdalene's confrontation with the resurrected Christ in the garden (Luke 10:38-42). The writer was confronted with the hope and light that came to Mary Magdalene in the midst of her pain and sorrows when she made the choice to Turn Around and See the Lord. The revelation that came out of that story transformed Joy's life as it did Mary's. The writer was moved with such compassion that she could not keep it to herself, but shared it with an urgency that those who read it will be impacted, changed and transformed just as she was. Like the four leprous men who found bread to save their lives and did not keep the good news to themselves but shared it with the children of Israel (2 Kings 7:3-11), the Reverend Joy Vassal writes with this compassion in sharing her treasure to save lives.

Motivated by the story of Mary, Joy has expanded the principle of Mary's story by sharing what happened when other Bible characters made the choice to Turn Around and See the Lord. All the characters in her book experienced life-changing blessings when they turned around. Joy makes it clear that whatever situation a reader might be going through in his or her life, applying the principle of Mary will make the difference. By turning around and seeing the

Lord, they will get a perspective that will change their lives and give them purpose.

In this wonderful book, the Reverend Joy Vassal tells the reader that if they follow the principle of Mary by turning around and seeing the Lord, they too will find the answers for their situation and gain insight to their call. Mary turned around and her disbelief was removed, her hope restored, and her joy overflowed. That was not all. Because Mary turned around and saw the Lord, she was commissioned to take the good news of Christ's resurrection to the other disciples.

Reading this book will help you in your time of despair to turn around, or turn away from your pain, to see what God is saying to you and for you to do. I do believe that your life will be changed when you read this book. I believe that, as the Reverend Joy Vassal was touched and changed by Mary's transformation when she turned around and saw, you too will be changed as you read and see the impact of the various biblical characters transformed by turning around to see. As you read this book, get ready for a turnaround in your life, because that is the goal of the author.

Daniel J. Vassell Sr. DMin
Coordinator of Cross-Cultural Youth and Single Adult Ministries,
Cleveland, TN,
and author of The Love Factor in Marriage and
Living the Blessing Filled Life NOW

TABLE OF CONTENTS

Chapter 1: Mary Magdalene: The Grief-Stricken Woman............15
Chapter 2: The Turning Point in My Life 27
Chapter 3: You Can Run But You Cannot Hide From God 35
Chapter 4: I Am Who I Am by the Grace of God 45
Chapter 5: He Turned Aside to See This Great Sight 53
Chapter 6: Hannah's Peninnah Led Her to Turn to the God of
            Her Salvation 63
Chapter 7: Elizabeth: A Woman of Prayer and Prophecy 69
Chapter 8: All Generations Shall Call Her Blessed 77
Chapter 9: A Man After God's Own Heart....................................83
Chapter 10: Are You a Supplanter?..91
Chapter 11: Hell 97
Chapter 12: Heaven..109
Chapter 13: Instruments for His Glory: Hannah and Anna
             of Phanuel 121
Chapter 14: Fear...129
Chapter 15: Jehovah's Presence With Power and Fire................135
Chapter 16: Proclaiming the Power of Pentecost 145
Chapter 17: A Fresh Anointing Is Flowing Our Way..................157
Chapter 18: Jesus' Blood Is on Our Souls 165
Chapter 19: The Power of Prayer..175

Chapter 20: The Prodigal Son	185
Chapter 21: The Seed of Sarah	191
Chapter 22: The Transforming Power of God	201
Chapter 23: There Is a River of Life Flowing in the House of God (Ezekial 47:1-12)	209
Chapter 24: Though We Are Sometimes Dead and Dry, We Can Be Resuscitated by the Word of God (Ezekiel 37)	219
Chapter 25: Demons Are Real	229
Chapter 26: It Is Finished	239
Chapter 27: Young Men, I Call Upon You for You Are Strong	247
Chapter 28: Sanctify Yourselves and Eradicate the Accursed Thing	253

CHAPTER 1

MARY MAGDALENE: THE GRIEF-STRICKEN WOMAN

In this chapter we will learn about some prominent women who loved Jesus and stayed in sync with His ministry. Among such women were Mary Magdalene and Martha. They loved Jesus very much, but Martha at one point thought it was unfair to do all the catering for Christ. On the contrary, Mary, the vessel who anointed Jesus' head at Bethany, spent quality time at the feet of Christ. She was so engrossed with the dynamic ministry of Jesus that she purposed in her heart to cling to Him through thick and thin. A vivid account of these prominent women can be found in Luke 10:38-42.

Despite the fact that women were considered less important in biblical days, they played significant roles in Jesus' ministry, especially Mary Magdalene, the woman who used the expensive perfume to prepare Jesus' body for His burial. A miniature image of the loyalty of these women is depicted in John 19:25: "Now there stood by the cross of Jesus his mother, and his mother's sister, Mary the wife of Cleophas, and Mary Magdalene" (KJV). Mary the mother of Jesus is a woman to whom God entrusted His greatest gift. She had one of the toughest assignments in history. In Luke 1:28 the messenger of God calls her "highly favored" and "blessed." Out of her mouth came these words of faith and confidence: "All generations will call me blessed" (Luke 1:48). Amazing!

Even though Jesus did not count it robbery to mention to onlookers that the words He spoke were not His words but those of His Father who sent Him, He is in fact the Word of God. His earthly ministry and teachings were characterized by great power, and were delivered with impeccable authority. Through His word many were healed of diverse sicknesses and diseases; even those who were under demonic oppressions were delivered and set free. The integrity and effective work of Jesus' word and power could be buttressed by the testimonies of these women, should we delve into their experiences with the Lord as mentioned in the Gospels.

Are you despised and expecting a touch of Christ, hoping to use that to turn your life around for the best? It would therefore be edifying to take a thorough look at Mary Magdalene, the woman who was also despised in life. But do this with the expectation that her experience with Christ, which shaped her life and gave her a memorable name, will encourage you to also turn your life around and see the Lord. This is part of the reason that Matthew spent quality time to testify about her despised experience with the world of her age.

But Mark states in 15:40-41, 47 of his book that "some women were watching from a distance. Among them were Mary Magdalene, Mary the mother of James the less and of Joses, and Salome. In Galilee these women had followed Him and cared for His needs. Many other women who had come up with him to Jerusalem were also there. . . . Mary Magdalene and Mary the mother of Joses saw where he was laid." In these two expositions we are informed of the precious time and resources Mary Magdalene gave Christ, which brought about her remarkable transformation despite the treatment she received from her world. Because Christ cast seven demons out of her, some people called her an adulterous woman, while others called her the filthy woman. Even her sister Martha counted her unworthy to sit at the feet of Christ. Nevertheless, these ridicules did not break her love, faith and confidence in Jesus Christ. There is therefore a spiritual nugget in the life of these women that I believe will grasp our attention, especially Mary Magdalene, since she is our test subject.

But who was this woman? Was she the secret wife of Jesus, as some have claimed, or simply his faithful disciple? There is so much falsehood about Mary Magdalene today concocted by liberal theologians in books such as *The Da Vinci Code*, and the Gnostic Gospels that there needs to be a reverent restudy of the original and canonical Gospels to obtain a true and full picture of the historical Mary and her place in the ministry of the Lord Jesus Christ on earth. Her name indicates that she probably came from Magdala, on the southwest coast of the Sea of Galilee. Mary Magdalene is mentioned thirteen times in the original and canonical Gospels. It is crystal clear in all these verses that the relationship between Jesus and Mary was not one of husband and wife, but Master and disciple.

Mary Magdalene would have been horrified to know how she has been scandalously used to defame her Lord and Saviour because, according to Mark 16:9 and Luke 8:2, Mary became a devoted disciple of Jesus Christ after He had cast seven demons or devils out of her. If you have ever been subjugated or possessed by devils and Jesus has delivered you, you can probably identify with this woman's situation and understand why she was so close to Christ. Better still, should we discover the deity of Christ as Mary Magdalene perceived, we would dedicate our entire life to the worship of Jesus, as she did.

We would do so even more if we earnestly pay attention to the purpose of the first coming of Jesus into the world, what he mentioned to His disciples about His earthly ministry, death, burial and resurrection as recorded in Matthew 26:2, "As you know, the Passover is two days away—and the Son of Man will be handed over to be crucified." And reading Luke 24:7, which says that "the Son of Man must be delivered into the hands of sinful men, be crucified and on the third day be raised again," we would understand why Mary's name was magnified. Nonetheless, the past life of Mary Magdalene before she met Jesus was nothing good to write about; it was simply terrible. She had a miserable life and was a great sinner who was possessed by seven demons. Jesus had compassion on her, and cast out all the demons in her, which made her, believe on the Lord.

He actually forgave her of her many sins. What a great and wonderful thing the Lord did for her. Appreciatively, Mary did not forget. She was deeply grateful to the Lord, and showed her gratitude by anointing Jesus with precious and expensive perfume, according to Luke 7:36-50.

If Mary Magdalene were here today to share her testimony, what would she tell us? We can fantasize that she might encourage us to believe on the Lord Jesus Christ, for He is the Son of God and the only Saviour of the world. But Mary is not the only sinner, for we are told by Paul that Adam's sin has made all of us sinners and we all have come short of the glory of God. We are all born in sin and we sin every day. We are living in Satan's world of lustful temptations and sinful pride. On the contrary, 1 John 2:15-16 commands us, "Do not love the world or the things in the world. If anyone loves the world, the love of the Father is not in him. For all that is in the world—the lust of the flesh, the lust of the eyes, and the pride of life—is not of the Father but is of the world" (NKJV). We may not be actually possessed by demons like Mary, but if we are obsessed with the things of the world, then we are in a sense possessed by the devil because we have allowed his ungodly principles and worldly methods to fill our hearts and minds.

The Lord tells us to do good things, but Satan says, "No, go steal or kill." Scripture says the good we desire we can't do, but the evil we do not want, that is what we do because evil is always present when we want to do good. Nevertheless, should Christ intervene into our deplorable situation and deliver us, we could magnify Him, as Mary did. There is a good deal of scholarship on the identity of Mary Magdalene. But despite the erroneous belief that society has formulated about her as a prostitute or the sinner woman, the Bible shows that it was because of the act of adultery that she was despised and nearly stoned. Even though Christ found her devotional gift good, her past filthy life tainted the sacred act to the extent that her very sister, Martha, could not appreciate that Christ spent time with her.

Fornication, adultery and prostitution are abominable acts that society abhors. In reality, the cost of criminal acts is a serious issue, and one that requires a strategic and meaningful community response. It's commonly known in human community that prostitution existed during the Egyptian, Greek, Roman and Byzantine Empirical eras. Nevertheless, during these periods special protocols were developed to deal with sexual relations. But in our generation each nation has its own system for dealing with the sex trade. While in Singapore sex is openly traded for money, Denmark and The Netherlands have confined places where prostitutes are allowed to ply their trade so long as it is not their sole means of income. Unlike in England and Wales, where prostitution is limited to individual providers, Canada, France and Mexico allow it.

It is only in the United States, with the exception of a few states, where prostitution is illegal. Besides prostitution, obscene practices such as homosexuality are acts that seriously arouse God's wrath to a people and a nation. Scripture states thus:

> For although they knew God, they neither glorified him as God nor gave thanks to him, but their thinking became futile and their foolish hearts were darkened. Although they claimed to be wise, they became fools and exchanged the glory of the immortal God for images made to look like mortal man and birds and animals and reptiles. Therefore God gave them over to the sinful desires of their hearts to sexual impurity for the degrading of their bodies with one another. They exchanged the truth of God for a lie, and worshipped and served created things rather than the Creator— who is forever praised. Amen. Because of this, God gave them over to shameful lusts. Even their women exchanged natural relations for unnatural ones. In the same way the men also abandoned natural relations with women and were inflamed with lust for one another. Men committed indecent acts with other men, and received in themselves the due penalty for their perversion. Furthermore, since they did not think it worthwhile to retain the knowledge of God, he gave them over to a depraved mind, to do what ought not to be done. They have become filled with every kind of wickedness, evil, greed and depravity. They are full of envy, murder, strife, deceit and malice. They are gossipers, slanderers, God-haters, insolent, arrogant and boastful; they invent ways of doing evil; they disobey their parents; they are senseless, faithless, heartless, ruthless. Although they know God's righteous decree that those who do such things deserve death, they not only

continue to do these very things but also approve of those who practice them (Romans 1:21-32).

I have witnessed such deplorable acts on many occasions around my school and have wondered why certain nations permit such activities to thrive. God have mercy!

In societies in which male chauvinism is predominant, women have not received fair treatment. Even though recent history shows women are making great gains in most cities, they are found as housewives instead of having political power or voice. A small number of civilizations now honor women, yet women have never been able to achieve equal status with men. They are even victimized the more due to prostitution, which is seen as an avenue through which women commit crime. No matter how one looks at fornication, adultery and prostitution, the fact remains that Mary Magdalene did not receive Christ's favor as a sinner until she cultivated the faith, hope and repentance that Christ alone could end her degraded experience and deliver her from the yoke of bondage that had caused her a life of ridicule.

I believe that the human world could mitigate the stones of life, the hatred other nations have against the Church as well as against the United States and Canada, which has made us a target of terrorist plots and attacks and has also made us lose our salty taste. Remember, the good Lord said that when the salt of the earth loses its taste it is no longer good for anything except that men throw it out and trample upon it (Matthew 5:13). Men will trample God's chosen people and nations down, but Jesus can transform them to maintain their memorable name and to establish their security.

It was unfortunate that none of Jesus' disciples had a full grasp of the message of His death. Had they understood, they would have been joyful instead of bewildered, but they were grief-stricken when they learned of His death. Even so, if we would understand the death of Christ for us as a people and a nation, we would turn from our sinful, idolatrous, adulterous and obnoxious life and look unto Jesus for salvation and security. According to the Scriptures, there was a time for Jesus to die so that He was led as a sheep to the slaughter. They crucified Him. Unlike the disciples, this precious woman, Mary Magdalene, did not give up when Jesus was arrested and crucified (John 19:25). She continually stood at the cross until He died. Oh, how painful it was for her to see His suffering and to listen to His last words, "It is finished!" Her heart must have been pierced through and through when Jesus bowed His head and gave up the ghost.

Mary's devotion comes as a challenge to remind those who are unfaithful to the Lord to turn to the Lord. We are suddenly shifting our society from Christ-centered principles to secularism, preferring to please men rather than remain loyal to God like Mary. All too soon we have forgotten that it is Christ-centered principles rather than secularism and human philosophies, ideas and wisdom that have made Judeo-Christian nations wealthy and prosperous. It is not too late, however, to turn to the Lord for Him to solidify our position in this universe.

Joseph of Arimathea, an honorable counselor who was also waiting for the kingdom of God, might have been at the cross with Mary while Jesus was dying. He went boldly to Pilate and asked for the body of Jesus. Mark 15:46 tells us that Joseph bought fine linen, took Jesus down, wrapped Him in the linen, laid Him in a sepulcher that was hewn out of a rock, and rolled a stone unto the door of the sepulcher. In verse 47, Mary Magdalene and Mary the mother of Joses beheld where he was laid. Later in chapter 16, the Word of the Lord tells us that when the Sabbath was past, Mary Magdalene, Mary the mother of James, and Salome brought sweet spices so that they might anoint Him. My God, even when He was in the grave she still loved Him and remained faithful to the Lord!

When she and the other women arrived at the tomb they saw that Jesus was not in His grave. What a frightening moment that must have been for these women, especially Mary Magdalene. To her astonishment the stone was rolled away, and what was most disappointing, the body of Jesus could not be found. She might have thought the wicked men who killed her Lord had come for His body, which she could probably use to comfort her soul. It so happened that at the sight of witnessing the disappearance of the Lord's body, her comfort, joy and hope sapped immediately from her innermost being, casting her instantaneously into grief. Have you ever been in a situation when you needed God the most and it appeared He was not around?

Unlike most of us, during that moment in Mary's life she never turned her back to the Lord. Mary testifies to us as a people and a nation to not turn our back to the Lord even though we attempt to seek Him and He appears not to be there. For He said, "I will never leave you nor forsake you. Behold, I am with you always." Nevertheless, in that devastated mood and overwhelmed with grief, Mary Magdalene ran hastily to Simon Peter and John, the disciple Jesus loved, and said, "They have taken the Lord's body out of the sepulcher, and we do not know where they laid Him" (see John 20:2).

This is what most of us do when we are found in serious predicaments. Instead of turning to the Lord for comfort and salvation, we run to pastors and church leaders. I am a minister, and I therefore know how important faith-leaders are to the body of Christ. But it's not always good to turn to vessels the Maker uses for miracles instead of to the Creator himself, who is abundantly able to fulfill the promises of all those who put their trust in Him. The two disciples Mary turned to, however, hurried to the tomb with her and saw the strips of linen lying there, and the napkin that was about His head wrapped together in a place by itself. The disciples had still not grasped the Scriptures that said Jesus had to die and rise from the dead.

And then they went back home. Even so, the women stood outside the tomb and wept. I must confess I do not believe that weeping is necessary or appropriate at times, even though I can identify with Mary's dilemma. One ought to discern the times in order not to confuse moments to rejoice with moments of grief, for Paul has said that in all things we must give thanks, for it is the will of God in Christ Jesus.

But at some point in our lives, we respond to death and miserable situations as did Mary and these women. Our world is in a time of grief with wars and rumors of war all around us. We find our men and women facing bullets in war-torn countries, and the coffins of our beloved parade our cities, so that people ask whether there is any hope for us. May His soothing name be our portion, and it would be if today we would turn to Him as a people and a nation. Amazingly, the Lord opened my spirit to discover and understand the spiritual significance of Mary's cries. Discernment and revelation knowledge created an impression in my heart, which made me believe Mary's cries were not sensual or earthly. I saw her cries as devoid of any parochial interest. It was a cry that needed divine attention and consolation, for it touched the heavens and motivated the Ancient of Days to take action.

The eye of my understanding was enlightened and was informed that someone must cry for the release of the resurrection message. Someone must cry for the disciples to know that their Lord and Savior has risen and is alive. Someone must cry for Israel to know that death, Hades and hell can never hold the Messiah. Someone must cry for the nations to turn and see the Lord. The absence of the apprehending ministry in our time necessitates a cry for its release because the need of such acts in our generation cannot be overemphasized. Our age is very advanced in knowledge, yet it appears the simple Gospel means little to us.

Besides, the rate at which scientific and technological development is advancing in our days, as well as the proliferation of arms and wars, making the world and the mind of man continually evil, necessitates a cry to the Lord to attend to the prayer of His people. These thoughts spontaneously buckled my knees to the floor, and instinctively cries began to gush out of my spirit with words inexplicable. Nonetheless, like the disciples and these women, there have been times when we have read the infallible Word of God without having a precise understanding of what we were reading. Most of the times when we are confronted by our Goliaths or mountainous situations, we do not know how to respond appropriately to the Word of God. We have shrunk back and succumbed to the grave of confusion, and we begin to waver in our faith.

We have been anxious and easily agitated instead of being at peace or rejoicing in the Lord who has power to quiet the storms of life. Even so, this grief-stricken woman, Mary Magdalene, wept for not seeing her Lord. But while she kept weeping, she looked into the tomb and saw two angels sitting where Jesus had been laid, one at the head and the other at the feet. These angels asked her a very important question, which was, "Why are you weeping?"

She answered, "They have taken my Lord away, and I do not know where they have put him" (see John 20:13). Even though the whole scenario looks very sad, we can, through the eyes of God's Spirit, lay hold of spiritual nuggets of truth that Mary Magdalene experienced with Jesus.

In today's world we are prone to experience unnecessary stress, and sometimes we perish in the process because of a lack of knowledge and a spirit of discernment when the blessings the Spirit might be pouring into our lives have been overshadowed by persisting troubles.

But if we would love Jesus with Mary's love, her memorial reward will also be our portion. But the death and resurrection of Jesus were imperative. In 1 Corinthians 15:15, 17, the apostle Paul tells us the reason: "More than that, we are then found to be false witnesses about God, for we have testified about God that he raised Christ from the dead. But he did not raise him if in fact the dead are not raised. . . . And if Christ has not been raised, your faith is futile; you are still in your sins." Nonetheless, Mary, still overshadowed and bent over with grief, turned around and saw Jesus standing nearby, but could not recognize Him. Her eyes were darkened by grief, so Jesus said to her, "Woman, why are you weeping, and who is it you are seeking?"

She, ignorantly figuring she was talking to a gardener, confronted Jesus, demanding that He tell her where they had laid her Lord's body. Is this not a heartrending story? But this is exactly how we at times respond to God during the crucial moments in our lives. More often than not, we miss the mark and fail miserably. We have missed out on countless God encounters or interventions, and subsequently have missed his wondrous glory and deliverances. But today God is calling us to turn back to Him for life and hope. Mysteriously, it takes the voice of Jesus to make us turn. Accordingly, Jesus called Mary by her name.

He said, "Mary!" Immediately she turned toward Him and cried out in Aramaic, "Rabbi!" (which means master or teacher). It took the voice of Jesus to quicken the mortal body of this woman to see and recognize Him. That is what Jesus does all the time to us. Listen to His wonderful word, for "the sheep know the voice of the shepherd" (see John 10:4, 27). Jesus said to Mary, "Do not touch me, for I have not yet returned to My Father." He said to her, "Go instead to my brothers and tell them I am returning to My Father and your Father, to my God and your God" (see 20:17). But you see, when Jesus called out to Mary Magdalene, her life was transformed and she was commissioned to be a vessel or instrument of the resurrection message.

This was a moment of blessing and promotion for this once despised woman. She was despised first of all because she was a woman, and secondly because she was possessed by seven devils. Jesus cast these devils out of her and gave her a brand-new life. More so, she was the first person or woman the Lord showed Himself to after His resurrection. Is this not wonderful? The resurrected Lord appeared first to this once despised woman.

Is this not fascinating? The resurrection message was fire in her innermost being, and she ran to the disciples and said to them, "I have seen the Lord. And these are the words He spoke to me" (see v. 18). Can you be imaginative for a moment? These men did not believe, but no one could have robbed her of the message she delivered. She saw Him! His disciples were scattered when Jesus was crucified, but Mary stayed close and watched what her Lord was facing. They were locked away in a room, but this woman was looking for her Lord. This is awesome; her waiting was not in vain. She saw the Lord!

What a significant role she played in being the conveyer, the evangelist, for such a moment as that. She was faithful, and amidst her turmoil she was steadfast and the Lord blessed her. Now if you could hear His voice and turn to Him, He can make you who are despised to have a new name, a new glory and a testimony. As a matter of fact, you will also see Him and become a custodian of the resurrection message. May His name be praised!

Prayer: Almighty God, the One who is Omniscient, though we your children may be considered despised or base, You know how to exalt the humble. Despite our low estate or situation, help us to listen and recognize when You are speaking to us. May we know Your voice and turn around to bring Your resurrection message to all people, in Jesus' holy name. Amen.

> I must confess I do not believe that weeping is necessary and appropriate at times, even though I can identify with Mary's dilemma. One ought to discern the times in order not to confuse moments to rejoice with moments of grief, for Paul has said that in all things we must give thanks, for it is the will of God in Christ Jesus.

CHAPTER 2

THE TURNING POINT IN MY LIFE

In Isaiah 45:22 the Lord declares, "Turn to me and be saved, all you ends of the earth; for I am God, and there is no other." Our Lord said, "I am the Alpha and the Omega" (Revelation 1:8). He has therefore planned our lives already before the beginning of all ages. Paul says in Colossians 3:3 that our life is hidden in Christ and in God; Luke adds, "For in him we live and move and have our being" (Acts 17:28).

His words are also true, for they are "yea" and "amen" (see 2 Corinthians 1:20). In the light of the preceding statements—better still, the above quoted scriptures—I was aided to discover how God has patterned my life in Him. Meanwhile, it's interesting and reassuring for us to know the significance of our spiritual life, the inspiration we can draw from our predecessors, and also the impact we can pass on to our successors.

In this chapter, I hope you will find this understanding and the veracity of God's Word through the testimony of my life, His plan for your life, and why and how you can also turn to Him and be saved. Do you remember how the apostle Paul, the great ambassador of the gospel of Jesus Christ, wrote to Timothy, his spiritual son, in 2 Timothy 1:5-7, reminding him not to be timid but to emulate the unfeigned or sincere faith of his grandmother Lois, which was also in his mother, Eunice?

As an outstanding and anointed mentor, Paul not only reminded Timothy, but prayed and impacted his faith into his heart and spirit, having this confidence that Timothy would not only keep the treasure he had deposited in him but would pass it on to others. It was the advice of Paul to Timothy to emulate his predecessors and the relationship they built that brought to my mind thoughts about my lineage. The memories were personal discoveries about my family, how the members of my family were created, and destined, to serve the body of Christ in different capacities. It was quite fascinating to me to know that my fore-parents, like those of Timothy, had strong faith in God, a faith which has been passed on, or transferred to, a considerable number of persons in my family.

In addition, it was pleasing to me also to learn how the efficacy of Christ's work has blessed my family with dynamic preachers, teachers, deacons, singers, drummers, and authors. Truthfully, in the good old days I never went to bed without my parents reading the Word of God and praying for me and my entire family. I can vividly remember those sacred moments of evening devotions when one ought to be still because Mom and Dad were about to enter or take us to the throne of grace. Despite my family's affinity for Christianity when I reached the age of accountability, I knew I was different from my siblings.

Spiritually, there was a strong urge in me to pursue higher religious studies in order to improve upon the religious teachings we had received from our parents. But little did I know at that time that the urge was a literal hunger for the written Word of God (the Logos), which ultimately led me to the living Word who is Jesus Christ, my Lord and Savior. In the area of education, although B was my G.C.E. O-Level grade at school, my score was always A. These successes made me proud of myself without the foggiest idea that the Almighty God was ordering my steps.

Do not forget what the psalmist writes concerning the vessels of God in Psalm 37:23: "The steps of a good man are ordered by the Lord, and He delights in his way" (NKJV). But could you please permit me to digress a bit from my testimony to share with you a few things about dreams and visions and how they reshaped my life for God? Prior to my acceptance of the Lord as my personal Savior, there was something quite phenomenal taking place in my life. I realized that almost anything I dreamt of came to pass. Moreover, thoughts about God's servants who were dreamers, such as Joseph and Daniel, brought great comfort to me. While dreams like that of Joseph seem very nonsensical to some people, that's the way God at times speaks to His people.

Have you, however, come to the place of asking yourself whether God really speaks through dreams, and whether today dreams do help us to know God's will? Personally, I believe that apart from hearing His voice audibly, dreams are a means that God uses to demonstrate something of great importance to His servants and followers.

Rare incidents do occur when one is led by a vision or a dream. God used visions and dreams to communicate with most of His messengers throughout the Bible, from the time of Abraham to the time of John the Revelator. For instance, the Lord says in Genesis 15:1, "After this, the word of the LORD came to Abram in a vision: 'Do not be afraid, Abram. I am your shield, your very great reward.'" Also, in Revelation 1:9-11 it is written, "I, John, your brother and companion in the suffering and kingdom and patient endurance that are ours in Jesus, was on the island of Patmos because of the word of God and the testimony of Jesus. On the Lord's Day I was in the Spirit, and I heard behind me a loud voice like a trumpet, which said: 'Write on a scroll what you see and send it to the seven churches: to Ephesus, Smyrna, Pergamum, Thyatira, Sardis, Philadelphia and Laodicea.'" May it be so in your life that God will shape your dreams and visions for your ways to be brighter and for you to achieve your maximum best.

Now back to my testimony. The family devotions my parents offered to the Lord for our entire family and for me especially, the successes in my education, and the experiences I had through dreams and visions, convinced me that the Lord had called me from birth to be a vessel of honor to serve Him.

I also believe that it was the Holy Spirit who led my mom to give me my name because the name Joy has had a great significance in my life. It comes from the Latin word *gaudia*, which means "joyful in the Lord." Joy in the Word of God is an attribute of deity. (A deity is often referred to as a supernatural being, who is always of significant power, worshipped, thought holy, divine, or sacred, held in high regard, or respected by human beings). Joy is also listed as

TURN AROUND AND SEE THE LORD

one of the nine fold fruits of the Holy Spirit and imparts strength to all believers. Thanks be to God that His joy is our strength! It is important to mention that the joy of the Lord working through me has given many of God's people exceeding great joy. To God be the glory and the praise!

Even though my parents gave me the necessary help to comfortably serve the Lord, at one point in my life the desire to gratify the dictates of the flesh grew very strong in my heart. These carnal traits caused me to backslide from the faith. Probably my sudden shift from the Lord somewhere in my life may sound strange to some of you, having testified of the strong Christian upbringing my parents cultivated in me. During the prime time of my life, I harbored a reluctance to succumb to the call and will of God for me. Perhaps it was due to stubbornness or a degree of ignorance of the plan of God for my life. In any case, I found myself not interested in yielding to God, and refused to listen to sound instructions offered to me by my parents. I eventually saw myself making wrong decisions, which led me to marry a man who was not compatible with me.

The decisions I made brewed afflictions far beyond my ability and comprehension. Even though the elongated hand of God was extending to me, I could not reach out to Him and lay hold of His unflinching hand. A cycle of raging storms overshadowed and cleaved to me with huge intensity, as if help was nowhere to be found. I felt so shattered that I could not even remember the days of the week. It was the mercies of God that kept me and also assured me that my time to depart from this world had not yet come.

Praise be to His name! Indeed, God had a purpose for my life. He has structured it according to His will and according to what heaven has ordained. His ways are past finding out. This supernatural being we serve does at times allow adverse and diverse situations in our lives as a means of getting our attention. At times the stormy clouds drive us between the rock and the hard place. When we are caught in such situations, our focus should be turned toward the hills of God. Even so it was the intensity of the unbearable situation life brought to me, as I have testified in my first book, *Demons Are Real,* that caused me to run away from my former husband and my two beautiful girls. It was the most difficult thing that I have ever done. However, I found a place of refuge with a cousin in the city of Toronto.

This dear cousin began to tell me about the Jesus my parents introduced to me but whom I had thrown away. She dramatically attested to how this Jesus could deliver me from all my predicaments. The soothing words of my cousin urged me to follow her to church one Sunday. The message that day amazingly reminded me how dangerous it is to live in sin and in this world without Christ, and fearing the devastating consequences the pastor preached that day, I humbled myself to the promptings of the Holy Ghost and accepted Jesus as my Lord and personal Savior again.

Nevertheless, I initially lived a very stubborn Christian life, very disobedient to the voice of God due to ignorance of the Word of God, specifically the teachings of Christ for my life. I saw my lifestyle as almost identical to that of the children of Israel. Israel's lifestyle was a cycle of disobedience and afflictions. However, when they turned from their wicked ways and cried out to God, they were always delivered. Part of the memorable facts of my past life that were similar to those of God's chosen people occurred when sin pushed me far from the peaceful shore of God's domain; the Holy Ghost snapped my attention with the privileges one could enjoy in Him.

During such moments, the Merciful One led me and showed me quite vividly how His hand upon me adhered to the call of His chosen people. Once upon a time He brought to my memory His instructions to the Israelites, which said that if they obeyed His word they would be blessed exceedingly, but if they chose not to listen to His word or obey all that was written therein, a curse would accompany them and overtake them. God's voice was audible, but I still turned deaf ears to Him. I was more interested in gratifying the desires of the flesh. I knew God was not impressed with my lifestyle, nonetheless He did not withhold from me His outreached hand. What a loving and faithful God and Father we serve!

The turning point was inevitable. My father had an accident. He was riding his donkey to a field when he fell and injured his head. The concussion he received caused him to behave like a two-year-old child. I was devastated about that news, but because sin still had dominion over me in that when I desired to do right

I did wrong, the devastation could not break me down. Because I was so much enslaved to sin like a cancer, my entire being was affected. Apparently my mind was still not focused on the things of God. Ironically, all the pleasures of life that caught my attention the most could not supply any internal peace in my heart and mind, yet I could not serve God wholeheartedly.

Then one day I got a call that my dad's health had deteriorated and he had been hospitalized. Within a few days I got the call no one is prepared to hear. It was a call from my uncle in the States saying that my dad had passed away. This was the knell that brought home the true turning point. My reaction was like Jonah's in the whale's gut. I fell on my knees and cried with a loud voice. I felt as if a part of me had died and nothing or no one could comfort me. I cried out to God. I said to Him, "When You did not allow me to see my father, you got my attention."

My dad was the most precious father who had ever walked the face of this earth. He was a spiritual man of God who loved to sing and whistle spiritual songs or hymns. He was an exceptional and loving daddy to his special girl. I can remember the days when my dad would watch me comb my hair. Can you believe it? I can still see in my mind's eye the glow on his face. There was a wonderful bond between us—as a matter of fact, there were times I even thought he respected me more than my mom, for he never made any major decision without my presence or approval even though my mom was in agreement with everything.

Do not get the wrong impression, for my mom is very humble and ladylike. She is a distinguished vessel of honor, a woman called after God who knew that the relationship between my father and me was that of a caring parent to a child. While mourning for the death of my father, I heard the still small voice of the Holy Spirit calling me to come up higher. He used Jeremiah 33:3 to turn me to Him: "Call to me and I will answer you and tell you great and unsearchable things you do not know." I also heard distinctly that my steps are ordered by the Lord: "If the Lord delights in a man's way, he makes his steps firm" (Psalm 37:23). He further spoke to me through his Word in 1 Corinthians 6:20: "You were bought at a price. Therefore honor God with your body."

While these divine messages were coming to me, my face was still down with guilt and shame. I was in that mood for a long time, but I knew my life had been totally transformed by the touch of my father's death. That news had actually aided me to renew my mind and to serve God better.

I saw my mind now girded with truth as Paul admonished: "Let this mind be in you, which was also in Christ Jesus" (Philippians 2:5 KJV). Later on, these admonishing words quickened my soul to turn away from my wicked ways. This was the time when determination took absolute control of me with a decision to walk before Him and to be perfect. I was now careful to begin observing the Word of God. I therefore laid hold of two verses of Scripture the great apostle Paul states in Romans 12:1-2: "Therefore, I urge you, brothers, in view of God's mercy, to offer your bodies as living sacrifices, holy and pleasing to God—this is your spiritual act of worship. Do not conform any longer to the pattern of this world, but be transformed by the renewing of your mind. Then you will be able to test and approve what God's will is—his good, pleasing and perfect will". The death of a loved one could be a turning point in some people's lives.

We are aware of the saying that death is inevitable, for it is appointed unto man once to die, and then judgment. The death of my father caused me grief, sighs and tears. It affected my whole anatomy and physiology. It's true, the death of a loved one affects the light that shines in the eyes. Even the brain at times ceases to function properly. The depths of death can affect one's being and can cause one to be broken and to become pliable. During this moment of bereavement it's imperative that one reach out for the joy and comfort that comes from the omnipotent Father who is full of mercy and grace. Yours might not be death, but no matter how deplorable your situation might be, lay aside your troubles by turning to Him, and I promise you, your life will never be the same!

That is why when my father died I reached out for God with all of my being (body, mind, spirit), and I surrendered to Him completely. My heart began to make melody unto the Lord, and I began to sing, "Consecrate me, Lord, for your service. Only then will I lift up." I sang this song unceasingly—I just could not stop—

and I asked the Lord why. Later, I heard the still small voice of the Holy Ghost saying, "I have brought you through great sorrow, and I have given you a song." The anointed songwriter wrote: "Some through the waters, some through the flood, some through the fire, but all through the blood; some through great sorrow, but God gives a song, in the night season and all the day long."

God gave Joy a song! It's a powerful song that is now a special piece for an outstanding choir. God is able to do the same for you. Here is a word of encouragement, strength and edification for you. In 2 Corinthians 1:3-4, the word of the Lord declares, "Praise be to the God and Father of our Lord Jesus Christ, the Father of compassion and the God of all comfort, who comforts us in all our troubles, so that we can comfort those in any trouble with the comfort we ourselves have received from God."

Prayer: Omnipotent Father of mercy and grace, we are at times disobedient and stiff-necked, not wanting to yield to Your perfect will. May being caught between a rock and a hard place or Your holding pattern cause us to turn to You. Help us to surrender to You and lean not on our own understanding. Amen.

This supernatural being we serve does at times allow adverse and diverse situations in our lives as a means of getting our attention. At times the stormy clouds drive us between a rock and a hard place. When we are caught in such situations, our focus should be turned toward the hills of God.

CHAPTER 3

YOU CAN RUN BUT YOU CANNOT HIDE FROM GOD

This chapter is devoted to another biblical character, Jonah. His story is told in a manner that will benefit those of you whose current experience in life has little to do with my testimony and the magnificent relationship Mary Magdalene cultivated for the Lord. It is my hope, however, that the information in this story will help you turn to the Lord and to be equally blessed as well. The Book of Jonah the prophet provides a wonderful source for spiritual contemplation. In this chapter our objective is to be beneficial and not to debate, therefore our approach is purely spiritual instead of theological. But here is a question for you before we delve into Jonah's story.

Does God the Omnipotent One always pursue those who run from Him? Not necessarily! God the Omniscient One knows that often people who run away from Him will eventually turn back to Him when faced by the cares of this world and the troubles of this life. The Prodigal Son in Luke 17 is a typical example. We all face death and miseries. Are you among those whom God could count on to return to Him? Harden not your heart if you hear Him calling you right now!

Now, the story of Jonah the minor prophet is a wonderful and inspirational story. It's a story that we have heard over and over again, but the way the story is told is intended to create a different meaning in your spirit and also have a unique impact in your life for good.

Jonah in Hebrew is *Yonah*, which means "dove, warmth and affection, lovable, passionate, and fruitful of God." Nonetheless, the meaning of Jonah's name had little significance to do with his call to preach repentance to Nineveh. He was a reluctant prophet who turned his back to God's mission for Nineveh, a city in Assyria. That was to preach a message of repentance to the Ninevites, warning them of the impending destruction the Almighty had thought to unleash upon them. Now, Jonah was very judgmental. He had thought of the sins of Nineveh and had concluded that they deserved the impending punishment of God. Moreover, being judgmental, he was not interested in delivering a message that would turn away God's wrath from that city for peace and prosperity.

Some of us, like Jonah, have the tendency of taking matters into our own hands. We fail to remember God's word that He is the King of Glory, strong and mighty in battle! He says in Hebrews 10:30, "For we know him who said, 'It is mine to avenge; I will repay,' and again, 'The Lord will judge his people.'" Jonah had a selfish and undermining attitude toward other nations, like some preachers, or should I say people. He did not believe that Nineveh should be given a chance for repentance or salvation. So stiff-necked was he that he attempted to escape by taking passage on a ship to Tarshish. It's interesting to note that Tarshish was a city in Spain, opposite in direction to Nineveh (this place was very far). This shows that Jonah did not only turn from the Lord spiritually, but also physically.

Invariably, what goes on in the spirit is parallel to what goes on in the physical. Thus, the one who turns his back to the Lord physically has equally turned his back to God spiritually. Therefore, those who fail to walk in their calling are not only turning away from the Lord physically, but spiritually as well. However, God, the Omniscient One, knew that if Jonah yielded to Him and proclaimed the message to these wicked people, the word would affect their hearts and they would turn to Him. God's words have power to penetrate racial barriers or prejudices, circumstances or troubles. It can also turn around everything for those who love Him and are called according to His purpose. He works in mysterious ways! He is gracious as well and compassionate; He uses the extraordinary or the unusual to grasp the attention of His people. How peaceful and blissful this world would have become if we had not failed to love and had preached the un-grafted message of salvation to those we think are so wicked, condemned and rejected by God. The apostle John says, "For God did not send his Son into the world to condemn the world, but to save the world through him" (John 3:17).

In Jonah 1:2, the word of the Lord came to him, saying, "Go to the great city of Nineveh and preach against it." One may ask the question, how did God send His word to Jonah? You know, God's ways are past finding out! God could have used one of the many mediums such as visions, dreams, or the signs in nature I mentioned in the earlier chapter. Simply put, He could have also spoken to him directly. Why did God send Jonah and not anyone else to preach against the Ninevites? According to the author of the Book of Jonah, Israel's northern kingdom regained its influence by Jeroboam II. The Assyrians, whose capital was Nineveh, were asserting themselves in increasingly menacing ways. Their wickedness had come up to God's nostrils with a very bad stench. He had chosen Jonah to preach repentance to the Ninevites because he was capable of bringing about a great conviction.

But judgmental Jonah, realizing his responsibility challenged the very core of his life, decided to run from God. What was he afraid of? Perhaps he was afraid of these wicked people, thinking they might be terrorists who fueled the Assyrians to make war against Israel with war machines.

Maybe he wanted God to favor Israel alone. Was Jonah egocentric? Did he fall into the Jews' belief that they were the only chosen people to whom one day all the other peoples would be subordinate? Pride is a major enemy of God's Word. Anyone with such a swollen ego may have difficulty in submitting to authority and in acknowledging scriptural authority. Disappointingly, our society is permeated with egocentric people who proudly believe they have a corner on the truth. Western egocentrism is defined as the highest stage of imperialism, conglomeration, and liberal egocentrism. It's a struggle against nature that tries to blend Christian theology and sociological description. There are some social psychologists who describe the approach to the American Dream as cultural self-centering and call it ethnocentrism.

Today world egocentrism has created the pursuit of human wisdom, which is believed by some as the standard against which everything should be measured. Such intellectualism is the product of the higher criticism and rationalism of the last century, and it destroys the truth. This fallacy empowers the Gnostics to question the veracity of the miracles in the Bible because they don't seem reasonable to them.

Other by-products of egoism have caused thousands of churches here in North America not to get along. The Church is fractured and fragmented, and there's a lack of spiritual leadership. Such confusion makes the Word of God lose its significance. Tragically, Christendom has replaced sound doctrine and study of the Bible with social programs and activities. Christendom spends most of its time resources dealing with these social problems and neglects the real priority of the Word.

Therefore entertainment, psychology, and a variety of other distractions have captured people's interest. The egocentric way is the most immature way to live, which often leads to the deification of personal development. We should cast off egocentrism and embrace theocentrism, a perspective that makes us grow up to Christian maturity: "Grown-ups are people who understand 'It's not about you. It's about something bigger than you."

It is about some larger purpose or mission, project or vision. It is about the work. It is about the whole and not just the individual parts. There's something at stake that transcends me. Here, God's will challenges our natural tendency to egocentrism (self-centeredness) and calls us to a God-centered perspective of life.

We tend to harbor the illusion that the world revolves around us and our desires. After all, our experience is more real to us than anything else. This causes us to be skeptical and dismissive of what we do not experience. Tragically, this is our sin. God's will, on the other hand, invites us to live for something greater than ourselves—that is, His kingdom. As a matter of fact, because Jonah failed to rightly focus on a God-centered perspective of life, he looked toward the seaport northwest of Jerusalem. There he found a ship, paid his fare, and went aboard, not looking back. I do not believe he thoroughly laid hold of or grasped the words of the great anointed king of Israel, David.

For David had written in Psalm 139:7-10: "Whither shall I go from thy spirit? Or whither shall I flee from thy presence? If I ascend up into heaven, thou art there: if I make my bed in hell, behold, thou art there. If I take the wings of the morning, and dwell in the uttermost parts of the sea; even there shall thy hand lead me, and thy right hand shall hold me" (KJV). In light of this, God's righteous right hand was kept on this vessel and there was absolutely no hiding place for Jonah. He, however, went below deck and comfortably sank into a deep sleep. Here is the perfect time for the One who never slumbers nor sleeps to show this man of God that He is Omnipresent.

Spiritually Jonah had failed to succumb and present his body (a vehicle of His grace) a living sacrifice, holy and acceptable unto God. God therefore sent a wind on the sea. So violent was the storm that it threatened to break up the ship and cause loss of lives. The sailors were sore afraid, because they had never seen the sea this violent. They began to cry out to their gods, but the raging storm grew more severe. They threw out pieces of cargo to lighten the ship, but the wind was persistent and fierce.

What was very odd about all this was the fact that all this time Jonah was deep in sleep while everyone else was awake and disturbed by the storm. The captain, puzzled by Jonah's docility, proceeded to question him. Under these circumstances, I'm sure your interest and anxiety would propel you to question any person in your ship acting as awkwardly as Jonah. But instead of reprimanding him, they asked him to get up and summon his God to stop the wind so that they would not perish.

They were convinced that they were caught in the middle of a wind caused by the wrath of God; it was therefore imperative that they find out who caused such a calamity. Lots were cast and Jonah was found guilty. Spiritual giants, are you hearing the voice of the Righteous calling you to rise up out of your sin-sleepy mood? Awake and shine, for the Lord of all lights has come! I hereby pray the people of God not go through all the predicaments Jonah faced before turning to the divine call of God for his life and for Nineveh.

I believe that the rate at which our children and youth are dying through gun violence and crime, the leadership confusion that brings destruction instead of peace, and the terror around our borders should be sufficient to wake us up from slumber or death for us to see the light of Christ and proclaim the true words of liberty and freedom divinity has given us for the human society. The sailors, however, continued by asking Jonah the cause for such a divine wrath. They also asked him about his country of origin and his occupation. Jonah responded, "I am a Hebrew and I worship the Lord, the God of heaven, who made the sea and the land" (1:9). The sea became rougher and rougher, so they asked what they must do to calm the sea.

It seemed Jonah found the appropriate answer. He told them to throw him overboard, admitting that he was the cause of this raging storm. The men did not desire his blood on their hands, so they tried to row back to land. But the sea got wilder. They cried out to the Lord concerning Jonah, then they threw him overboard and immediately the sea was calm. Fear gripped their hearts because they realized that Jonah's God was omnipotent, affirming what the Scriptures say in Hebrews 10:31, that it is a terrible thing to fall into the hands of the living God. The Word of the Lord says in Jonah 1:16, "At this the men greatly feared the Lord, and they offered a sacrifice to the Lord and made vows to him."

Meanwhile God had already prepared a way of escape for His prophet so that His will would be fulfilled. The Word of the Lord tells us in 1 Corinthians 10:13, "No temptation has seized you except what is common to man. And God is faithful; he will not let you be tempted beyond what you can bear. But when you are tempted, he will also provide a way out so that you can stand up under it." God provided a great fish to swallow up Jonah and keep him in God's holding pattern for three days and three nights. It must have been hell in the darkened and slimy gut of this fish. Jonah was hedged in, and I can imagine how every turn he made in that fish's belly brought thoughts about his wayward ways, which made him cry out to the God of salvation.

I would like you to be imaginative for a little while. Just imagine what would happen to a man inside the fish's digestive system. Let's also think about how Jonah breathed in the fish's digestive system;

the hand of God was on him in His holding pattern. I believe that enzymes are released to work on any kind of food substances that may be swallowed by the fish, and here Jonah was the food. I believe that the enzymes worked on the skin and caused some kind of skin discoloration. If you understand how digestion occurs, how food is broken down into simpler products so that the body can absorb its nutrients, then you can imagine the painful condition Jonah was in. In such desperate moments he might have remembered the mercies of God, leading him to turn to the Lord in the belly of the fish. The affliction actually challenged him to approach the throne of grace and cry unto God for grace and salvation.

God sometimes uses unpleasant conditions to get our attention and to build our faith in Him. Unusual or miraculous events are inexplicable. They show how mysterious God is. He used this great fish in a dramatic way to change Jonah's stubborn attitude. Jonah's prayer was one of gratitude. He might have thanked God in advance for saving his life. He might have thanked God for His goodness toward him and perhaps made a vow to God for his salvation. Let us grasp some spiritual truth from this story. He was broken and pliable in the hands of the Potter. But when he turned from his wicked ways and disobedience, God heard his cry and delivered him.

God, knowing how important Jonah's life meant to him, commanded the fish to vomit Jonah onto the dry land. I do not believe that Jonah was interested in how he looked at that moment. He immediately went to the wicked pagan city, and for forty days he preached to Nineveh to turn to the Lord. The preaching was so convicting that there was a citywide repentance in sackcloth and ashes. These wicked people embraced the word of God and entreated God to remove their sentence. The king at that time had to yield to the word of God. He arose from his earthly throne, took off his royal robes, and covered himself with sackcloth; he sat in the dust.

The king was now in God's holding pattern and was compelled to do God's bidding. He decreed a revival for man and beast, herd and flock. I thought about the animals. They do not sin; they are not complex organisms like us who will give an account for their sins. They cannot respond to God as we do. So why force animals to be religious? The Scriptures have shown how animals were used to express the sincerity and depth of repentance in a city. Causing animals to go without food and water and to wear sackcloth was a symbolic gesture of mourning. So when God saw that the people had turned from their wicked ways, He had compassion on them.

He did not bring upon them the destruction they deserved. I pray for the day that people everywhere will emulate Nineveh. Just as they and their animals repented and saw the favor of God, may we, like Nineveh, also have that true peace and security for us and our children. The story of Jonah and the whale is a type and shadow of the death of Christ, His burial and His resurrection. If you can identify yourself with Jonah's story and you are caught in God's holding pattern, turn around and see the Lord. He is your salvation. Pray in God's holding pattern, for He is willing to send to you His perfect will. Advisably, do not be anxious about the holding pattern. It may be very painful, but continually give thanks to God, for only He is capable to deliver you. If you are a preacher or an evangelist, or whatever your calling might be, please remember Jonah and turn toward where God is sending you.

Egocentrism and the pursuit of human wisdom are causing us more harm than good as people and a nation. Our society has become a target of terrorism, and there is the temptation that if this danger is not corrected our children may lose the coveted place we once enjoyed. But while time remains, if we can turn to God and focus our efforts to building universal love and peaceful cohabitation where equal rights are encouraged and respected, we would, like Jonah, see God, who can give us security and salvation.

Prayer: Abba Father, we are at times very stubborn and do not want to succumb to Your plan and Your purpose for our lives. Help us to listen diligently to Your voice at all times, and may we rise from the bottom of the ship where we are comfortably sleeping and find ourselves on the peaceful shore doing Your perfect will. Amen.

> God sometimes uses unpleasant conditions to get our attention and to build our faith in Him. Unusual or miraculous events are inexplicable. They show how mysterious God is. He used this great fish in a dramatic way to change Jonah's stubborn attitude. Jonah's prayer was one of gratitude.

CHAPTER 4

I AM WHO I AM BY THE GRACE OF GOD

We live in a world in which people have diverse opinions about the existence of God. The mere fact that man cannot see God even with the aid of a telescope, and the belief that He is not made of a graven image, causes men to disbelieve that He exists. Atheists assert that there is no God, and agnostics say they cannot tell whether there is a God or not. The materialist, however, boasts that he does not require a God. But according to the infallible Word of God, "The fool says in his heart, 'There is no God'" (Psalm 14:1; 53:1).

Lack of knowledge may also be a contributing factor for some to say there is no God, meanwhile, it's written in God's Word that lack of knowledge makes God's people perish (Hosea 4:6). It's not impressive, but the hard fact is people turn to God when they are faced with difficulties. Many have also rejected the Gospel due to the same perception, and such erroneous belief has caused some to attempt to destroy faith in Christ Jesus. But the foundation of the Lord stands strong, and the light of God still shines brightly for whosoever decides to turn to Him for the knowledge of Him and for salvation.

In order for us to comprehend the veracity of God's existence and acquaint ourselves with the profound knowledge of Him, we are challenged to study about a biblical character whom I describe as a peculiar man of God and who counted himself as an ambassador or envoy of the good tidings of the great joy and the life in Christ Jesus. He was bold enough to declare, "I am who I am by the grace of God." This peculiar man and great intellectual was a student of the renowned Jew Gamaliel. This was the man who initially tried to destroy the faith that he later built.

He was one of the greatest missionaries who ever walked on the face of this earth. He was an apostle commissioned by Christ Jesus. He was advanced in the knowledge of Judaism far beyond many Jews of his age, extremely zealous in following the traditions of his father. The word of the Lord tells us in Philippians 3:5 that this man was circumcised on the eighth day, he was of the stock of Israel, of the tribe of Benjamin, a Hebrew of the Hebrews; in regard to the law, a Pharisee; concerning zeal, persecuting the Church; as for legalistic righteousness, faultless. This man persecuted the believers of the Way and created havoc for the Church, entering into people's houses and committing men and women to prison.

The Gospel he initially tried to destroy was hidden from him, for the god of this world had blinded his mind. 2 Corinthians 4:3-4 says, "And even if our gospel is veiled, it is veiled to those who are perishing. The god of this age has blinded the minds of unbelievers, so that they cannot see the light of the gospel of the glory of Christ, who is the image of God." This man was hostile about the Gospel because sin had dominion over him. He acquired letters from Jerusalem to Damascus saying that if he found any of the believers of the Way, whether they were women or men, he might bring them bound to Jerusalem.

But God had planned that this man should have an encounter with the light of the world. Acts 9:3-4 says that as he journeyed he came near Damascus, and suddenly there shone round about him a light from heaven, and he fell to the earth and heard a voice saying to him, "Saul, Saul, why do you persecute me?" What we the saints of the living God have to bear in mind is that the light that met Saul on the road to Damascus penetrates through the hearts and minds of all people and brightens the life of every individual who turns to Him.

In effect, the glory of this light can cause men and women to fall prostrate before the Father of all lights. The power and authority of the light does not only cut into the interior parts of our hearts, but can eradicate the desires of the flesh and produces renewal and transformation of life. John gave us a little insight regarding this light. He wrote in 1:9 of his book that this true light lightens every man who comes into the world. This was the light that questioned, apprehended and arrested Saul for the Lord.

When the light arrested him, he turned around and immediately hearkened unto the call of God for his life. Momentarily he asked for the purpose of the encounter, saying, "What would you have me to do?" Most of us by now have discovered that the above story is about Saul, who later became Paul. Most Christian commentators believe that Saul suffered from what is commonly known as doctrinal delusion. It's a delusion often anchored by obsessive ideas and used in everyday language to describe a belief that is either false or fanciful, usually the result of deception.

It also refers to false belief that stems from the misrepresentation and misapplication of sound biblical teachings or doctrine. But it was not only Saul who was caught with this feverish syndrome, but almost all religionists, including Christians, are plagued with this malady. In these days of strong delusion, there are those who have developed "itching ears" who seek to validate their belief by surrounding themselves with teachers who will tell them what they want to hear. It's in this delusive ideology that the progenitors of occultism and all devilish worshipers have their roots.

The issue surrounding my displeasure with these movements such as occults and diviners has little to do with their founders, or who or what is their definition. It's also not my intent to approach it with doctrinal intensity but to bring to our attention the misuse of Scripture to justify their cause and to also take off the veil that is covering our eyes from seeing these movements as modern-day idol worship. I believe it's for some of these fallacies that Galatians 1:6-10 sent this caution:

> I am astonished that you are so quickly deserting the one who called you by the grace of Christ and are turning to a different gospel—which is really no gospel at all. Evidently some people are throwing you into confusion and are trying to pervert the gospel of Christ. But even if we or an angel from heaven should

preach a gospel other than the one we preached to you, let him be eternally condemned! As we have already said, so now I say again: If anybody is preaching to you a gospel other than what you accepted, let him be eternally condemned! Am I now trying to win the approval of men, or of God? Or am I trying to please men? If I were still trying to please men, I would not be a servant of Christ.

It's therefore my prayer that the good Lord who apprehended Saul would extend His apprehending mission toward His people and all places, that this light of the Lord will take away the blindness from our eyes so we might receive the true light and be saved. This was the light of God that struck Saul to the ground. When he arose from the earth, his eyes were blinded. He saw no man, so he was led by hand and brought to Damascus. Three days he was without sight, neither did he eat or drink. This magnificent light demonstrated to Saul of Tarsus that God had power to blind the natural eyes and to restore them.

This was a dramatic encounter in the life of Saul, and there is no doubt at all that God was performing spiritual surgery in his calloused heart. I believe that God had knowledge of this man's potential to advance His kingdom, so He prepared this earthen vessel for the Master's use. Accordingly, the Lord summoned a disciple named Ananias to go to the Straight Street and enquire about Saul. I find the name of this street to be interesting, because it was at this very street that this vessel began to pray to the light of his salvation. It was at this street that Ananias, the anointed chosen vessel of the Lord, laid his hand on Saul of Tarsus and he received his sight. Ananias was not interested, however, in delivering Saul; he figured, more or less, that he deserved the punishment upon his life, considering the havoc he had brought to the Church. Thus, he complained to the Lord that this wicked man had brutalized the believers of the Way.

But the Lord said to him, "Go your way, for he is a chosen vessel unto Me, to bear My name before the Gentiles, kings, and children of all men. I must show him the great things he must suffer for My sake" (see Acts 9:15-16). In verses 18-20, we learn that Ananias listened to the Lord. He therefore went and prayed for Saul to receive his sight, and later Saul arose and was baptized. He also ate some meat and was strengthened. He, however, spent a few days with the disciples at Damascus and proceeded fearlessly with the proclamation of the Gospel about the man Christ Jesus.

He declared to the Romans, "I am not ashamed of the gospel of Christ: for it is the power of God unto salvation" (1:16 KJV). He also went to synagogues and preached that Christ is the Son of God, compelling the Jews to turn to Christ. Soon the Jews wanted him dead, fearing that Saul's dynamism would convert more Jews to faith in Jesus. Everywhere Saul went there were riots and confusion! So his name was changed from Saul to Paul. What a turnaround for this vessel who was destined for greatness! Paul was transformed from wickedness to righteousness, from an old way of life to a new way of life.

The Word of the Lord tells us in 2 Corinthians 5:17, "Therefore, if anyone is in Christ, he is a new creation; the old has gone, the new has come." I also believe it was for that reason his name was transformed from Saul to Paul the apostle. He was the great missionary, the herald, the teacher, the preacher, the bond servant, the spiritual father and mentor. What a remarkable man of God he turned out to be, which made him to declare, "I am an ambassador for Christ." In Galatians 1 he declared that God set him apart from birth. He was chosen by God even before he became a Christian but his commission as apostle was not confirmed until he was converted. Paul mentioned that God called him by His grace and he was least among the apostles because he persecuted the Church. It was God, however, who entrusted the Gospel to Paul. He revealed His Son to him so that he might preach Jesus to the gentiles.

The apostle Paul wrote about the mystery of the Gospel made known to him through revelations. What was this mystery? It is not a myth or a secret. Ephesians 3:5 refers to it as a spiritual insight or revelation from God unknown to the previous generations. The Old Testament revealed that Gentiles would be saved, but only in the New Testament was the method of salvation made clear and the mystery disclosed. Paul was rooted and grounded in the things of God. The word of Christ dwelt in him richly.

God entrusted him with revelations which could not be uttered to man. He wrote to the Corinthians saying, "And lest I should be exalted above measure through the abundance of the revelations, there was given to me a thorn in the flesh, the messenger of Satan to buffet me, lest I should be exalted above measure" (2 Corinthians 12:7 KJV). What awesome work the Light had done in the life of this anointed man of God. He was enriched with the Gospel, the good tidings of great joy. The Gospel dwelt richly in him with all the treasures of wisdom and knowledge. He called himself a bond servant, for even in prison and being chained, he continued with declaring the Gospel, maintaining that the Gospel is unchainable. He was an encourager to many churches. He wrote to the Colossians, "Let the word of Christ dwell in you richly as you teach and admonish one another with all wisdom, and as you sing psalms, hymns and spiritual songs with gratitude in your hearts to God" (3:16). The apostle Paul not only boasted in the Lord saying, "I am who I am by the grace of God," but he also made known to all this special grace which was given to him, the least of the apostles, to preach the unsearchable riches of Christ.

Let us look keenly at what is in this man who initially reacted with hostility to the Gospel of Jesus Christ. He was a murderer and consented to Stephen's death. He had anger, pride and wickedness in his inward parts and was destined for destruction. The Word of the Lord says in Mark 7:21-23, "For from within, out of the heart of men, proceed evil thoughts, adulteries, fornications, murders, thefts, covetousness, wickedness, deceit, lasciviousness, an evil eye, blasphemy, pride, foolishness: all these evil things come from within, and defile the man" (KJV). In essence, Saul was the old man of sin destined to destruction. But Paul is the new man who turned to God through Christ and was fully dressed to show forth the power of God. His encounter with the light performed spiritual heart surgery, and he turned from his wicked ways to do the works of the Potter who created him.

Here is another important question to ask: Who was it that indwelt him? It was the Word of Christ, the double-edged sword, the perfect law of liberty, the royal law, the good tiding of great joy that was at work in him. The indwelling Word in him caused him to have great inspiration and motivation, which I believe quickened him to do the good works. He began to pen letters to the churches that needed to be encouraged. He wrote to the Corinthians, the Romans, the Ephesians, the Galatians, the Colossians, the Thessalonians, to Timothy, Titus, and Philemon and to the Hebrews to admonish, rebuke and correct God's people. He desired his brothers to also mortify the old man for this new way of life. It's therefore imperative for all God's people to be cleansed or sanctified for the new way, so that Christ may dwell in their hearts by faith. This is what is called the renewal or transformation of the heart and the spirit.

This spiritual exercise is interspersed in many of Paul's writings. In Philippians 2:5 he wrote, "Let this mind be in you, which was also in Christ Jesus" (KJV). In Colossians 3:2 he wrote, "Set your affection on things above, not on things on the earth" (KJV). This is advice that you need to keep inwardly, think and meditate about. Besides, it could assist you to direct your mind toward heavenly things. Moreover, it's gratifying to seek everything in the light of eternity. The saints of Jesus Christ must be heavenly, not worrying about earthly things. In Philippians 4:7 Paul said, "And the peace of God, which passeth all understanding, shall keep your hearts and minds through Christ Jesus" (KJV). He said, "Finally, brothers, whatever is true, whatever is noble, whatever is right, whatever is pure, whatever is lovely, whatever is admirable—if anything is excellent or praiseworthy—think about such things" (v. 8). Meditate on these things day and night; be careful to observe all that is written so that God's goal is accomplished in you.

It's noteworthy that all these noble qualities were exemplified in Christ and are graces of the Holy Spirit. Paul was more instrumental than all the apostles in encouraging all believers to suffer for Christ. Even so, his life was one of great suffering that brought the Gentiles to Christ. I thank God for the penetrating light that affected the mind and heart of Paul. This encounter inspired him to pen words of doctrine, admonition, rebuke, and correction to equip God's people thoroughly. Will you also turn around and take heed to the call of God for your life? Will you give Him your body, which is the temple of the Holy Ghost? Turn around for the Lord so that you can be that woman or man of God that has the glory of God in its earthen vessel.

Prayer: Lord, sometimes we are so stiff-necked and ignorant regarding Your call on our lives, but let the penetrating light from above pierce our spirit, soul, and body so that we will blurt to the God of heaven, "What would you have me to do?" May we be pliable for the light to do heart surgery. Amen.

> God is to be praised for the penetrating light that affected the mind and heart of Paul. This encounter inspired him to pen words of doctrine, admonition, rebuke, and correction to equip God's people thoroughly. Will you also turn around and take heed to the call of God for your life? Will you give Him your body, which is the temple of the Holy Ghost?

CHAPTER 5

HE TURNED ASIDE TO SEE THIS GREAT SIGHT

With our carnal mentality, finite human beings cannot fathom or understand the supernatural God whom we serve. The Word of the Lord declares that His ways are past finding out! However, attempts have been made by most humans to figure out what God intends to do in our lives, but the conclusions have fallen short of God's unfathomable mysteries. We have not been able to put the pieces of the God-mystery together, except when by grace God takes us to that place of power, authority, promotion, favor and blessing in Christ Jesus.

So God has delivered some of His people from diverse and adverse situations and has eventually assigned them to a particular person, people or nation for divine protection and prosperity. For instance, we can say God has delivered some of us from our "Egypt" for a season since there is that propensity that some of us could return to "Egypt" to deliver those who are held captive because of their sin. There are a few traces in the Bible character whom we will learn about in this chapter that allude to the above scenario. His relationship with God and life experience is very interestingly designed to help us draw spiritual food for our well-being.

This person is Moses, and his name means "drawn from the water," even though there is a great deal of scholarly discussion about the meaning of his name. How intriguing it is that the very

Nile which was meant for his destruction turned out to be a haven for him. Even though I believe Moses was born at the right time, Egyptian history rather revealed that time to be a troublesome moment for the people of God. It was quite evident that the Hebrew children who were sold into slavery were multiplying rapidly, thus the ruling king, Pharaoh, feared that, should there be a war, the Egyptians would be outnumbered by these Hebrew children and they might defeat them. He therefore instructed the taskmasters to oppress the Hebrews severely so that they would not find the time to procreate. Despite this plan, their "biological clocks" were not affected, for God did promise that He would multiply their seed as the stars of heaven and as the sand on the seashore. He did what He said He would do because He is faithful.

Moses' story unfolds as follows. In Exodus 1:22 we are told that Pharaoh ordered all his people to throw every Hebrew baby boy into the river Nile. But thanks be to God that the girls were saved! What would have happened to Moses if these girls were not spared? How would Miriam shepherd Moses? Or his mother nurse her own son in the house of Pharaoh? God always knows how to create a way of escape for His people. Is He not wonderful? Oh, what a Savior!

The intriguing part of the Moses story is that it was during this perilous time that he was born. Therefore God had to orchestrate every detail of his life. I can imagine the moments of intensity in the life of Jacobed, but she was a woman who feared God, and I believe she was inspired to perform every strategic moment in the life of her son. She made him a special basket pitched with tar and placed it among the reeds along the bank of the Nile. What was her expectation? That Miriam would be assigned to watch baby Moses. But miraculously God ordered the steps of the king's daughter to take a walk down the Nile because His future deliverer must be delivered and protected so that His plan would come to fruition.

God's plan was perfect. He allowed the boy's mother to nurse him, and she was paid to do so. Doesn't God know how to take care of His own? Accordingly Moses' mother, being a true worshipper of Jehovah God, taught her son the fear of the Lord. He was brought up in the way he should go, never to depart from what he learned. Time passed and Moses was taken to Pharaoh's court where he was trained and educated for forty years. It is my belief that Moses had not fully comprehended God's plan for his life during this period. Besides, history showed him to be quite an impulsive guy!

Once upon a time, he saw an Egyptian mistreating a Hebrew man and he intervened, killing the Egyptian. He struck him dead and hid his body in the sand, not knowing that his deed had been witnessed by someone. So one day when he saw two of his people fighting and attempted to resolve their problem, the one who saw his mischief objected with hostility, asking who made him a judge or ruler over them. He said, "Do you want to kill us like you killed the Egyptian?"

Moses was astonished. Fear gripped his entire being and the adrenalin in his body began to circulate rapidly. He therefore ran for his life to a place called Midian, a place of importance, because it was at this place that he met the love of his life. Here he met his future wife, Zipporah, who introduced him to Jethro, her father. Jethro was also a very important person. He was a priest whom God used to better the plan of Moses, the fugitive. Interestingly, Jethro became Moses' father-in-law, whom he served as a sheep-man. Nevertheless, it did not cross his mind at that time that God had saved him to fulfill His covenant with the people of Israel.

So on the far side of Mount Horeb, he took a lowly job tending the sheep of his father-in-law. The processes of God's work in one's life seem demeaning and insignificant at times. This is because we cannot fathom the spiritual or physical preparatory processes of our divine life and calling. The training process for our future can be very frustrating when we appear ignorant of God's ways. In a similar circumstance Moses spent forty years caring for the flocks and learning survival under a harsh climate totally opposite to what he had known in Egypt.

As mentioned earlier, Moses was a sheep-man, or shepherd, which means he was tending very dumb animals. It was probably also important for Moses to learn about how to survive in a desert, given that the Israelites would sojourn in a desert for forty years. Sheep require more attention than any other livestock, endless attention and meticulous care. Why was Moses a sheep trainer? This is interesting because the behavior of sheep and that of humans are similar in many ways. Our mass mind (mob instinct), our fear and timidity, our stubbornness, our stupidity, and our perverse habits are parallel to those of sheep, which has profound importance for our character study.

When you think for even a little while about the Israelites' stubbornness, disobedience and unbelieving attitudes in their walk with God, especially during the days of their wilderness journey to the Promised Land, you may be tempted to agree that the above illustration is a perfect picture of the Jews. So for Moses to become that leader who could tolerate, comprehend and handle the behavior of the Jews and to lead them to their Promised Land, God had to instruct him through the vocation of a shepherd.

It's therefore my prayer that God will raise up leaders in whatever portfolio—spiritual, political, economical, social and cultural—who have the wisdom and the experience to handle with care our lives which we have willingly submitted unto them either through votes or by the far side of Mount Horeb. What is the meaning of the word *Horeb*? It means "drought" or "desert." Again, I diligently thought about the far side of the mountain. While doing this mental exercise I concluded that the far side of the mountain could mean shortsightedness.

In other words, it's the inability for one to see what's happening ahead. The far side of the mountain could also be a place of infertility or unproductivity. It is a place of dryness, alienation, loneliness, rejection and insignificance. God loves to take control of the lives of His people at this point in life. What is quite interesting about this type of visitation from God is that He continues to show up until such a time when we can hear, listen, and obey His voice.

Once Moses had been trained, tested and tried, God assumed readiness to commission him. He appeared to Moses after He saw that He had passed the experience of the rugged and rough life of going after stray sheep. Moses had learned how to defend himself and the sheep from ferocious animals. He was now ready to be the prominent leader for God's chosen people held under Egyptian captivity. What a journey from sheep-tending to being one of Israel's greatest leaders and deliverers. This is how God will design your life if you turn to Him.

God's appearance to Moses was also quite strange. He appeared in a bush that was on fire yet was not consumed. Is this sight not exceptionally peculiar, for the truth is that fire burns and changes things? This odd phenomenon attracted Moses' attention. So he turned aside to take a good look at it, only to come face to face with Jehovah God.

It was one of the most important events in Moses' life. God spoke to him about his assigned task, that of delivering His people from bondage. How many of us would not appreciate God granting us such an encounter? But Moses saw his task as being very challenging, for he thought he was incapable of accomplishing God's plan. He therefore tried to back out of God's plan, lamenting to God about his weaknesses (Exodus 4:10-11). But the Lord told Moses that He had indeed seen the misery of His people, that He had heard their cry and was concerned about their suffering, and had chosen Moses to be the one to deliver Israel from Egypt. Moses would have to confront Pharaoh and tell him to let God's people go so that they could worship God in the wilderness.

As you may be aware, Moses found the task and the time of the commission very difficult, so it was imperative to him that he finds answers to a few questions from God. Thus, he asked the Lord, "Who must I say sent me?" God told him, "I Am that I Am." Again, Moses complained, "But the Egyptians will not believe me." Therefore God recommended to him to show forth His amazing power to Pharaoh by using the rod in his hand.

Let's take a moment to look at the significance of the rod. I believe the rod was a representation of failure in the life of Moses, for he gave up the splendor of Egypt and fled as a murderer to take the rod of a shepherd, a very low-standard life compared to his life at Pharaoh's palace. More often than not, the significant use of a rod is to drive off vicious preying animals. It's also used to beat or drive away snakes and other creatures disturbing the flock.

Nevertheless, when the Spirit of God came upon the rod, it was turned from a symbol of failure into a rod of victory. It became a symbol of strength, power, and authority as exhibited in Pharaoh's palace when Moses encountered the magicians of Egypt. Prior to that encounter, God told Moses to throw down his rod to the ground and it became a snake. I believe initially he was frightened out of his wits, but the Lord instructed him to take the snake by the tail and it returned into a rod. Therefore Moses discovered how powerful and wonderful the Spirit of God over the rod could be, and he used it to perform miracles before the hard-hearted Pharaoh and also to divide the impassable Red Sea.

As Christians, we also have what it takes to get the job done. We must endeavor to use the rod of God's Word when faced by mountainous situations. There is no substitute for the Scriptures when coping with the complexities of life. Jesus used the words "It is written" when Satan came tempting Him in the wilderness, therefore in every situation we will have to use the rod of God's Word to meet or master the difficulties of life. Nevertheless, Moses continued talking to God about his weaknesses. Exodus 4:10 says, "Moses said to the Lord, 'O Lord, I have never been eloquent, neither in the past nor since you have spoken to your servant. I am slow of speech and tongue.'" God encouraged and instructed Moses to go and He would be with him.

After God had provided Aaron the brother of Moses as a helper, he finally obeyed and decided to confront Pharaoh, who later finally freed the Jews after God had sent a series of plagues on Egypt. Now that the Jews were finally set free and were on their journey to the Promised Land, God instructed Moses to speak to His people. God instructed the people to turn and encamp before Pihahiroth, between Midgol and the sea over against Baalzephon. His presence was with the Israelites through a cloud by day and a pillar of fire by night. Also, the Lord reassured them of His presence, guiding them and providing for them while they camped by the sea. There were many obstacles, but God was faithful to His people. For instance, after Israel had left Egypt, God hardened the heart of Pharaoh and the Egyptian officials. They changed their mind from allowing Israel to leave their land and pursued them, for which cause God opened the Red Sea, which became salvation to Israel but destruction to Egypt.

Today if your enemies are pursuing you, decide to turn your life to God and He will open the "Red Sea," that impassable and insurmountable situation before you. That unbearable situation shall become a means of salvation to you but destruction to your enemies.

For the apostle Peter said, "If this is so, then the Lord knows how to rescue godly men from trials and to hold the unrighteous for the day of judgment, while continuing their punishment" (2 Peter 2:9). All the same, can you imagine the Israelites' plight when they lifted up their eyes and saw the Egyptians coming? They were sore afraid. Sensing they were between a rock and a hard place, they cried out to God. They then grumbled against Moses, but this great leader was not perturbed, for he had learned how to offer comfort when shepherding his father-in-law's disgruntled flock.

In fact, to him it was rather a time to take charge. In this regard, he became a comforter to these panic-stricken folks: "He said to them, fear not, stand still and see the salvation of the Lord, which He shall bring you today. For the Egyptians you see today, you will never see them again. The Lord shall fight for you. You shall hold your peace" (see Exodus 14:13). Later Moses cried out to the Lord for the salvation of His people. But God, the ever-present help in time of trouble, said to Moses, "Why are you crying out to me? Speak unto the children of Israel that they go forward" (see v. 15). God saw that moment too as a time for action, so He told Moses to lift up his rod and to stretch his hand over the sea.

That action divided the water for the children of Israel to cross the sea on dry land. It was indeed a miraculous intervention! During a time of action, God will show those who turn to Him or put their trust in Him a word that can save them from all dangers and attacks of Satan and his cohorts. During the act of this salvation, the waters became a wall unto the Jews on their right and on their left. But when the Egyptians continued to pursue them, God instructed Moses to stretch out his hand over the sea to engulf the Egyptians, their chariots and their horsemen in the Red Sea.

While Moses maintained his stretched out hand over the sea, all the Egyptians drowned, and the Israelites, seeing their bodies upon the seashore, feared the Lord and put their trust in Him and in Moses his servant. Moses and all the Israelites were inspired to sing unto God, who had defeated their enemies and had given them the victory. In fact, there are many songs that were penned while the authors of such songs were in great sorrow and peril. In the oracles of God, we are informed to make melody in our hearts unto the Lord when we are faced with adverse situations and even when victory seems not to be in sight. For it's significantly edifying to use what you have to glorify God.

After this victory, Moses and God's people continued their journey to the Promised Land, but they had to face other obstacles. For instance, while they journeyed in a sun-parched land, they desired water but there was none. The water they found was bitter, which agitated them to complain heavily against Moses and his God. He therefore lifted up his voice and cried unto the Lord, who instructed him to put the leaves of a tree into the water, and behold, the water was made sweet. This was their Marah (or bitter water), but God intervened.

In today's world the cross of Christ can take the bitterness of life out of all of your experiences, just as God provided the Hebrews with food they had not known and victory over the Amalekites. From one experience to another, they journeyed to Reph-i-dim, and when they came to the desert of Sinai, they pitched their tents in the wilderness and camped there in front of a mountain.

It was a time to hear from God, and He spoke to Moses about how special His chosen people were. He told Moses that He brought His people out of Egypt on eagles' wings to be His treasured possession. He therefore directed Moses to gather the elders and all the people and to sanctify them for three days, and on the third day He would come down on Mount Sinai for the people of Israel to see Him. Exodus 19:14 says that Moses went down from the mountain and sanctified or consecrated the people and they washed their clothes.

What did it mean to sanctify or consecrate the Israelites? It means that the Israelites were supposed to be called from their worldly business to religious disciplines, meditation and prayer, that they might receive the Law from God's mouth with awe and devotion.

One author says, "They were to be made ready since they might have gathered wondering thoughts, impure affections and disquieting passions which ought to be suppressed so that their hearts would be engaged to approach God". Here God is teaching His children the attitude they ought to cultivate when approaching His throne for divine instructions and to worship Him. The apostle James said, "Therefore, get rid of all moral filth and the evil that is so prevalent and humbly accept the word planted in you, which can save you" (James 1:21).

What was the significance for them to wash their clothes? God had little regard for their clothes, but He knew that while they were washing their clothes they would be thinking of washing their souls, an act of repentance from the sins they had contracted in Egypt. It's significant in our society for us to appear in clean clothes when approaching great men, so all the more this awesome God whom we serve. Similarly, pure hearts and clean hands are required in our attendance to this awesome God, who is omniscient. Nothing is hidden from Him; everything is laid bare before His eyes that soar throughout the universe.

On the third day after the Israelites had experienced the turning of the bitter waters into sweet, the people sanctified themselves and washed their clothes. There was thunder and lightning and a thick cloud upon the mountain. Exodus 19:18 says, "Mount Sinai was covered with smoke, because the Lord descended on it in fire. The smoke billowed up from it like smoke from a furnace, the whole mountain trembled violently." The Lord descended on the top of Mount Sinai and called unto Moses, and he ascended.

A sermon was preached which has never been preached before nor which will ever be preached again, because it was God Omnipotent preaching. It was a preaching that came to God's people in the wilderness. Deuteronomy 4:33 says, "Has any other people heard the voice of God speaking out of fire, as you have, and lived?" I believe the message was unique because the preacher here was God himself! The Lord descended on Mount Sinai and the Shekinah, or the glory of God, appeared in the sight of all the people. What a sight! According to the Scriptures, the congregation was called together by the sound of a trumpet, exceedingly loud, which waxed louder and louder. The service was introduced by thunder and lightning, and the sounds and sights were designed to strike awe upon the people and to engage their attention should they be sleeping.

The thunder came to awaken them should they be gazing or looking in another direction. I believe the lightning would engage them to turn their faces toward Him who spoke to them because they needed a face-to-face encounter with God, as Moses did, for them to see that God meant what He said. It's noteworthy to know that thunder is the voice of God and lightning the fire of God which, when used properly, will engage the eyes of our understanding, giving us spiritual insight. It's through our senses that we receive much information. It was on this mountain of God that Moses said that the Ten Commandments were written by the fingers of God on stone tablets. Moses reported in Exodus 33:11 that God spoke to him face to face. What an awesome account of God's providential care regarding His chosen vessel of honor!

Moses was a destiny child who was born in a perilous time, but God was with him every step of the way directing, protecting and providing for him. Amid diverse situations, this outstanding leader never sought the attention of others for advice but cried out to God at all times, and God was faithful to him. It is therefore imperative that we turn aside and pay attention to the Lord at all times. If Moses had not turned aside or not taken heed to the call of God, we would not have had the Pentateuch, or the first five books of the Bible, nor his songs. I hereby admonish you to turn aside or around and see what the Lord God of Hosts has for you, also what He will enable you to do.

Prayer: Our Father who art in heaven, holy is Your name. Forevermore You are God, and so we desire to turn aside or around to see You and look upon Your face. May we stay at the far side of our Horeb until we are commissioned by You. Help us to fulfill our destiny despite the many mountainous situations we may face as we journey on this pilgrim's pathway. Amen.

Different phases of one's life may seem demeaning and insignificant at times. This is because we cannot fathom the divine or physical preparation of our divine life and calling. The training process for our future can be very frustrating when we appear ignorant of God's ways.

CHAPTER 6

HANNAH'S PENINNAH LED HER TO TURN TO THE GOD OF HER SALVATION

Without any shadow of a doubt, you will agree with me that when the cares of life pin you down, our initial response may not be courageous. As a matter of fact, sometimes when you are pinned down it seems impossible to undo the bands or strongholds that hold you strong. One's turning to God will be comprised of inward stamina and a choice to cry out to the Lord. In this troubled world full of complexities and stress, it is natural to sulk and complain, to shrink back and be devastated when faced with diverse temptations. More so, as humans we lack what it takes to make us identify with the Word of the Lord during times of trial, even though we have been admonished by the apostle James: "Consider it pure joy, my brothers, whenever you face trials of many kinds, because you know that the testing of your faith develops perseverance. Perseverance must finish its work so that you may be mature and complete, not lacking anything" (James 1:2-4).

Also, 1 Peter 4:12-13 says, "Dear friends, do not be surprised at the painful trial you are suffering, as though something strange were happening to you. But rejoice that you participate in the sufferings of Christ, so that you may be overjoyed when his glory is revealed." There are many Christians who cannot accept these comforting scriptures when under trials, and the question they frequently ask is, "Why?" There are other people who believe that Christians should live a test-free life, forgetting that even Jesus was tested, as evidenced in his prayers He turned to God the Father for support.

Christ's earthly life is an exemplary life intended to edify, to comfort and to strengthen all saints in Christ and also to illustrate the availability of God's grace that helps when we boldly approach His throne. So in order for us to comprehend and rectify some of these negative tendencies and numerous challenges, 2 Timothy 3:16-17 asserts that "all Scripture is God-breathed and is useful for teaching, rebuking, correcting and training in righteousness, so that the man of God may be thoroughly equipped for every good work."

Hannah, a devout woman of God, is a perfect model in the Old Testament from whom we can learn and draw inspiration to teach us how endurance can help us turn to God for salvation. Despite the fact that this woman was just and righteous, she had a domestic or family problem, and the way she handled that problem presents an example that virtuous women of God have to emulate should they be faced with their mountainous situations. Hannah had a husband, El-ka-nah, who was married to another woman, Peninnah. Please take note, polygamy was permitted in those days. Peninnah was very fertile and bore El-ka-nah's children, but Hannah, the woman El-ka-nah loved, was barren.

What made the situation worse was that her rival provoked her into deep depression. There were times that the ridicules, the insinuations and the domestic pressures from her rival left her without any desire to eat food, and she wept bitterly continually. There were also times her husband had made several attempts to comfort her, but she was inconsolable. Should we, for a moment, try to empathize or wear this woman's shoes, especially how she overcame her mountainous situation, we would grasp precious spiritual nuggets from this interesting account. Hannah's rival had successfully pinned her down into utter despair, but her provocation rather turned out for Hannah's good. Eventually she rose up one day and found her refuge in the temple of the Lord. She knew no one could help, so she turned to the hills of God, the One who made the heavens and the earth and had the capability of touching her infertile womb and causing her to procreate as depicted in 1 Samuel 1:10. I may not be able to give that picture vividly, but the scripture says she was in bitterness of soul and prayed unto the Lord and wept sorely. In verse 13 the Word of the Lord says that she spoke in her heart; only her lips moved, but her voice was not heard.

If you were a spectator you might think this woman was more or less a nut-head. So did Eli, the priest of the Temple, who thought she was drunk and thus scolded her. But this outstanding woman of God maintained her integrity and humbly told the priest that she was not drunk. "Would it not look awkward should I be drunk at this hour of the day?" she said. "Besides," Hannah said, "I am a woman who is deeply troubled. I have not been drinking wine or strong drink; I was pouring out my soul to the Lord. Do not take your servant for a wicked woman. Rather, it's because anguish and grief have eaten me up that you see me offer this manner of prayer" (see 1 Samuel 1:15-16).

Hearing this, Eli discontinued scolding her, and with sympathy and confidence blessed her. He told her to go in peace and may the God of Israel grant her what she had requested. Hannah responded, "May your servant find favor in your eyes" (v. 18). With her faith now built up, she arose and ate some food to brighten her face. That morning she joined the family to worship the Lord and later went back home to Ramah. Thereafter, El-ka-nah lay with her and the Lord remembered her. She conceived and gave birth to a son, whom she called Samuel, saying, "Because I asked the Lord for him" (v. 20).

Hannah's story is very emotional as well as inspirational. It shows us how imperative it is for us to always turn aside or around and focus on the Lord despite our diverse and insurmountable situations. Hannah's prayer was effective; it touched the heart of God and brought about the realization of her specific request. She made a vow unto the Lord and faithfully kept it by offering her only son unto the Lord to serve Him all the days of his life.

Again, Hannah's story is a wonderful lesson for us. It teaches us not to be anxious about anything, but in everything, by prayer and supplication, we are to make our request known unto the Lord, who is able to do much more than we can imagine. God does not want us to remain barren or unproductive. So He has provided us a throne room where we can enter boldly and offer our requests for salvation and deliverance. Although one may be provoked or misunderstood during desperate times, prayer is the key that brings our desire to reality. You see, persistence in prayer pays off.

1 Samuel 2:1-11 offers us a model which enables us to look at the significance of Hannah's prayer. Her prayer or conversation with the Lord was not overshadowed with her personal needs but was full of praise and thanksgiving to God for the things He had done for her. She sang, "My soul rejoices in the Lord." An echo of this verse occurs in Philippians 4:4, which says, "Rejoice in the Lord always. I will say it again: Rejoice!" Hannah had all the reason to rejoice, for she was now blessed with the blessing of motherhood, which all women long for. She said, "My horn is lifted high," which symbolizes strength. Just as an animal's strength is concentrated in its horn, so Hannah laid her strength in the Lord's goodness for the son He gave her.

This portion of her prayer, "Neither is there any rock like our God," is a favorite simile among Israel-inspired poets, since the rocks of Sinai and Palestine supplied an ever-present picture of God's unchangeable majesty and of the eternal safety found in Him. The term *rock* was first applied to God by Moses in his song of salvation, which indicates that Hannah might be acquainted with the national hymn of Israel's greatest lawgiver. She also described the Lord as a God of knowledge by whom actions are weighed. Here it's important to observe that the Lord clearly and perfectly sees the inward character of every person and gives knowledge and understanding to those who seek Him.

Hannah discovered that the God she was praying to reverses human conditions. That is, He can bring low the wicked and exalt the righteous. The focus of this woman's prayer amplified God's justice and caused Him to balance the scales, giving God no other choice than to lift her up. To make it even more enchanting, at the conclusion of her prayer the magnification of the Lord's sovereign wisdom and power in dealing with humanity was made vivid, which also implies that by human strength shall no man prevail. It underlines the truth that whosoever opposes the Lord will be defeated. Hannah's prayer is an interesting prayer to meditate or reflect on. Her testimony is a challenge to everybody, even Christians. It's intended to motivate all to seek God regardless of what their situation might be.

Prayer is incomprehensible. It is a force that brings hope, but since it's a spiritual exercise, we cannot see with our physical eyes how God brings to pass the materialization of the intended answers to our prayers. Let us bask in this force for a little while to build up our most sacred faith. Before we conclude, let us consider this first: What is prayer? I believe it is the most powerful force in the world available to us and the greatest means at our disposal to fulfill the great commission. According to one writer, "Prayer is the match that is used to ignite the explosive power of the Holy Ghost in the affairs of men".

E. M. Bounds wrote, "Prayer may well be defined as that which vitalizes and energizes the Word of God to enable us to take hold of the promises of God." It is indeed awesome that we have this wonderful privilege through which we can make our request known to God. Oh what a consolation it is for us to have this privilege! He who has promised us is faithful and will answer all our prayers if only we would pray according to His will.

In conclusion to this wonderful account of Hannah's story, here are two verses of Scripture from 1 John 5:14-15 that I hope will keep your spirit alive and high until your desire and hope materializes: "This is the confidence we have in approaching God: that if we ask anything according to his will, he hears us. And if we know that he hears us—whatever we ask— we know that we have what we asked of him." Why not rise up now, turn, and enter the throne of grace and talk to your Father?

Prayer: Father, may our prayer reach up into Your bosom and cause You to shift Your attention to us. We thank You for access to the throne of grace to make our requests known unto You. When others do not understand what we are wrestling with, may we humble ourselves and behave wisely before God and men. For You are faithful to do much more than we can imagine. Amen.

> God does not want us to remain barren or unproductive. So He has provided us a throne room where we can enter boldly and offer our requests for salvation and deliverance. Although one may be provoked or misunderstood during desperate times, prayer is the key that brings our desire to reality. You see, persistence in prayer pays off.

CHAPTER 7

ELIZABETH: A WOMAN OF PRAYER AND PROPHECY

I will attempt in this chapter to deal with the erroneous conception that a child of God must always walk uprightly, godly and circumspectly to the finish line, and that everything pertaining to his/her life should be balanced for his/her dreams to be fulfilled.

To justify the above statement, we need a critical survey of the Scriptures. That is, we must look at the Word of God from beginning to end, realizing that all those wonderful Bible characters we have read about and admired had elements of trouble during their time on earth. So although we may pray effective prayers, like the prophet Elijah there will be areas in our lives for the potter to break, mold and melt until we are made into a masterpiece for the Master's use.

What I would also like you to bear in mind is that no man was ever created with the capacity to fathom God's ways. But He is more than capable of helping us to understand why we experience certain things in our lives. Let us therefore delve into the life of Elizabeth to pull out some spiritual nuggets to help us build our faith. According to the Word of the Lord, Elizabeth was a righteous woman. She was a woman of prayer, as was her husband, Zechariah. In Luke 1:6 the Word of the Lord says that both of them were upright in the sight of God, observing all the Lord's commandments and all regulations blamelessly.

This very outstanding woman was married to a priest, and priests in those days prepared the sacrifices to be offered up to God. Zechariah, Elizabeth's husband, spent two weeks serving the Lord in the Temple. He had the unique opportunity to offer incense before the Holy of Holies. The picture I am drawing is intended to bring to your imagination the righteousness or uprightness of this couple before God. Isn't it therefore incredible that this righteous couple, Elizabeth and Zechariah, failed to procreate despite their earnest quest to have children? Indeed, according to the Scriptures Elizabeth was barren and stricken in age. What this means biologically is that Elizabeth would have a problem with childbearing, even though God the Creator of all things later intervened miraculously.

What was His plan behind the challenges of this devout couple? Dearly beloved, have you ever paid a little respect to the challenges you are currently facing to comprehend the precious enterprise you are about to establish for which cause you have to go through these disciplines?

God got involved with the couple's problem because He intended to make a pathway for the introduction of Jesus, His Son, who was in His bosom but would be revealed as a ransom to take away the sins of all mankind. It's after you have been tested and tried that you can be trusted. God will never entrust into your hands the life and destiny of His people until you have proven your worth. Remember what Paul told Timothy concerning such disciplines: "No one serving as a soldier gets involved in civilian affairs—he wants to please his commanding officer. Similarly, if anyone competes as an athlete, he does not receive the victor's crown unless he competes according to the rules" (2 Timothy 2:4-5).

Just as God at the appointed time sent Gabriel with a message to Zechariah, so will He visit at the time He has predestined for you. You see, Zechariah was ministering in the Temple when he had the angelic visitation. It is therefore quite interesting for you to note this: Whoever labors diligently for the Lord will be rewarded by Him. God knows all our desires and He is able to bring them to pass.

According to God's Word in Luke 1:8-17, Elizabeth's husband was offering incense in the Temple when he had an angelic visitation. When the angel appeared at the right side of the altar, Zechariah was gripped with fear, but the wise angel consoled him. He told him not to be afraid, because his prayer had been heard.

What was the priest's request? It could have been his long-standing request for a son or his general petitions for the coming Messiah, or both. The fact of the matter is that both were shortly accomplished. The angel revealed to Zechariah that his wife would bear a son and his name would be called John. The angel said that this boy would not be an ordinary child, but he would be a joy and delight to him and many would rejoice because of his birth. He told Zechariah that this special boy would be great in the sight of the Lord. He instructed that John was never to drink wine or fermented drink, and the most interesting thing that gripped my attention is the fact that he would be filled with the Holy Spirit from birth.

John was born to be a vessel for a special purpose. He was destined to bring back many of the flock of Israel to the Lord. The sacred Book of the Lord tells us that John would precede Jesus and would carry the power and spirit of Elijah to turn the hearts of the fathers to their children and the disobedient to righteousness—to make ready a people prepared for the Lord. Naturally speaking, the news was very mind-boggling. It therefore clouded Zechariah's spiritual mind with earthly issues that jostled his faith. Therefore he fleshly asked the God-sent messenger how this was going to be, considering that he was old and his wife was also stricken in age. Gabriel responded, "I stand in the presence of God, and I have been sent to speak to you and to tell you this good news" (Luke 1:19). Furthermore, he told Zechariah that because he did not believe his word, he would be dumb and would not be able to speak until the day the child was born.

Frankly, I have thought about Zechariah's saga over and over again, and I'm assuming you may have also pondered several times the very interesting issue of why God made Zechariah mute. I have wondered if the angel's rebuke was too harsh since Zechariah's saga was just lack of faith.

Doubts marred his mind and heart, for which cause he was given a period of silent reflection that lasted until his son was born. Or was it God's intention to place Zechariah into that state for him to lay hold and grasp what God was doing in his life?

Probably, God was teaching him how to trust Him more even though he was a righteous man. I'm trying to convince myself that the period of silence may have caused him to think, meditate or ponder over the goodness and marvelous work of God. I believe those days brought to his senses reasons why it's not helpful for one to doubt the works of God. I also believe that this experience might have increased his faith to inwardly accept the fact that God is able to bring His promises to pass.

The Word of the Lord tells us in Luke 1:23-25 that when Zechariah's time of service was completed, he returned home. Later his wife Elizabeth became pregnant and for five months remained in seclusion. I believe Elizabeth was joyful with her pregnancy, because being barren in those days was considered a disgrace. She said, "Look what the Lord has done," and again, "The Lord has done this for me in these last days; he has taken away my disgrace among the people." Imagine for a minute or reflect on Elizabeth's pregnancy with her husband. This woman at her youthful age has sought for a child but to no avail.

Don't you agree that becoming pregnant in her old age, Elizabeth would have had very good reasons to express her emotions and joy to her husband? How terrible it must have been to go through that experience. On the other hand, it's also reasonable to believe that Elizabeth might have spoken to her husband since there are other ways her husband could respond to her, but not with a speech to console her. Interestingly, it's when a woman is pregnant that she needs all the attention and tender, loving care from her husband, but in Elizabeth's case it was different. The problem was that Elizabeth's beloved soulmate was dumb.

What would she be thinking about during these trying times? What kind of peace had God given her to carry this ordeal? When a woman is pregnant her whole anatomy and physiology are affected. It's apparent that this woman would need faith to bear the condition she found herself in. You will probably agree with me that this situation was a real test of faith for Elizabeth, but God was in control. She had no choice in such circumstances but to turn to God and truly believe that His hand was upon her life.

She had been told that she carried a destiny child, but the morbid conditions she was in needed specific answers to bear it. Therefore God had to perform a greater task in this situation. According to Paul's first letter to the Corinthians, the purpose of prophecy is to edify, exhort and comfort. Could it therefore mean that Elizabeth needed a word of prophecy to edify, exhort and comfort her? What did God have in mind for her in that situation? Lo, there was another woman very close to Elizabeth whom God thought of using to inspire His daughter. What is quite interesting about this other woman is that she was Elizabeth's relative. Her name was Mary, the future mother of Jesus.

She knew that Elizabeth was pregnant, but Elizabeth did not know that Mary was pregnant. The God we serve is wise and perfect. This supernatural Being of perfection orchestrated a meeting for these two precious vessels. Again, let's see what we can grasp from this encounter! The Word of the Lord says that when Mary became pregnant, she hurried to Judea to visit Elizabeth. Mary was excited and full of joy to see Elizabeth, so she greeted her, and lo and behold, something supernatural happened. Baby John the Baptist, filled with the Holy Ghost from birth, leaped in his mother's womb, and instantly she also was filled with the Holy Ghost.

Now the one who rather needed prophecy to edify, exhort and comfort herself began to prophesy to Mary, who also needed a word from God to boost her faith. She had to be convinced that her unusual situation was from God. So, with a loud voice Elizabeth prophesied to Mary, saying: "Blessed are you among women, and blessed is the child you will bear!" (Luke 1:42). But since she did not have all the answers, she questioned God in her prophecy: "Why am I so favored, that the mother of my Lord should come to me?" (v. 43).

Let's not blame the poor woman for her utterance since we have also acted unspiritual under similar circumstances, especially when we find ourselves in situations where we fail to understand the puzzles of life or figure out the process that God might be taking us through. Elizabeth, however, told Mary that as soon as the sound of her greeting reached her ears, the baby in her womb leaped for joy. This is exciting and interesting. The mother of the forerunner of Jesus Christ was used mightily by God to bring words of comfort to the woman charged with bringing forth the plan of salvation for the world.

In this scenario the significance of the role of prophetess in the body of Christ was magnified. Therefore, if God has raised you up to be that woman, present yourself a living sacrifice unto Him, which is your reasonable service. I need to bring to your attention this outstanding prophetic gift. The apostle Paul wrote to the Corinthians saying, "Follow after charity and desire spiritual gifts, but it is better that you prophesy" (see 1 Corinthians 14:1). But who is a prophetess?

There is a biblical commentary that teaches that a prophetess was a woman who exercised the prophetic gift in ancient Israel or in the early Christian church. In general, a prophetess is any woman who possesses the charismatic gifts and powers of a prophet. In the Old Testament there are four women who have this designation. Miriam, the sister of Moses (found in Exodus 15:20); Deborah, another outstanding woman (Judges 4:4); Huldah (2 Kings 22:14); and the unnamed wife of Isaiah, who bore him children (Isaiah 8:3). According to biblical commentary, prophesying was extensively done in the early church. It was a spiritual gift that supernaturally empowered or built up God's family. Those with this gift either proclaimed to God's people new truth from God or challenged them with existing scriptural truths. 1 Corinthians 11:4-5 says that both men and women prophesy.

I believe it is important to take a look at another prophetess in the New Testament. This woman was Anna, the daughter of Phanuel. She was a widow of great age. The Word of the Lord tells us that she was eighty-four years old, and she departed not from the Temple but served God with fasting and prayer day and night. Anna's gift functioned when Mary and Joseph took Jesus to Jerusalem to present Him to the Lord. It is written in Luke 2:38 that she gave thanks to God, and in that instant she spoke about Jesus to all those who looked for redemption in Jerusalem. Prophecy functions as a consolation for the body of Christ. The believer needs comforting words for the journey to the finish line, and since a word of prophecy amplifies one's faith and allows one to lay hold of the word or promise of

God, the gift of a prophetess cannot be overemphasized. Let this be a word of encouragement for the believers of Christ.

You are destined for greatness, and God desires to use your mind and heart to comfort the comfortless in times of need. Give birth to that prophetic ministry and let no one despise you. Your life may be in turmoil, but you are a vessel that can be used for the Master Potter. What I would like you to bear in mind is the truth that the prophecy of Elizabeth caused Mary the mother of Jesus Christ to sing praises unto God. This is a joyful thing and it is marvelous. Walk before God blamelessly and purpose in your heart to pray without ceasing. God is the Rewarder of those who seek Him diligently.

Prayer: Lord Jesus, raise up prophetesses and prayer warriors in your Body to encourage, edify and comfort believers. Fan into flames the gifts of prophecy that have remained dormant, and let there be an explosion and manifestation of the needed ministry or gift in the Lord's name. Amen.

> The believer needs comforting words for the journey to the finish line, and since a word of prophecy amplifies one's faith and allows one to lay hold of the word or promise of God, the gift of a prophetess cannot be overemphasized.

CHAPTER 8

ALL GENERATION SHALL CALL HER BLESSED

Hebrews 13:4 states that marriage is an honorable institution. Thanks be to God for this noble institution and for His Word, which shows that He instituted marriage for both man and woman and for their maximum pleasure. However, what is marriage? Marriage is an intimate union to which a man and woman consent, continuously nourished by sexual intercourse in a lifelong partnership of mutual love and commitment. According to *Zondervan's Pictorial Dictionary*, it is also a social institution regulated by the Word of God and by laws and customs developed by society to safeguard its continuity and welfare. It is also an order of creation. The Creator made man and woman, projecting His full image as both man and woman.

This is awesome, and the wise and perfect God whom we serve made man for woman and woman for man, that their essential natures would complement one another and bring both of them into oneness. Genesis 2:24 says, "Therefore shall a man leave his father and mother, and shall cleave unto his wife: and they shall be one flesh" (KJV). Matthew 19:4-6 says, "'Haven't you read,' he replied, 'that at the beginning the Creator "made them male and female," and said, "For this reason a man will leave his father and mother and be united to his wife, and the two will become one flesh"? So they are no longer two, but one. Therefore what God has joined together, let man not separate."

Marriage is a formal religious rite or act and in some religious traditions, such as Roman Catholicism, is known as a sacrament. Most Protestant traditions do not see it as a sacrament. It is therefore appropriate to say that marriage is a sacrament of human society. Under it, husband and wife share and perpetuate their happiness in bearing and raising a family within the sphere of their own love. One writer says, the unity of husband and wife is of God's creative will, and from Him come the love and grace which enable the couple to grow together in life comradeship, to beget children, and to fulfill their responsibilities toward their children and to society as a family unit.

Marriage is a desirable institution or state and involves every nation of God's people. Ceremonies may be varied, but marriage was instituted by God. God is to be praised for ordaining marriage, and the first performance was in the very beginning with our first fore-parents, Adam and Eve. Throughout the Bible, one can see quite vividly that marriage was an honorable act among God's people. In the New Testament, we read about a poor peasant girl who reached the age of accountability and maturity to marry. The Word of the Lord declares that this girl was espoused to a man named Joseph.

Being espoused or betrothed is what we now call engagement. It is interesting to note that unlike in the twentieth century, first-century engagement was a binding premarital contract leading to marriage. During the period of engagement, the couple behaved like husband and wife (except that they did not live together or have sex). To break off or annul such an engagement, a divorce was required. I believe this young woman lived a life of expectancy, joyfully waiting for her marriage to be consummated. I believe she very much desired to be with Joseph to love him and bear his children, but she did not know that God had something else in mind. God the Omniscient One, the Creator of mankind, saw that the marriage that He had instituted to be pure, perfect and binding was in disarray.

The first marriage in the Garden of Eden had failed, and sin's invasion had caused man's relationship with God to be broken. Now God, desiring a relationship and fellowship with His people, told

Satan in Genesis 3:15, "And I will put enmity between you and the woman, and between your offspring and hers; he will crush your head, and you will strike his heel." The apostle Paul also wrote to the Galatians concerning the relationship God intended to raise through the offspring of this woman, saying, "But when the time had fully come, God sent his Son, born of a woman, born under the law" (4:4). This particular woman of God was a chaste vessel; in fact, the Word of the Lord declares that she was a virgin. However, God foresaw that this chaste virgin was planning a wedding that would disrupt His desire for the human world.

God also knew that the time before the child's birth would be a trying time for the virgin and her betrothed, so He summoned Gabriel and sent him with a message to this chosen woman of God. Gabriel told her she was highly favored and the Lord was with her. I believe she was shaken and felt nervous as she wondered about the angel's salutation. She was surely troubled, but the wise angel comforted her, saying, "You are favored by God and will indeed give birth to a son, and you shall call His name Jesus" (see Luke 1:30-31).

This would be quite frightening news to any woman of God. So the angel said to her, "[Jesus] will be great and will be called the Son of the Most High. The Lord God will give him the throne of his father David, and he will reign over the house of Jacob forever; his kingdom will never end" (vv. 32-33). But humanly speaking, wouldn't this be very disturbing news to Mary? It might sound like a fairy tale. Naturally, she knew this method of childbearing would not be possible, for she was a virgin. So she proceeded to ask a very important question: "How will this be . . . since I am a virgin?" (v. 34).

Therefore the angel answered Mary that the Holy Ghost would come upon her and the power of the Most High would overshadow her, so the Holy One to be born would be called the Son of God. This was more than she could comprehend! She could not swallow this word at that moment, for it was too profound, so the angel began to testify to her since her faith needed to be boosted. Therefore God's angel inspired Mary's relative, Elizabeth, who was stricken in age and once was barren but now pregnant, to let Mary see the big picture. Thus, when she visited Elizabeth with that expectation, she was told, "With God nothing is impossible."

Mary believed and ceased leaning on her own understanding regarding the situation. Luke 1:38 indicates that after her initial questions, she immediately acquiesced to God's will, turning to God and saying, "I am the Lord's servant, may it be to me as you have said. Be it unto me according to your word." I believe it was that moment that the process for the Word of God to become flesh began in her womb. God garbed himself in flesh to redeem mankind from their sins. What a journey from heaven to earth! What a great sacrifice!

At the time Mary went to visit her relative, the Word of the Lord declares that she went down to Judea hastily and greeted Elizabeth, and lo and behold, baby John leaped for joy in the womb of his mother. There is no reason to question this leap for joy, for the baby was anointed with the Holy Ghost, and the angel also said that this John would cause joy and gladness and many would rejoice at his birth. The leap for joy that took place in the womb of Elizabeth caused her to be filled with the Holy Ghost, and she who had not prophesied before began to prophesy.

Luke 1:42-45 says, "In a loud voice she exclaimed: 'Blessed are you among women, and blessed is the child you will bear! But why am I so favored, that the mother of my Lord should come to me? As soon as the sound of your greeting reached my ears, the baby in my womb leaped for joy. Blessed is she who has believed that what the Lord has said to her will be accomplished!'" Something awesome happened to Mary: she was relieved of her anxiety, confusion, fear and disbelief, and her faith culminated within her and the eyes of her understanding were enlightened. The Word of the Lord declares that faith comes by hearing, and hearing by the Word of God.

Mary understood the word of prophecy and she laid hold of it. It was the word she heard that released the praise of God. Instead of bewilderment, she was now wearing the garment of praise. This song of praise she sang is known as the *Magnificat* and it is recorded in Luke 1:46-55. When the appointed time came for her to give birth, she brought forth her firstborn, Jesus of Nazareth, the Savior of the world. Jesus became the good tidings of great joy which was for all people. Israel, including Simeon, had long waited for the birth of the Messiah. Simeon was a devout man of God. Luke 2:26-35 declares that he was waiting for the consolation of Israel: "And the Holy

Ghost was upon him. And it was revealed unto him by the Holy Ghost, that he should not see death, before he had seen the Lord's Christ" (KJV).

He came by the Spirit into the Temple when the parents of Jesus brought Him to the Temple to do for Him after the custom of the law. Simeon took the child Jesus in his arms and blessed God. He said, "Lord, let now Your servant depart in peace, according to Your word: for mine eyes have seen Your salvation which You have prepared before the face of all people. This salvation is a light to lighten the Gentiles and the glory of Your people Israel" (see vv. 29-32). This special Seed, the Word, the boy of this woman, was no ordinary child. Luke 2:40 says, "And the child grew and became strong; he was filled with wisdom, and the grace of God was upon him." Jesus increased in wisdom and stature and in favor with God and man. At the age of twelve, he debated with the teachers of the law and they were baffled at His wisdom and great understanding. This woman's seed, or child, was up for the big question! The Bible tells us that the onlookers asked questions about Mary's seed.

This was the Light John spoke of that would lighten the path for all people and bring glory, honor and praise to God. Jesus knew who He was and read His mission statement about Himself. This fact can be found in the Luke 4:16-22 and Isaiah 61:1-2. Your plan may seem imperfect, but the Word of the Lord declares that the Lord has a plan to prosper you and not harm you, a plan to give you hope and a future. We will not be able to understand all that He desires to do, and we may at times respond just like Mary and any other Bible character when we hear of the amazing things God intends to do with and for us.

However, let us surrender and say, like Mary, "I am the Lord's servant; be it unto me according to Your word." Then our pliability will change to strength because of the word of God, which is life and light. It's active and sharp enough to cut into the heart, where it will abide. If you allow it to be planted in your spirit, it will develop in you, and then at God's appointed time, you will give birth to your promised baby. No matter how painful it is to birth your baby, push it out for the world to see. Let your baby be a blessing to those who see it, and they will give praise to God.

Prayer: Father in heaven, though we may not understand Your plan for our lives, help us to surrender and listen to the still small voice of the Holy Spirit at all times. May we say with confidence, "I am the Lord's servant; be it unto me according to Your word." Lord, help us to give birth to that ministry, because somebody's life depends on it. Amen.

> Your plan may seem imperfect, but the Word of the Lord declares that the Lord has a plan to prosper you and not harm you, a plan to give you hope and a future. We will not be able to understand all that He desires to do, and we may at times respond just like Mary and any other Bible character when we hear of the amazing things God intends to do with and for us.

CHAPTER 9

A MAN AFTER GOD'S OWN HEART

There is a human tendency to look at the cover of a book and make an instant evaluation. Nevertheless, it's inappropriate for us to make a judgment on the basis of outward appearance. Also, sometimes it doesn't seem as if there is anything of importance documented in some books, but when the contents are reviewed they truly amaze us. More so, sometimes a person does not seem to be capable of doing a particular job, but the gifts and potential deposited in the inward part only need to be ignited or fanned aflame or discovered to magnify one's workmanship. God is very selective when it comes to the clay that He chooses to mold and shape into His vessel of honor.

The apostle Paul understood this selection when he wrote to the Corinthians. In 1 Corinthians 1:26-28 the Word of the Lord says, "Brothers, think of what you were when you were called. Not many of you were wise by human standards; not many were influential; not many were of noble birth. But God chose the foolish things of the world to shame the wise; God chose the weak things of the world to shame the strong. He chose the lowly things of this world and the despised things—and the things that are not—to nullify the things that are." 2 Corinthians 10:7 declares, "You are looking only on the surface of things. If anyone is confident that he belongs to Christ, he should consider again that we belong to Christ just as much as he." Also in 1 Samuel 16:7, when the Merciful One was speaking to Samuel, He said to him, "Do not consider his appearance or his height, for I have rejected him. The Lord does not look at the things man looks at. Man looks at the outward appearance, but the Lord looks at the heart." The saying of the Lord to Samuel came at a time when Israel demanded a king instead of God as their king. That king, whose name was Saul, had failed, hence God decided to find a man after His own heart. It's significant to note, however, that the period when God rejected Saul was a very disappointing time in the life of the Israelites; they wanted to be like other nations. They desired a human king to go into battle before them. They rejected the Omnipotent Father of mercy and grace fighting for them. In 1 Samuel 8, God explains to Samuel all that the king would do to them. Samuel repeated all he heard in the ears of the people, but they said, "Give us a king." Samuel, being their prophet, or seer, was very disappointed, but God spoke to him and said, "They have not rejected you, but Me."

God therefore chose Saul, a man from the tribe of Benjamin, and the prophet Samuel anointed him to be the first king of Israel. Initially he listened to the instructions of God, but as time progressed he leaned on his own understanding. He was not the obedient king anymore, and the account of his disobedience can be found in 1 Samuel 15. God was not impressed with King Saul. In fact, He was rather upset. He instructed Samuel to go and anoint one of Jesse's sons to be king. God had desired that the chosen king of Israel this time should be a king after His own heart. Samuel, who was always obedient to the command of God, was sent to accomplish this all-important task.

He went up to Bethlehem to anoint one of Jesse's sons to be king over God's people. Jesse called all his children together, and Samuel, when he saw who seemed to be the perfect candidates for the position, would have anointed Eliab, Abinadab and Shammah, but God rejected them. Jesse made seven of his sons pass before Samuel, but God did not choose any of them. Therefore, the prophet asked Jesse if these were all of his children. Jesse answered that there was another, but he was the youngest and was tending the sheep. I believe the prophet knew that when the Lord speaks, He watches over His word to perform it or hastens His word to perform it. So Samuel said to Jesse, with great assurance, "Bring this lad to me."

When they brought the youngest son, David, the Lord told Samuel this was the one and instructed him to arise and anoint him.

Though David was anointed as king of the Israelites, he did not begin to reign as king; he went back to take care of the sheep because, I believe, he needed training and experience with those wayward, stubborn animals in order to be an effective king over God's people. King David needed to be tested so that his testimony would be profound when God's appointed time to deliver arrived. David had to learn to defend and protect the sheep from predators. But why should David be a sheep trainer? Sheep here are being likened to the body of Christ. As we saw in the story of Moses, aren't people like dumb animals at times? We tend to mass together, rebel and disobey. Sheep were used to give David the hands-on experience he needed, for he was to rule over God's people as a mighty commander and warrior. God had to show David that without His supernatural strength, he would not be able to put to death the wild beasts of the field. God was indeed at work in David's life, building up his faith and his testimonies.

Let's take a look at his first test! One day as David tended the flock, a lion and a bear snatched one of his sheep. The anointed man of God laid hold of the lion and delivered his sheep from his paw. Here is something of great interest that we need to take into consideration. Because the enemies of Israel were skillful warriors, this anointed vessel of God had to be swift and watchful. Thus, God taught him how to defend his people through the attack of the bear and the lion against his flock. According to God's Word, David grabbed the lion by the whiskers and tore it into pieces, doing the same thing to the bear. Now, the lion was the king of beasts. The lion here is also symbolic of great strength and power. However, because God's plan was to make out of David the Lion of the tribe of Judah, He allowed him to kill this ferocious animal. This was the beginning of David's awesome testimony and assured him that he possessed the strength of a lion.

What we also experience on our journey to the Promised Land will make our testimonies effective even before those who are in authority. Then, when they listen to our testimonies, they will know that we are the women and the men for the job. God is wise and knows when to act or respond on behalf of His people. He will not delegate or commission you if He has not equipped you. When the fullness of time came for David's kingship to begin, God began to quicken different persons so that the king He had chosen would be ushered into His position. First, David's father, Jesse, called upon him to take bread, grains and cheese to his brothers and commanders.

He also requested that he bring back a report of the well-being of his brothers. David obeyed his father's instructions. He gathered the grains, cheese and other goodies and went to see his brothers. When he got to E-lah, the Philistine Goliath was challenging Saul, the king of Israel. He even defied the God of Israel and said, "Why are ye come out to set your battle in array? Am not I a Philistine, and ye servants of Saul? Choose you a man for you, and let him come down to me" (1 Samuel 17:8 KJV). In 1 Samuel 17:10 he said, "I defy the armies of Israel this day; give me a man, that we may fight together" (KJV). God, I believe, was impressed with this request because He had chosen a man of valor to kill and behead this great champion of the Philistines.

David heard of Goliath's challenge against God's chosen people, and he saw how terrified they were. The people fled from their opponent, but David asked what would be given to the man who killed this Philistine and took away the reproach from Israel. David also asked who this uncircumcised Philistine was that he should challenge or defy the armies of the living God. The men he questioned rehearsed in the ear of David the things this man would receive if he succeeded in killing Goliath. When E-li-ab, David's senior, heard of his request he rebuked him sharply. Nevertheless, David moved on to ask another person the same question until the word reached the ears of King Saul, who was anxious to see this man who dared to fight the giant, for no one had ever won the battle against this champion. He therefore sent for David. When God's chosen king approached the rejected king, he looked at David and came to the conclusion that David was not capable of fighting the giant.

Samuel was looking at the outward appearance when he went up to Bethlehem, but the Lord spoke to him and he was enlightened. We do possess the "can-do" power in Christ which cannot be seen with the naked eye. One's gift or potential cannot be seen until it is manifested. David was confident. He said to the king, "Let no man's heart fail because of this uncircumcised Philistine." He said, "Your servant will go and fight the giant" (see v. 32). King Saul said to David, "You are not able to go against this Philistine to fight him. For you are a youth, and he is a man of war from his youth."

I therefore urge you, just as David refused to be intimidated by the king's fears and utterances, do not allow any man to despise you because you are young, but be an example of the believers in word, in charity, in spirit, in faith, in purity. God has His eyes on you because you are chosen and strong. However, David perceived that this was the opportune time for him to testify about his King of Glory. He said to Saul, "I am a shepherd over my father's sheep, even though I am young. But one day the king of the beasts and a bear took one of my father's sheep. I went after him and smote him and delivered the sheep out of his mouth. Then he got angry and turned on me, and I caught him by the beard and killed him. Your servant killed both these ferocious animals, and this uncircumcised Philistine will be no exception, seeing he has defied the armies of the God of Israel" (see vv. 34-36). David exalted his God; moreover, he said, "The Lord who delivered me from the paw of the lion and the paw of the bear will deliver me from the hand of this Philistine" (v. 37).

King Saul had no choice, for God was in control. So he commanded the young man to go, and he spoke with confidence these words, "Go, and the Lord be with you" (v. 37). King Saul offered David his armor and David tried them on, but he could not wear them. David's armor was not physical. His was spiritual might, through God, to the pulling down of strongholds. David stood firm to fight this battle. His loins were girded with truth.

One writer says, belted around his thighs were the military bands of integrity and sincerity, which held the tunic and scabbard in place. Truth is revealed in the Word of God. David had on the breastplate of righteousness, both of his character and conduct, which protects the vital organs in the chest area from the assaults of the enemy. Without this protection, he would have been vulnerable, disgraced and defeated. Every single part of the armor of God is of great significance to God's children.

When the champion saw that David was but a youth, he despised him. He asked, "Am I a dog, that you come at me with sticks?" (v. 43). He cursed David by his gods and he told David that he was going to kill him and give his carcass to the fowls of the air. David, the anointed, militant warrior of the Lord of Hosts, said to the giant, "You come against me with sword, and spear and javelin, but I come against you in the name of the Lord Almighty, the God of the armies of Israel, whom you have defied" (v. 45). He added, "Today the Lord will deliver you into my hand, and I will smite you and cut off your head and give your carcass to the fowls of the air and the beasts of the earth, that the earth may know that there is a God in Israel. All this assembly will know that the Lord saves not with a sword or a spear: for the battle is the Lord's, and He will give you into my hands" (see vv. 46-47).

Now David was swift on his feet. He was prepared and ready to do battle with Goliath, the champion of all time. The army of the Philistines drew nigh to meet David; therefore he hastened toward the army to meet Goliath. He exercised his God-given faith by placing his staff in his hand, and he selected five stones from the brook.

Girded with the power of God, he took one of the stones and smote the giant in the forehead. The manner in which David prevailed over the Philistine with the sling and with a stone was calculated to bring glory to God. The anointed king then ran and beheaded the stunned Philistine, and his followers fled. The Israelites pursued them and won a great victory. David then took the head of the giant to Jerusalem.

Please bear in mind that even though David was a man after God's own heart, there was a time in his life when he allowed the Enemy to invade his life. We cannot give the Enemy any room, or a foothold, because he will use the opportunity to devastate our lives. That unfortunate day, David should have gone to battle, but he remained at home while his commander in chief, his soldiers and all Israel were on the battlefield. Later as David walked on his roof, he saw a beautiful woman bathing herself. Although he had many wives, he was captivated by this woman's beauty. The beauty of the woman enticed him, and he was drawn away by lust.

Furthermore, when he allowed the lust to be conceived in his heart, he went on and committed the sin of adultery and even murder. This is what the Word of the Lord says in James 1:14-15: "But each one is tempted when, by his own evil desire, he is dragged away and enticed. Then, after desire has conceived, it gives birth to sin; and sin, when it is full-grown, gives birth to death." Sin affects the mind and the heart, and there is no telling what one's action or response will be. David later slept with this woman, the wife of Uriah, and she got pregnant. David knew he was the father of the seed in the woman. How was he going to get out of this trouble? Sin began to wage warfare in his mind and heart, leading him to devise a cunning plan.

Uriah was at war fighting, so David sent for him and told him to go home to his wife. Uriah, a cool, calm and collected man, said he could not enjoy being at home with his wife when all the men of war were on the battlefield. He therefore refused to accept David's offer. Bent on carrying out his devious act, David got Uriah to be intoxicated, hoping his plan would come to fruition, but the man slept at his door. The consequences of sin are inevitable, and sin at work in one's life can spread like a cancer. David again devised another plan to eliminate this man. He wrote a letter and gave it to Uriah to deliver to the commander in order that he would be placed in the heat of the battle.

Uriah was killed and David took his wife for himself. This act displeased the Lord. Therefore God sent the prophet Nathan to David to tell him how distasteful his action was. This account can be found in 2 Samuel 12. Nathan framed a story about the incident and narrated that to David. He listened attentively to the story but got extremely angry with the act of the man in question. Therefore he said this man deserved to be dead. The prophet then said to him, "You are the man!" (v. 7). David said to Nathan, "I have sinned against the Lord." Nathan replied, "The Lord has taken away your sin. You are not going to die" (v. 13). David repented and prayed a prayer of confession in Psalm 51. David wrote, "Have mercy on me, O God, according to your unfailing love; according to your great compassion blot out my transgressions" (v. 1). We need the Omnipotent Father of mercy and grace to wash us thoroughly of our iniquities, and we also need to be cleansed of our sins.

Our transgressions and sins are ever before Him, and we have sinned against the Lord and done evil in His sight. In verse 5, David wrote, "Surely I was sinful at birth, sinful from the time my mother conceived me." Verse 7 says, "Cleanse me with hyssop, and I will be clean; wash me, and I will be whiter than snow." Verses 10-12 says, "Create in me a pure heart, O God, and renew a steadfast spirit within me. Do not cast me from your presence or take your Holy Spirit from me. Restore to me the joy of your salvation and grant me a willing spirit, to sustain me." David therefore turned from his wicked way and laid hold of God's Word which was sweet for meditation. Because he allowed the Word to dwell in him richly, he found an inspiration which made him write songs of praise, deliverance, victory and worship. In the conclusion, the anointed king wrote, "I have hidden your word in my heart that I might not sin against you" (Psalm 119:11). The Word can guide us into all truth. Let us therefore also purpose in our hearts to be people after God's own heart, that the Word can guide us into all truth, which can set us free (John 8:32).

Prayer: Lord Jesus, help us to be people after Your own heart. May we obey and inquire of You all things. Lord, though we have the tendency to stumble and fall into sin, help us to surrender and repent of our wicked ways. We thank You that You are able to blot out our transgressions, and that You know how to throw it into the sea of forgetfulness where You remember it no more. Amen.

What we also experience on our journey to the Promised Land will make our testimonies effective even before those who are in authority. Then, when they listen to our testimonies, they will know that we are the women and men for the job. God is wise, and He knows when to act or respond on behalf of His people. He will not delegate or commission you if He has not equipped you.

CHAPTER 10

ARE YOU A SUPPLANTER?

It is my belief that one's entire being can be affected by family traits which are transferable from one generation to the next. The person we turn out to be, good or bad, can be traced back to the traits we receive from our parents. Some people may have had parents who were liars and thieves, and their traits or attitudes were instilled in their children and then into the lives of their offspring.

Sometimes the traits passed on can become problematic. For this reason it is of paramount importance to train our children in the way they should go so that when they get older they will not depart from it. The Bible is like a schoolteacher; it shows both good and bad characters so that we can learn from their lifestyles as to how to stand or respond to certain situations. We hereby follow an interesting account of two outstanding Bible characters, Jacob and Esau. We can learn much from their story.

The Bible tells us about how these two boys jostled each other when they were in Rebecca's, their mother's, womb. However, during the delivery Jacob's brother, Esau, was born first, with Jacob's hand grasping Esau's heel. The Bible tells us that Esau was a skillful hunter, while Jacob stayed at home. Jacob was an industrious lad who liked to cook delicious food. One day after Jacob had cooked, Esau came home very famished and tired. He therefore desired to eat some of Jacob's food.

During the moments of his brother's vulnerability, Jacob used that opportunity to display his craftiness. He told his brother that he would give him some of the stew, only in exchange for his birthright. Esau was at the verge of death, so he did not think about the implication of selling his birthright. He said, "What good is the birthright to me?" (Genesis 25:32). This was a very foolish statement, because you will later see his reaction to this great deception. Jacob commanded him to swear an oath to him to authenticate his willingness to sell his birthright.

Putting immediate gratification before long-term interests, Esau swore the oath, foolishly giving up his inheritance or rights that favored him as the firstborn son of Isaac. These rights involved a greater share of the inheritance, privileges and responsibilities of family leadership. It so happened that their father had reached old age and his eyes were dim. He therefore called his older son, Esau, and gave him instruction to prepare for the bestowal of the blessing. Meanwhile, a seed of deception had entered into the heart of his mother, Rebecca, for she heard what Isaac said to Esau.

So she hastily instructed her favorite son, Jacob, on what he needed to do to receive the blessing. Why would she scheme to steal Esau's blessing? She was probably biased, or maybe it was because she loved Jacob and Isaac loved Esau. That answer is not important for now since Rebecca had already received the message from God that the elder would serve the younger; this might seem to justify her motive. Often we have good intentions, but our actions to fulfill them twist the virtues, bringing forth disastrous consequences. The preacher therefore said, "Trust in the Lord with all your heart and lean not on your own understanding; in all your ways acknowledge him, and he will make your paths straight. Do not be wise in your own eyes; fear the Lord and shun evil" (Proverbs 3:5-7).

Strangely, Rebecca's plan, according to Genesis 27, worked out very well. She helped Jacob to prepare the venison, and then she dressed him with furs of animal hair. Jacob beguiled his father with his mother's help and received the deathbed blessing. After Jacob had received the blessing, Esau came home, prepared his father's meal, and went in to be blessed. Both father and son were shocked out of their wits. Esau could not believe what he heard, and Isaac was dumbfounded. This incident must have caused his heart to beat faster and the adrenalin must have affected his whole body. Genesis 27:33

says that Isaac trembled violently, explaining to his son that someone had received the blessing and that someone was indeed blessed.

Esau became very bitter, so he cried out loudly saying, "Bless me too my father!" (see v. 34). This must have been very devastating, for it was impossible for Esau to receive the blessing his brother had already received. He asked, is there not another blessing reserved for me? Esau, I can imagine, was disturbed because his brother had taken his birthright and had now robbed him of his blessing. In Genesis 27:39-40 we learn that Isaac said to Esau, "Your dwelling will be away from the earth's richness, away from the dew of heaven above. You will live by the sword and you will serve your brother. But when you grow restless, you will throw his yoke from off your neck."

Angrily Esau planned to kill his brother, but Rebecca learned of the plot and once again intervened. She decided to send Jacob away to her brother Laban in Haran. Isaac blessed Jacob and commanded him not to marry a Canaanite woman, so after the instructions, Jacob set out on his way to his uncle's place. Even though Jacob was a deceiver, God was with him, ordering his steps, throughout his journey to and from Haran. After meeting his relatives, Jacob worked for his uncle and fell in love with his younger cousin Rachel. He asked for her hand in marriage, but the seed of deception was in the heart of his uncle also, so after Jacob worked seven years to earn the right to marry Rachel, Laban tricked Jacob into marrying Leah instead.

Once Jacob realized what had happened, he bargained with his uncle to work for him for another seven years to earn Rachel as his wife. God blessed the work of Jacob's hand. In fact, there was such an increase in his uncle's flock as well as Jacob's that they decided to depart from one another. The Bible tells us that there was feuding between the herdsmen of Jacob and the herdsmen of his uncle. I believe that was the opportune time for Jacob to return home. Jacob desired to go back to his mother's land. He had acquired great wealth, so he gathered everything he possessed and began his journey. He could not help thinking, however, about his brother Esau and how he could appease him. He decided to send gifts ahead of him to soften his brother. Jacob, I believe, was very restless and quite afraid.

He needed inner peace. Genesis 32:22-32 states that he rose up that night, took his two wives and his two women servants and his eleven sons, and he passed over the ford of Jab-bok. Jacob sent everything over the brook, but he was left alone, and there he wrestled with a heavenly being until the breaking of the day.

This was an unusual encounter, for Jacob wrestled with this being and prevailed. According to Genesis 32:25, the heavenly being touched the hollow of Jacob's thigh and his thigh was out of joint. This was the Lord of Hosts that Jacob wrestled with. Jacob held on to this heavenly being despite his cry to let him go. By this time Jacob knew whom he was holding onto, so he said with boldness, "I will not let you go unless you bless me" (v. 26). A question was directed to Jacob: "What is your name?" And he said, "Jacob," which means "deceiver" (v. 27). His name was therefore changed from Jacob to Israel, because he struggled with God and with men, and prevailed.

Later, Jacob asked his opponent his name and he answered, "Why are you asking for my name?" Even though he did not give Jacob his name, he blessed him. This place was of great significance to Jacob, so he named it Peniel (meaning, "For I have seen God face to face, and my life is preserved"). It's appropriate for one to consider this phase in Jacob's life as being very important and remarkable. This was a time of change, or turnaround that was marked with a blessing. Psalm 51:5 states that we were shaped in iniquity, and in sin did our mothers conceive us. Our bloodline is sinful, but thank God for the precious blood of Jesus Christ which flowed from His veins. Through that we can plunge beneath the blood of Jesus and lose all our guilty stains.

This is a very interesting story that we need to meditate on. It teaches us that we can inherit the Promised Land if we would truly seek the face of God. God promised that He will bless us if we seek Him with all our heart, soul and mind. The Word of the Lord tells us that the blessing of the Lord makes rich, and it adds no sorrow with it. It is imperative that we, the body of Christ, wrestle at the place of uncertainties until we mortify the desires of the flesh. When there is a mortification of the old man, everything about us is changed and renewed, and this is all for the glory of God.

Transformation is a most important process in the life of a child of God, and if we have to plead and beseech this awesome God of ours, we must do so until the blessing is pronounced upon us. We must grasp the truth available in the life of this biblical character Jacob. He perceived that he held onto a supernatural being and determined to never let him go until the blessing was bestowed on him. Thank God he did not give up but endured to the end and even with a limp received the blessing of the Lord.

Thereafter, Jacob left to meet with his brother, who met him without animosity. They hugged each other and wept. Isn't this awesome? I give praise and worship to my God for this truth: that where the blessing of Almighty God is, the desires of the flesh will not be gratified.

Prayer: Almighty God, You are the only One who can bring transformation into our lives. Let there be awareness or an acknowledgement that we need to lay hold of You until change comes. May we turn around and see, do, and say the things that are necessary to bring us to the finish line. You have made us vessels or instruments for your glory. Amen.

Here is a very interesting account that we need to meditate on. It teaches us that we can inherit the Promised Land if we would truly seek the face of God. God promised that He will bless us if we seek Him with all our heart, soul and mind. The Word of the Lord tells us that the blessing of the Lord makes rich, and it adds no sorrow with it.

CHAPTER 11

HELL

The flame of hell is eternal; its gates are wide open, and many are those who travel through them because worldly attractions and pleasures have blindfolded their eyes, subjecting them to utter darkness and preventing them from seeing the Light of life. Simply put, sin has blindfolded most people, preventing them from seeing the portals of heaven. In fact, such persons are drawing close to the pit of hell, where it will be too late for them to turn around and see the Lord.

Fortunately, now is the appointed time for them to turn around and see the Lord. Also, now is the time for them to set all their affections on the One whose place of abode is peace forevermore, even to Jesus. It is therefore my prayer for all, especially the disobedient and the ignorant, to turn away from the flames of hell and lay claim to the pearly white city. Humankind has two destinations: hell and heaven. It is therefore up to us to choose which place we prefer for a destiny or to live forever. For this cause, those who believe in Christ are chosen of God to assist those who are seeking for a way of escape.

It is therefore our prerogative to serve God wholeheartedly as a believer and to work for the salvation of all people until the end of time. Then our assurance of escaping the flames of hell will be solidified and our name will be kept in the Lamb's Book of Life. Those whose names are written in the Lamb's Book of Life are those who will escape the lake of fire. According to Zondervan's *Pictorial Bible Dictionary*, hell is the abode of the damned. It's in the world's lower region, a place of vice, misery and torture. The word *hell*, defined by the King James Version of the Bible, carries a connotation of doom, hopelessness and futility.

Psalm 9:17 says, "The wicked shall be turned into hell, and all the nations that forget God" (KJV). Job 21:13 says, "They spend their days in wealth, and in a moment go down to the grave" (KJV). Again, Psalm 139:8: "If I ascend into heaven, You are there; if I make my bed in hell, behold, You are there" (NKJV). Therefore, hell may also be defined as the grave, or the abode of the unbelieving dead. The New Testament word for "hell" is *Hades*, which corresponds to Sheol. There are many schools of thought about Hades. Some believe it represents the grave, while others say it's a definite place of conscious punishment.

But all these differences could be laid to rest if one carefully studies or examines Luke 16:23-24; Revelation 1:18; and 1 Corinthians 15:55. However, there are other places of eternal torment prepared as a designation for the devil and his angels (Matthew 25:41). They are listed as follows:

Gehenna: "But I tell you that anyone who is angry with his brother will be subject to judgment. Again, anyone who says to his brother, 'Raca,' is answerable to the Sanhedrin. But anyone who says, 'You fool!' will be in danger of the fire of hell" (Matthew 5:22). "If your hand causes you to sin, cut it off. It is better for you to enter life maimed than with two hands to go into hell, where the fire never goes out. And if your foot causes you to sin, cut it off. It is better for you to enter life crippled than to have two feet and be thrown into hell. And if your eye causes you to sin, pluck it out. It is better for you to enter the kingdom of God with one eye than to have two eyes and be thrown into hell, where 'their worm does not die, and the fire is not quenched'" (Mark 9:43-48). "The tongue also is a fire, a world of evil among the parts of the body. It corrupts the whole person, sets the whole course of his life on fire, and is itself set on fire by hell" (James 3:6).

Eternal damnation: "But whoever blasphemes against the Holy Spirit will never be forgiven; he is guilty of an eternal sin" (Mark 3:29).

Outer darkness: "But the subjects of the kingdom will be thrown outside, into the darkness, where there will be weeping and gnashing of teeth" (Matthew 8:12).

Resurrection of damnation: "Those who have done good will rise to live, and those who have done evil will rise to be condemned" (John 5:29).

Second death: "He who has an ear, let him hear what the Spirit says to the churches. He who overcomes will not be hurt at all by the second death" (Revelation 2:11). "But the cowardly, the unbelieving, the vile, the murderers, the sexually immoral, those who practice magic arts, the idolaters and all liars—their place will be in the fiery lake of burning sulfur. This is the second death" (21:8).

Everlasting destruction: "The wicked return to the grave, all the nations that forget God" (Psalm 9:17). "They will be punished with everlasting destruction and shut out from the presence of the Lord and from the majesty of his power" (2 Thessalonians 1:9).

Blackness of darkness: "God did not spare angels when they sinned, but sent them to hell, putting them into gloomy dungeons to be held for judgment" (2 Peter 2:4). "They are wild waves of the sea, foaming up their shame; wandering stars, for whom blackest darkness has been reserved forever" (Jude 1:13).

The curse of God: "All who rely on observing the law are under a curse, for it is written: 'Cursed is everyone who does not continue to do everything written in the Book of the Law'" (Galatians 3:10).

The wrath of God: "Whoever believes in the Son has eternal life, but whoever rejects the Son will not see life, for God's wrath remains on him" (John 3:36). "The wrath of God is being revealed from heaven against all the godlessness and wickedness of men who suppress the truth by their wickedness" (Romans 1:18).

Worm of conscience: "It is better for you to enter life maimed than with two hands to go into hell, where the fire never goes out" (Mark 9:43).

Unending torments: "And the smoke of their torment rises forever and ever. There is no rest day or night for those who worship the beast and his image, or for anyone who receives the mark of his name" (Revelation 14:11).

The lake of fire: "But the beast was captured, and with him the false prophet who had performed the miraculous signs on his behalf. With these signs he had deluded those who had received the mark of the beast and worshipped his image. The two of them were thrown alive into the fiery lake of burning sulfur" (Revelation 19:20). "If anyone's name was not found written in the book of life, he was thrown into the lake of fire" (20:15).

Those who have indulged in sin will be brought to shame, for the wages of sin is death, even the second death and hell (Revelation 21:8). I have drawn the meaning of sin from various languages. For instance, the Hebrew words for "sin" are *hattath*, which means "missing"; *pesha*, which means "transgression"; *awon*, which means "perversion"; and *ra*, which means "evil in disposition." The Greek words for "sin" are *hamartia*, which means "missing the mark"; *parabasis*, which means "transgression"; *adikia*, which means "unrighteousness"; and *anomia*, which means "contempt and violation of the law." Doctrinally, sin may be defined as anything that a person does which does not express the holiness of God or is contrary to it. It can also be defined as anything that is not in conformity with or is in transgression of the law of God. 1 John 3:4 says, "Everyone who sins breaks the law; in fact, sin is lawlessness." Romans 6:23 says, "For the wages of sin is death, but the gift of God is eternal life in Christ Jesus our Lord."

One school of thought says it is quite unfortunate that there are many who dwell exclusively on the goodness of God. Some folks teach and preach only about prosperity and blessings, forgetting that goodness and severity are twin attributes of God. Romans 11:22 says,

"Consider therefore the kindness and sternness of God: sternness to those who fell, but kindness to you, provided that you continue in his kindness. Otherwise, you also will be cut off." Some do not want to hear about eternal punishment, as if the subject of hell is not in the Bible. Nevertheless, the Bible has made it clear that whoever lives in sin and does not turn to God from their wicked ways is on the road to destruction. Hell will definitely be a place of abode for those who choose to take up residence there.

Jesus says in Matthew 25:30 that there shall be weeping and gnashing of teeth in hell. There are lots of places in the Bible where Jesus spoke about hell, although He possessed the tender heart of compassion that ever pleads to mankind. Whenever He spoke about hell, He constantly alluded to a certain terrible unending suffering for those who die in sin. Galatians 5:19-21 tells us that if we commit adultery, fornication, idolatry, murder, drunkenness, witchcraft, hatred, variance, emulations, wrath, strife, seditions, heresies, envy and reveling, we shall not inherit the kingdom of God.

Jesus taught about eternal punishment with boldness, plainness and awful significance. We are hereby challenged as preachers to imitate the principle Christ used to teach about hell. That is, with a compassionate heart for the unsaved, seeing that God is not silent about the dreaded place called hell. The Bible speaks of unending felicity or happiness of the saved and the unending torment for the lost, urging the latter to flee from the wrath to come. The God whom we serve is no respecter of persons. Remember how He once destroyed all of His creation in the Book of Genesis.

Genesis 6:5-7 says, "The Lord saw how great man's wickedness on the earth had become, and that every inclination of the thoughts of his heart was only evil all the time. The Lord was grieved that he had made man on the earth, and his heart was filled with pain. So the Lord said, 'I will wipe mankind, whom I have created, from the face of the earth—men and animals, and creatures that move along the ground, and birds of the air—for I am grieved that I have made them.'" Solomon describes hell as the "grave": "The path of life leads upward for the wise to keep him from going down to the grave" (Proverbs 15:24). Whereas in the Gospels it's recorded that the devils besought Christ to command them to go into the deep.

Hell is in the deep! The wise Chrysostom warns us: "Let me not so labor to know where hell is, as how to escape it. I cannot tolerate the brilliance or the heat from the sun for too long. I holler and suffer pain when I am burnt by hot water, steam or anything that is heated. I felt the heat from the forces of hell and it felt as if I was placed into a fiery furnace at 400 degrees Fahrenheit. If these momentary experiences have such torment, we must escape it. Hell is hot, hot, and hot! To spend eternity in hell will not be comfortable; it is a place of suffering."

When we think about this dreaded place, the phrase that comes to mind is "eternal punishment." Matthew 25:46 states that those who die without Christ will go to hell. The Old Testament word for hell is *Sheol*, and it's used in a double sense. First of all, it represents the grave to which the righteous and the wicked will go (Genesis 37:35; 1 Kings 2:6, 9; Psalm 6:5). Sheol also stands for the place of future punishment (Isaiah 28:15-18; Proverbs 7:27; Psalms 9:17; 55:15). Jesus talked to His disciples about the reality of hell in Luke 16:19-31.

According to Jesus there was a rich man who dressed in the most expensive clothes and lived in great luxury every day. Into this rich man's domain was brought a poor man named Lazarus. This poor man was very sick. His body was covered with sores, and he hoped he could eat the crumbs of food that fell from the rich man's table. This must have been an awful sight, for the Word of the Lord says dogs approached him and licked his sores. I can imagine how inflamed his body was, exuding blood and pus.

Indeed, he was poverty-stricken and very sick, but the rich man offered no help. Christ's story was intended to educate people to help the poor and the sick, just as He and His disciples did. James 2:15-16 says, "Suppose a brother or sister is without clothes and daily food. If one of you says to him, 'Go, I wish you well; keep warm and well fed,' but does nothing about his physical needs, what good is it?" In this regard, the rich man had no true faith in God. If he had, he would have helped this poor man. We need the bowels of compassion for those who are poverty-stricken, sick, and oppressed by the devil and his cohorts. According to the Scriptures, this poor man died and angels escorted him into Abraham's bosom. We are informed by Christ that when a believer dies his soul and spirit are escorted by angels into the presence of God.

Therefore in 1 Peter it is written, "Dear friends, do not be surprised at the painful trial you are suffering, as though something strange were happening to you. But rejoice that you participate in the sufferings of Christ, so that you may be overjoyed when his glory is revealed" (4:12-13). The trial of this poor man's life on earth was fiery, but to God be the glory, he escaped the fiery furnace, the flames of hell, which would have tormented him forever. Therefore, no matter how fiery your trial is on earth, you must endeavor to work out your salvation with fear and trembling.

Think about heaven, that place prepared by Jesus, which is where your destiny should be. Somebody sang, "Are you feeling hot, hot, hot?" Well, my friends, hell is going to be hotter than that. What a hell of a time it is going to be if we do not make it to heaven. Thus, we must make it a priority to escape the wrath to come. But sadly, that was the place the rich man went. While in hell and in torment, the rich man lifted up his eyes and saw Abraham afar off and Lazarus in his bosom. Wherefore he cried, "I am in pain!" Beloved, hell's fire causes great pain. Furthermore, he cried out louder, "Father Abraham, have mercy on me." But it was to no avail. Once we reach the fire beneath, it is just too late to cry for mercy. There is no salvation in hell.

It will be too late, too late, and there is no mercy. Too late! Too late and judgment comes. Even so it was too late for the rich man to plead with father Abraham to send Lazarus that he might dip the tip of his finger into the water and cool his tongue. He exclaimed, "I am tormented in this flame." Folks, fire can be a cruel master! The first use of the word *fire* in Scripture is found in Genesis 19:24, where the fire from the Lord out of heaven destroyed the cities of the plain. The final destiny of the enemies of God is the lake of fire. In Revelation 19:20 we learn, "But the beast was captured, and with him the false prophet who had performed the miraculous signs on his behalf. With these signs he had deluded those who had received the mark of the beast and worshipped his image. The two of them were thrown alive into the fiery lake of burning sulfur." Also, Revelation 20:10, 14 reads, "And the devil, who deceived them, was thrown into the lake of burning sulfur, where the beast and the false prophet had been thrown. They will be tormented day and night forever and ever. . . . Then death and Hades were thrown into the lake of fire. The lake of fire is the second death."

Someday, according to 2 Peter 3:7-12, this world will be consumed by fire: "By the same word the present heavens and earth are reserved for fire, being kept for the Day of Judgment and destruction of ungodly men. But do not forget this one thing, dear friends: With the Lord a day is like a thousand years, and a thousand years are like a day. The Lord is not slow in keeping his promise, as some understand slowness. He is patient with you, not wanting anyone to perish, but everyone to come to repentance. But the day of the Lord will come like a thief. The heavens will disappear with a roar; the elements will be destroyed by fire, and the earth and everything in it will be laid bare. Since everything will be destroyed in this way, what kind of people ought we to be? We ought to live holy and godly lives as we look forward to the return of our Lord and Savior Jesus Christ. That day will bring about the destruction of the heavens by fire, and the elements will melt in the heat."

The fascinating and heartrending story of the rich man and Lazarus reminds us of the good life the rich man lived on earth, showing no thankfulness for his blessings, neither was he generous to the poor and the sick man. Thus, father Abraham said to him, "Just as you received good things on earth without torment, even so Lazarus who received evil things is now comforted and you are tormented." Therefore Lazarus received salvation instead of death, showing how significant it is for us to choose salvation today.

Furthermore, father Abraham portrayed the alarming and ugly picture of the separation between the righteous and the wicked when he said to the rich man that there is a gulf or deep pit fixed between us, so that those who want to cross over from here to there cannot do so, nor can anyone cross over to us from there to here. Therefore if peradventure you make it into hell that will be your place of abode forevermore. All opportunity for salvation is now, today, on this side of the grave. Purgatory is a fool's hope, for there is no such place.

When the rich man heard that message, he begged father Abraham to send Lazarus to his father's house where he had five brothers, saying, "Tell Lazarus to go and warn them so that they, at least, will not come to this place of doom." Hell is a place of torment! The rich man was not pleading for himself alone. He knew it was too late for him, he knew he was eternally lost, but his brothers had a chance to escape the flames of hell. It is easy to step into hell but impossible to step out. There is a fixed gulf that separates the wicked from heavenly bliss.

Therefore, it is imperative that the message of hell be preached and be taught from the pulpit to the street, over the hills and everywhere, so humankind may turn from their wicked ways. Abraham therefore said to the rich man, "Your brothers have Moses and the prophets, let them hear from them." The rich man said to Abraham, "That is not enough, but if someone were to rise from the dead and go to them, then they would turn from their sins."

On the contrary, that is impossible, for this is the truth and nothing but the truth: They ought to listen to Moses and the prophets, for they would not be convinced even if someone were to rise from the dead. We must heed the Word of God and turn from our sins. Let us not yield to temptation, for yielding is sin. Turn to God and He will carry you through. The fleshly desires must be mortified so that we are clad in the garment of the new man (Ephesians 4:17-32).

Needless to say, a spirit returning from the grave will not trouble or affect the wicked, especially when he or she is turned over to a reprobate mind. A person who does not heed the Word of God will not listen to someone who has come back from the dead. They will not believe a word, and they will figure more or less that it is foolishness.

The Bible lays emphasis on this in John 11, when it says that Jesus' friend Lazarus was raised from the dead and the Pharisees wanted to put Jesus to death. It's becoming abundantly clear that it's our prerogative to turn someone from the lake of fire which is designed to consume all those who enter hell. Revelation 20:14-15 says, "Then death and Hades were thrown into the lake of fire. The lake of fire is the second death. If anyone's name was not found written in the book of life, he was thrown into the lake of fire."

Revelation 21:8 says, "But the cowardly, the unbelieving, the vile, the murderers, the sexually immoral, those who practice magic arts, the idolaters and all liars—their place will be in the fiery lake of burning sulfur. This is the second death." The lake of fire is a place of conscious suffering. What doom awaits those who die without Christ (Revelation 2:11; 19:20; 20:10; Matthew 25:41, 46)? Revelation 2:11 says, "He who has an ear, let him hear what the Spirit says to the churches. He who overcomes will not be hurt at all by the second death."

An analysis of hell from the previous paragraphs show conscious unending torment in the lake of fire, torment which consists of two aspects. First, the punishment of separation: "Depart from me." As stated in Matthew 7:23: "Then I will tell them plainly, 'I never knew you. Away from me, you evildoers." The second aspect is the separation of loss: "ye cursed!" Matthew 25:41 says, "Then he will say to those on his left [the goats], 'Depart from me, you who are cursed, into the eternal fire prepared for the devil and his angels.'" I do not think you would like to have any of these two experiences. You are advised to escape from eternal punishment now. Today listen to Him if you hear His voice, for today is your day of salvation.

Acceptance of the finished work of Christ for sinners alone guarantees deliverance from the terrible doom depicted in the Scriptures. Once we accept Him as our Lord and Savior, all condemnation or punishment is removed. Romans 8:1 says, "There is therefore now no condemnation [guilt] to them which are in Christ Jesus, who walk not after the flesh, but after the Spirit" (KJV).

Isaiah 1:18-20 says, "Come, now, and let us reason together, saith the Lord: though your sins be as scarlet, they shall be as white as snow; though they be red like crimson, they shall be as wool. If ye be willing and obedient, ye shall eat the good of the land: but if ye refuse and rebel, ye shall be devoured with the sword: for the mouth of the Lord hath spoken it" (KJV). It should therefore be our reasonable service here and now to warn others to flee from the wrath to come. Turn from the pit of hell, for it will be a place of torment forevermore! We can quench our thirst in this life by drinking water, but in the pit of hell the flames will absorb all moisture. Seeing how devastating hell could be, it is not irksome for me to repeat that there are two roads to choose from. The choice is yours!

In Ezekiel 3:17-21 the oracles of God declare, "Son of man, I have made you a watchman for the house of Israel; so hear the word I speak and give them warning from me. When I say to a wicked man, 'You will surely die,' and you do not warn him or speak out to dissuade him from his evil ways in order to save his life, that wicked man will die for his sin, and I will hold you accountable for his blood. But if you do warn the wicked man and he does not turn from his wickedness or from his evil ways, he will die for his sin; but you will have saved yourself. Again, when a righteous man turns from his righteousness and does evil, and I put a stumbling block before him, he will die. Since you did not warn him, he will die for his sin. The righteous things he did will not be remembered, and I will hold you accountable for his blood. But if you do warn the righteous man not to sin and he does not sin, he will surely live because he took warning, and you will have saved yourself."

This message is not only for the lost alone, but is to also warn the righteous who turn from their righteousness. The righteous must be constantly warned or else many, if not most, will turn aside. Today and always, we must turn around and see the Lord. The message of hell is a challenging responsibility for all preachers. One must never fail to proclaim the message of hell. He who has an ear, let him hear what the Spirit of God is saying to the churches! *Lockyer* states, "If only there could be heard by them the groans and shrieks of the damned for one hour, how they would flee to Christ, for mercy is my prayer!" Ancient Anselm says: "I had rather endure all torments, than see the devil with bodily eyes. What a hell it would be to be shut in with a raging lion forever, and have the old red Dragon forever hiss and spit in your face!" All that comes out of a dragon's mouth is fire.

By now you might be wondering what you must do to escape this torment of hell. The answer is the same one that Jesus gave to Nicodemus. "In reply Jesus declared, 'I tell you the truth, no one can see the kingdom of God unless he is born again'" (John 3:3). Just as you were born physically, you must be born spiritually to reach the portals of heaven, for which cause Christ revealed, "I am the way and the truth and the life. No one comes to the Father except through me" (John 14:6). You are not promised another day on this earth. Tomorrow may be too late. Now is the time to do something about your lost condition. For the Spirit says, "I have heard thee in a time accepted, and in the day of salvation have I succoured thee: behold, now is the accepted time; behold, now is the day of salvation" (2 Corinthians 6:2 KJV). Your life might end before another hour passes, and your soul will be somewhere terrible for eternity. Will you receive Jesus Christ as your Lord and Savior and be confident of everlasting life?

Prayer: The flames of hell! The flames of hell! Help us, heavenly Father, that we may live a life that is holy and acceptable, which is our reasonable service. Help us to serve You with all of our heart, soul and strength, and may our names be written in the Lamb's Book of Life. We purpose in our heart to escape the place of torment which is hell, in Jesus' name. Amen.

> "I cannot tolerate the brilliance or the heat from the sun for too long. I holler and suffer pain when I am burnt by hot water, steam or anything that is heated. I felt the heat from the forces of hell and it felt as if I was placed into a fiery furnace at 400 degrees Fahrenheit. If these momentary experiences have such torment, we must escape it. Hell is hot, hot, and hot! To spend eternity in hell will not be comfortable; it is a place of suffering."

CHAPTER 12

HEAVEN

John 14:1-3 states, "Do not let your hearts be troubled. Trust in God; trust also in me. In my Father's house are many rooms; if it were not so, I would have told you. I am going there to prepare a place for you. And if I go and prepare a place for you, I will come back and take you to be with me that you also may be where I am." 1 Thessalonians 4:17 says, "After that, we who are still alive and are left will be caught up together with them in the clouds to meet the Lord in the air. And so we will be with the Lord forever."

The above scriptures whet the mind and resuscitate God's people to turn their eyes to the eastern sky, for our redemption is nearer than we thought. Unlike hell, the road to heaven is a narrow one and few people travel on it. There are many obstacles on the way that may cause the believer to detour, thus our eyes must be fixed on the things of God. Our focus must remain on the Lord as we make our way to our mansion that He has prepared for us, even those whose names are written in the palm of His hand and in the Lamb's Book of Life.

Jesus left the splendor of heaven knowing His destiny. He knew He had to become flesh in the womb of a woman. He would be born as a man and His ministry would be a short one. Also, he knew death was His destiny; however, He said that on the third day He would rise again. John 17:5, 24 tells about Jesus being exalted before He was born to be the propitiation for our sins: "And now, Father, glorify me in your presence with the glory I had with you before the world began. . . . Father, I want those you have given me to be with me where I am, and to see my glory, the glory you have given me because you loved me before the creation of the world." It's a majestic and an exalted position. Nonetheless, according to Philippians 2, Jesus surrendered all the glory He had to take on the form of humankind. This was the divine plan of the Father for Him that He could atone for sinful humanity. God's justice required a human being to atone for human sin. Part of the plan was Golgotha, which was a gruesome experience for Jesus. He did not resist but obeyed and was humiliated and died like a criminal on a tree in order to fulfill God's divine purpose.

The Bible teaches us that three days after His death, Christ arose. He appeared first of all to Mary Magdalene. He appeared also to the two on the road to Emmaus, His disciples, and later the five hundred. During his many discourses while on earth, he told His disciples about the significance of His going to the Father.

On one occasion He said, "But I tell you the truth: It is for your good that I am going away. Unless I go away, the Counselor will not come to you; but if I go, I will send him to you" (John 16:7). In Acts Chapter 1 He commanded His disciples not to depart from Jerusalem but to wait for the promise of the Father, which they had heard Him speak about. In verse 9 of the same chapter, the Word of the Lord states that "when he had spoken these things, while they beheld, he was taken up; and a cloud received him out of their sight. And while they looked steadfastly toward heaven as he went up, behold, two men stood by them in white apparel; which also said, ye men of Galilee, why stand ye gazing up into heaven? This same Jesus, which is taken up from you into heaven, shall so come in like manner as ye have seen him go into heaven" (KJV).

John says in 14:1-3 of his Gospel that Jesus comforted His disciples with these words: "Do not let your hearts be troubled. Trust in God; trust also in me. In my Father's house are many rooms; if it were not so, I would have told you. I am going there to prepare a place for you. And if I go and prepare a place for you, I will come back and take you to be with me that you also may be where I am." In fact, the Lord's word to His disciples about the prepared place called heaven is a blessed assurance for you and me. For He said, "And if

I go and prepare a place for you, I will come again, and receive you unto myself; that where I am, there ye may be also" (KJV).

Despite the many theological works and biblical exegesis on the doctrine of heaven, many are still asking this question: Is there a heaven? And if heaven is real, where is it? The simple answer to this question is anchored in the belief I have in God, for which cause I declare by faith that heaven is a prepared place, especially for those who believe in God.

Where is it? I believe it is above, for the Bible tells me so. In John 17:1 it's revealed that after He had spoken these words, He lifted His eyes to heaven. Acts 1:10-11 also says He went up. We have a similar suggestion in Luke 24:50-52, which paints the same picture, namely that Christ was carried up into heaven. Heaven is real; however, the Jews and most Christians believe that there are three heavens.

To them, the first heaven is the blue cloud or sky above, biblically known as firmament, the aerial or atmospheric nature we experience around us. This is where the birds fly, the wind blows, and the showers, mists, vapors and clouds are formed (Genesis 1:1, 7-8; Psalms 19:1; 103:11; Acts 1:11). The second heaven is the domain of Satan and his cohorts (Job 2:2; Ephesians 6:12). It's what Paul calls "the heavenly realms" in Ephesians 6:12: "For our struggle is not against flesh and blood, but against the rulers, against the authorities, against the powers of this dark world and against the spiritual forces of evil in the heavenly realms." In this spiritual dimension there are angelic forces and godly forces as well as demonic forces and powers. This second heaven, a spiritual atmosphere cohabited by both good and evil, is a very, very small part of the cosmos. In reality it just surrounds the earth, the only rebellious and sinful place in the whole cosmos.

The third heaven is the heaven of heavens. This is where God dwells, and is the region spoken of as the immediate presence of God. It is the region of divine glory and the dwelling place of angels and saints, as shown in 2 Corinthians 12:1-4.

But 1 Kings 8:30 says, "Hear the supplication of your servant and of your people Israel when they pray toward this place. Hear from heaven, your dwelling place, and when you hear, forgive."

Psalm 11:4 says, "The Lord is in his holy temple; the Lord is on his heavenly throne. He observes the sons of men; his eyes examine them." Psalm 15:1 says, "Lord, who may dwell in your sanctuary? Who may live on your holy hill?" *Dr. Herbert Lockyer* declares that, "Heaven is the temple of divine majesty where God's excellent glory is revealed most conspicuously. It's the habitation of His holiness, the place where His honor dwells". This prepared place is not a myth.

Men and women from different ethnic backgrounds have set their affections on it and have even written inspired songs about it, such as, "Heaven, heaven, heaven is the place I long to be. Heaven, heaven, heaven, where Jesus prepared for me. Come let us adore Him, for Christ is coming soon to take us home to heaven. Going home! I'm going home! There is nothing to hold me here. I caught a glimpse of my heavenly home and now I'm going home. Oh how I long to see Him, to look upon His face, there to sing forever of His saving grace. On the streets of glory, let me lift my voice, cares all past, home at last, ever to rejoice."

The Hebrew word for heaven is *shamayin*, and the Greek word is *quranios*.

Dr. Herbert Lockyer states, "Heaven is the final abode of those redeemed by the blood of Christ and regenerated by the Holy Ghost". We have to be redeemed to make it to the pearly white city. A songwriter wrote, "I'm redeemed, bought with a price. Jesus has changed my whole life. If anyone asks you just who you are, tell them, 'I'm redeemed.' He who has an ear to hear, take heed to what the Spirit is saying to the churches. One's relationship to Jesus Christ will determine one's eternal destiny and abode: "No one comes to the Father except through me" (John 14:6).

There are two roads and two destinies. We will all die one day, according to St. Paul: "Man is destined to die once, and after that to face judgment" (Hebrews 9:27). It's evident that there is a destiny after death. This destiny has been set down as one of two alternatives: heaven or hell. According to *Dr. Herbert Lockyer*, "Heaven is a state of unbroken peace and unflawed joy in the presence of God for the redeemed. Heaven is expressly spoken of as a definite place, as well as a state" (John 14:2-3). Heaven is a prepared place for the true Church. It's a prepared place for a prepared people, and to be heaven bound, you must be born again. But what does it mean to be born again? What does it require for someone to enter the kingdom of God?

To enter God's kingdom requires something that's impossible by human standards—that is, one must be born of water and of the Spirit (John 3:5). By this, Jesus refers to the work of the Holy Spirit breathing life into our sinful and dead spiritual nature. When we are born again, we become new persons. Our sins are forgiven and we are granted an intimate friendship with God. Bear in mind, Jesus answered Nicodemus, a ruler of the Jews, saying, "I tell you the truth, no one can see the kingdom of God unless he is born again" (v. 3). Verse 5 states, "Jesus answered, 'I tell you the truth, no one can enter the kingdom of God unless he is born of water and the Spirit.'" What does it mean to be born of water and the Spirit? There are many theological approaches to this text. While some believe it could refer to physical birth (accompanied by water breaking) and spiritual birth (the dawning of the spiritual awareness), others take it to be baptism (repentance symbolized by water) and life in the Spirit (awakening to the reality of God's Spirit working in a person's life).

But if you recall, Paul spoke of the bride of Christ, the Church, in Ephesians 5:26, that God will use the Word as water to cleanse the Church, "to make her holy, cleansing her by the washing with water through the word." Christ buttressed that in John 15:3, which says, "You are already clean because of the word I have spoken to you." He also used that symbolically in the discourse he had with Peter in John 13:6-10:

> He came to Simon Peter, who said to him, "Lord, are you going to wash my feet?" Jesus replied, "You do not realize now what I am doing, but later you will understand." "No," said Peter, "you shall never wash my feet." Jesus answered, "Unless I wash you, you have no part with me." "Then, Lord," Simon Peter replied, "not just my feet but my hands and my head as well!" Jesus answered, "A person who has had a bath needs only to wash his feet; his

whole body is clean. And you are clean, though not every one of you."

As soon as we are cleansed, we are sealed with the Holy Spirit:

> In him we were also chosen, having been predestined according to the plan of him who works out everything in conformity with the purpose of his will, in order that we, who were the first to hope in Christ, might be for the praise of his glory. And you also were included in Christ when you heard the word of truth, the gospel of your salvation. Having believed, you were marked in him with a seal, the promised Holy Spirit, who is a deposit guaranteeing our inheritance until the redemption of those who are God's possession—to the praise of his glory (Ephesians 1:11-14).

Not only are we cleansed with water and sealed by the Spirit, but through the Spirit we are translated into the kingdom of God, as described by Christ to Nicodemus in John 3:5. Paul's description simplifies the salvation experience man enjoys entering into the kingdom of God, "Giving thanks to the Father, who has qualified you to share in the inheritance of the saints in the kingdom of light. For he has rescued us from the dominion of darkness and brought us into the kingdom of the Son he loves, in whom we have redemption, the forgiveness of sins" (Colossians 1:12-14).

"When we all get to heaven, what a day of rejoicing that will be! When we all see Jesus, we will sing and shout the victory!" Our Father conveys the meaning that His abode has warmth, love and joy. Someone said it is a state of happiness infinite in degree and endless in duration. Another writer said the joys of heaven are without example, above experience, and beyond imagination. According to Hannah Moore, heaven is a place of perfect purity, fullness of joy, everlasting freedom, health and fruition, complete security and eternal life. It's referred to as a Kingdom with a King (see Matthew 18:1).

Heaven is a city with citizens. Hebrews 11:10, 16 says, "For he looked for a city which hath foundations, whose builder and maker is God. . . . But now they desire a better country, that is, an heavenly city: wherefore God is not ashamed to be called their God: for he hath prepared for them a city." In other words, heaven is a building with its dwellers. It's a building and mansion of God. Although the Bible tells us about this mansion, songwriter Ira F. Stamphill penned this concerning this mansion: "I've got a mansion just over the hilltop, in that bright land where we'll never grow old. And some day yonder, we will never more wander but walk the streets that are purest gold."

Dr. Lockyer states, "Heaven is eternal in duration as a home; it will never crumble and there will be no need for renovations. Heaven will not decay because of the ravages of time, storm or war. God's dwelling is as eternal as He is." No sin will enter the pearly white city, only the godly in Christ Jesus have the right of entrance into heaven. But all the wicked and Christ rejecters are disqualified for citizenship in this city without foundation. Galatians 5:21 tells us that those who participate in envy, drunkenness, orgies, and the like, will not inherit the kingdom of God. Ephesians 5:5 says; "For of this you can be sure: No immoral, impure or greedy person—such a man is an idolater—has any inheritance in the kingdom of Christ and of God."

Revelation 22:14-15 also says, "Blessed are those who wash their robes, that they may have the right to the tree of life and may go through the gates into the city. Outside are the dogs, those who practice magic arts, the sexually immoral, the murderers, the idolaters and everyone who loves and practices falsehood." To be a citizen of heaven, we must have a heavenly nature, which is what the Holy Spirit supplies when He makes the sinner a partaker of the divine nature. The road to heaven is not an easy one. We have been pressed out of measure, cast down, insomuch that we despaired even of life. We have had trouble on every side: perplexity, persecution, distress, famine, peril, sword, death, sickness and disease, but our eyes are on Jesus!

We have turned to Him when we accepted Him as our Lord and Savior, and we will continue to set our affection on Him. Who else can we turn to anyway? There is no failure with Him. Satan buffeted us! Demons, wicked human spirits, leaders, executives, chiefs, masterminds, controllers, strong men, witches and wizards fought against us, but we will soon be done with troubles and trials. When we get home on the other side, we are going to sit down and rest with the King of kings for eternity.

It is an opportune time to join with the heavenly host and give God the highest praise. Revelation 7:16-17 says, "Never again will they hunger; never again will they thirst. The sun will not beat upon them, nor any scorching heat. For the Lamb at the center of the throne will be their shepherd; he will lead them to springs of living water. And God will wipe away every tear from their eyes."

Let us thank God our Father, and Jesus Christ, the King of kings and the Lord of lords, that there will be no more sorrow, crying, and tears. All the curses of this world will forever be removed. There will be no sea, the emblem of unrest and dissatisfaction. Most of us are afraid to die, but thanks be to God Almighty that there will be no more death! The Word of the Lord says in 1 Corinthians 15:26 that the last enemy that will be destroyed is death and Hades. Revelation 20:14 says that death and Hades will be thrown into the lake of fire, which is the second death. There will be no night; all weariness will vanish.

What a day of rejoicing it will be when we all get to heaven! We will sing, "God, I am free! Praise the Lord, I am free! No longer bound! No more chain holding me! My soul is resting! It's just a blessing! I am free, praise the Lord, I am free at last!" Psalm 16:11 says there will be fullness of joy and pleasures forevermore.

Thank God a day is coming when there will be rest from weary labor. Hebrews 4:9 states, "There remaineth therefore a rest to the people of God" (KJV). Revelation 14:13 says, "Then I heard a voice from heaven say, write "Blessed are the dead who die in the Lord from now on. . . . They will rest from their labor, for their deeds will follow them." There will be unceasing service. They will be before Him day and night in the temple, and He who sits on the throne will spread His tent over them (Revelation 7:15). Revelation 22:3 says, "There shall be no more curse" (KJV). The throne of God and of the Lamb will be the city, and His servants will serve Him. There will be perfect knowledge: "For we know in part and we prophesy in part, but when perfection comes, the imperfect disappears. When I was a child, I talked like a child; I thought like a child, I reasoned like a child.

When I became a man, I put childish ways behind me. Now we see but a poor reflection as in a mirror; then we shall see face to face. Now I know in part; then I shall know fully, even as I am fully known" (1 Corinthians 13:9-12). There will be perfect beauty and safety.

There will be happy reunion with loved ones: "But now that he is dead, why should I fast? Can I bring him back again? I will go to him, but he will not return to me" (2 Samuel 12:23). This is what St. Paul states in 1 Thessalonians 4:13-18:

> Brothers, we do not want you to be ignorant about those who fall asleep, or to grieve like the rest of men, who have no hope. We believe that Jesus died and rose again and so we believe that God will bring with Jesus those who have fallen asleep in him. According to the Lord's own word, we tell you that we who are still alive, who are left till the coming of the Lord, will certainly not precede those who have fallen asleep. For the Lord himself will come down from heaven, with a loud command, with the voice of the archangel and with the trumpet call of God, and the dead in Christ will rise first. After that, we who are still alive and are left will be caught up together with them in the clouds to meet the Lord in the air. And so we will be with the Lord forever. Therefore encourage each other with these words.

Soon and very soon, we shall behold Him face to face with all His glory. Are we ready for the New Jerusalem? An insight of this city is worth living for! Revelation 21:1-10 states thus:

> Then I saw a new heaven and a new earth, for the first heaven and the first earth had passed away, and there was no longer any sea. I saw the Holy City, the New Jerusalem, coming down out of heaven from God, prepared as a bride beautifully dressed for her husband. And I heard a loud voice from the throne saying, "Now the dwelling of God is with men, and he will live with them. They will be his people, and God himself will be with them and be their God. He will wipe every tear from their eyes. There will be no more death or mourning or crying or pain, for the old order of things has passed away." He who was seated on the throne said,

"I am making everything new!" Then he said, "Write this down, for these words are trustworthy and true." He said to me: "It is done. I am the Alpha and the Omega, the Beginning and the End. To him who is thirsty I will give to drink without cost from the spring of the water of life. He who overcomes will inherit all this, and I will be his God and he will be my son. But the cowardly, the unbelieving, the vile, the murderers, the sexually immoral, those who practice magic arts, the idolaters and all liars—their place will be in the fiery lake of burning sulfur. This is the second death." One of the seven angels who had the seven bowls full of the seven last plagues came and said to me, "Come, I will show you the bride, the wife of the Lamb." And he carried me away in the Spirit to a mountain great and high, and showed me the Holy City, Jerusalem, coming down out of heaven from God.

After this I heard what sounded like the roar of a great multitude in heaven shouting: "Hallelujah! Salvation and glory and power belong to our God, for true and just are his judgments. He has condemned the great prostitute who corrupted the earth by her adulteries. He has avenged on her the blood of his servants." And again they shouted: "Hallelujah! The smoke from her goes up forever and ever." The twenty-four elders and the four living creatures fell down and worshipped God, who was seated on the throne. And they cried: "Amen, Hallelujah!" Then a voice came from the throne, saying: "Praise our God, all you his servants, you who fear him, both small and great!" Then I heard what sounded like a great multitude, like the roar of rushing waters and like loud peals of thunder, shouting: "Hallelujah! For our Lord God Almighty reigns. Let us rejoice and be glad and give him glory! For the wedding of the Lamb has come, and his bride has made herself ready" (Revelation 19:1-7).

In heaven, we will be giving the Lamb of God the highest praise, Hallelujah! *Hallelujah* comes from two Hebrew words, *hillēl* and *yāh*, and means "praise Yahweh."

Last, but certainly not least, heaven is full of God's presence and overwhelming joy. Revelation 4:1-11 says:

> After this I looked, and there before me was a door standing open in heaven. And the voice I had first heard speaking to me like a trumpet said, "Come up here, and I will show you what must take place after this." At once I was in the Spirit, and there before me was a throne in heaven with someone sitting on it. And the one who sat there had the appearance of jasper and carnelian. A rainbow, resembling an emerald, encircled the throne. Surrounding the throne were twenty-four other thrones, and seated on them were twenty-four elders. They were dressed in white and had crowns of gold on their heads. From the throne came flashes of lightning, rumblings and peals of thunder. Before the throne, seven lamps were blazing. These are the seven spirits of God. Also before the throne there was what looked like a sea of glass, clear as crystal. In the center, around the throne, were four living creatures, and they were covered with eyes, in front and in back. The first living creature was like a lion, the second was like an ox, the third had a face like a man, the fourth was like a flying eagle. Each of the four living creatures had six wings and was covered with eyes all around, even under his wings. Day and night they never stop saying: "Holy, holy, holy is the Lord God Almighty, who was, and is, and is to come." Whenever the living creatures give glory, honor and thanks to him who sits on the throne and who lives for ever and ever, the twenty-four elders fall down before him who sits on the throne, and worship him who lives for ever and ever. They lay their crowns before the throne and say: "You are worthy, our Lord and God, to receive glory and honor and power, for you created all things, and by your will they were created and have their being."

Let your destiny be God's place of abode! If your destiny is not the narrow road, now is the time to repent and redirect your steps in that direction, for heaven will be a place of rest. What a glorious day it is going to be should we make it to the pearly white city!

Prayer: Thank You, God, that Jesus gave the comforting words about that prepared place for those who trod the narrow road. To You, God, be the honor for preparing a place of abode for Your children to be with You forevermore. Father, many are distressed, but soon and very soon old things will pass away and all things will become new. Amen.

We must therefore continue to keep our eyes daily on the eastern sky, for our redemption draws nigh. Our focus must remain on the Lord as we make our way to our mansion that He has prepared for us, even those whose names are written on the palm of His hand and in the Lamb's Book of Life.

CHAPTER 13

INSTRUMENTS FOR HIS GLORY: HANNAH AND ANNA OF PHANUEL

There is turmoil in life, but no matter how unbearable or unexplainable our lives may appear, our Father's hand is not so short that He cannot save us. He can reach down into the miry clay and save us if our hope is stayed on Him. Therefore we must be built up, rooted and established in Him and in the faith in which we were taught, abounding in thanksgiving and not allowing anything to distort our vision. Let us therefore fix our eyes on Him, knowing who He is! Romans 6:13 says, "Do not offer the parts of your body to sin, as instruments of wickedness, but rather offer yourselves to God, as those who have been brought from death to life; and offer the parts of your body to him as instruments of righteousness."

From the very beginning of time, God created woman to play a significant role in His plan. Two remarkable women, Anna and Hannah, could have erred and delayed or hindered the plans of God in their lives, but they turned to God in prayer and fasting and they beheld with their eyes the handiwork of God. I know some of us are in a mess and we are being tested, but if we would take our eyes off the situation by turning our eyes upon God, He is able to do exceedingly abundantly more than we can ask or think. Because of His power that is working within me, I feel like taking a break and praising the Lord!

Do you feel that way as well? Then do it! Regardless of your situation, you are an instrument for His glory. You are destined for greatness because the Greater One and His anointing dwell in you. In you dwells the incorruptible Seed, the Word of Christ, but if you do not believe that it is so, check the Word of God which says in Colossians 3:16, "Let the word of Christ dwell in you richly as you teach and admonish one another with all wisdom, and as you sing psalms, hymns and spiritual songs with gratitude in your hearts to God."

The Word within you and me is to sanctify us. The written Word of God says, "Sanctify them by the truth; your word is truth" (John 17:17). The sanctified instruments for God's glory will do the work of the ministry. Such a vessel will prophesy, fast and pray, praise and worship God. In this chapter, our focus will be on a widow. As mentioned earlier, the Word of the Lord says in Luke 2:36-38, "There was also a prophetess, Anna, the daughter of Phanuel, of the tribe of Asher. She was very old; she had lived with her husband seven years after her marriage, and then was a widow until she was eighty-four. She never left the temple but worshipped night and day, fasting and praying. Coming up to [Joseph, Mary and Jesus] at that very moment, she gave thanks to God and spoke about the child to all who were looking forward to the redemption of Jerusalem." I would like you to bear in mind that the names *Anna* and *Hannah* mean "grace." These two women were instruments of God's unmerited favor or goodness. Let us focus on this widow woman first, however, and then we will conclude with Hannah, the childless woman of godly motherhood.

It is quite interesting that my middle name is Anna and, like the prophetess, I also believe in prophecy, fasting and prayer. The Word of the Lord says that Anna was a widow. Her husband died after seven years of marriage. Some of us would have been devastated if we were wearing the shoes of this woman. I believe she grieved for a while, but she did not allow herself to be grief-stricken like Mary Magdalene. She also did not grieve to the extent of not recognizing the plan of God in her life. As you know, God's Word says that this woman was a prophetess and in her old age she was doing the work of ministry. Psalm 92:13-14 reads, "Planted in the house of the Lord, they will flourish in the courts of our God. They will still bear fruit in old age, they will stay fresh and green." Therefore there is no excuse for the aged women or mothers of Zion to sit relaxed in the body of Christ saying, "I have finished the course, and I am waiting for my time of departure."

Aged women or mothers must be instruments for God's glory to teach the young women to be sober, to love their husbands, to love their children, to be discreet and chaste, keepers of the home, good, and obedient to their own husbands, so that the Word of God will not be blasphemed or mocked. Aged women or mothers of the body of Christ do not retire. They must re-fire to prophesy, pray and fast. For it is imperative to yield your members as instruments unto righteousness, prepared to do the Master's will as a woman.

When I entered Haughton Street Church of God, there was something peculiar about a wonderful anointed mother of Zion. She was one of the prominent mothers of that church. I did not know anything about her, but God knows who she is. She is a woman of fasting and prayer. One day, when we moved to West Toronto Church of God, she pulled me aside and said to me, "Do not be discouraged nor give up, and do not leave the Church. I am praying for you."

I was so excited and blessed when I heard those words of comfort; I was revived and decided to press on. She was in the house of God doing the will of God. Isn't it very interesting that she is a widow? Like Anna, she is in the house of God doing His will. However, listen, you do not have to be a widow to do the will of God. Every woman in the house of God must present herself as a living sacrifice, holy, acceptable unto God, which is her reasonable service. The Bible tells us that Anna was a prophetess and in her old age she was effective in the Temple. She was eighty-four years old when the infant Jesus was brought into the Temple to be dedicated; she recognized and proclaimed Jesus as the Messiah. We need women of this caliber in the body of Christ.

In you dwells the incorruptible Seed, the Word, to strengthen, comfort and edify. You have the gift of prophecy. Fan it aflame in the name of Jesus Christ of Nazareth. Trust me, there is somebody close to you who needs comfort, strength and building up, so rise up, prophetess, and do the work in the house of God. What is prophecy? One writer says, it is to speak with forthrightness and insight, especially when enabled by the Spirit of God. It is divinely inspired and anointed utterance as well as the proclamation of the supernatural in a known language. Prophecy, in other words, is a manifestation of the Spirit of God by the spirit, not the intellect. "All these are the work of one and the same Spirit, and he gives them to each one, just as he determines" (1 Corinthians 12:11).

It may operate in all who have the infilling of the Holy Spirit: "For you can all prophesy in turn so that everyone may be instructed and encouraged" (14:31), and in accordance to the will of God (12:11), by intellect and by faith, but its exercise is not intellectually based. Prophecy is calling forth words from the Spirit of God.

This woman by the name of Anna was doing precisely that. Remember, Jesus Christ was garbed in flesh and was nestled in the arm of Mary. What I would like you to bear in mind is the truth, and nothing but the truth, that Mary needed a word about this strange happening in her life. She had heard many things and had pondered them in her heart.

She had laid hold of the salvation plan, but going to Jerusalem to dedicate this Baby, she needed a word from God. It was at this moment in her life that Anna, an instrument of God's glory, presented herself to the holy mother of Jesus. The Word of the Lord says, "And she coming in that instant gave thanks likewise unto the Lord, and spake of him to all them that looked for redemption" (Luke 2:38 KJV). Indeed, you are also peculiar! You are an instrument of the incorruptible seed of Jesus Christ. I take it a pleasure in comforting, strengthening and building you up, because that "baby" that you are going to give birth to will be a blessing to your family, to society and to the world. Anna gave thanks to God for Mary's Baby and prophesied about this Baby.

I also have a kind of jealousy for God's people, for which cause I also prophesy over them, knowing that the Son of Man was manifested so that they too will become sons of God showing forth the glory of God. Your ministry may not be the same as Anna's but you were created to be an instrument for God's glory.

Remember that even though Anna was a widow, she served the Lord in the Temple. I thank God for her life of commitment and devotion. The Word of the Lord declares that she departed not from the Temple, but served God with fasting and prayer. If there was ever a time that the women of God needed to fast and pray, it is now.

What is fasting? One author states that a biblical definition for fasting is a Christian's voluntary abstinence from food for spiritual purposes. Since fasting is voluntary, it is not to be coerced. Fasting is more than the ultimate crash diet for the body; it is abstinence from food for spiritual purposes. Richard Foster defines fasting as "the voluntary denial of a normal function for the sake of intense spiritual activity."

So then, fasting does not always deal with abstinence from food. Sometimes during fasting we may need to abstain ourselves from involvement with other folks, or from the public, from the telephone, from talking, or from sleep or rest, in order to become more absorbed in a time for spiritual activity.

Isaiah 58:6 says, "Is not this the fast that I have chosen? To loose the bands of wickedness, to undo the heavy burdens, and to let the oppressed go free, and that ye break every yoke?" (KJV). There are yokes to be broken, bands, shackles, habits and strongholds to be broken and destroyed. Strongholds are things that hold you strong, but in the name of Jesus Christ you are going to be loosed.

Your spirit, soul and body must be loosed so that you will be that woman of destiny. The Word of the Lord says in Mark 9:29, "He replied, 'This kind can come out only by prayer'. "This kind" is referring to the casting out of the demon that possessed a lad in the above chapter. Fasting and prayer will cause the Enemy's neck to be broken on the same gallows he built for you.

Fasting and prayer caused Jehoshaphat's enemies' great defeat. They used the sword against each other to utter destruction. Fasting and prayer will cause the righteous to receive favor. Fasting and prayer will enable one to call forth a word from the Spirit of God. Fasting and prayer will cause the eyes of your understanding to be enlightened so that you may know Jesus better.

Fasting and prayer will enable you to be spiritual giants for the Lord, counteracting, contending with and pulling down every stronghold of the devil and his cohorts. The city of Nineveh declared a citywide fast. Every beast, man, boy and girl fasted, and there was citywide repentance. May it be so for our city and even among the nations!

Anna was a woman of prayer. She spent quality time talking to God. We must purpose in our hearts to be women and men of prayer. We must boldly turn and approach the throne of grace and have a little talk with Abba Father. You may have tolerated a situation for too long. You may be depressed because of the mess, but do not look back or you may become a pillar of salt like Lot's wife. Rather, turn to the Lord, and He can turn your mess into a message.

You may have wept many times and you may have lost your appetite, but it is time to rise up in the name of Jesus and turn wholeheartedly to the throne of grace, where you can find mercy and help in the time of need. We must be determined to tell Jesus; only Jesus can help us, only Jesus alone.

Cry if you have to! The Word of the Lord declares that there was a poor man who cried and God delivered him out of all of his situations. David the anointed psalmist wrote, "Hear my cry, O God; listen to my prayer. From the ends of the earth I call to you, I call as my heart grows faint; lead me to the rock that is higher than I. For you have been my refuge, a strong tower against the foe. I long to dwell in your tent forever and take refuge in the shelter of your wings" (61:1-4). I love the protection that I have under His wings. He who dwells in the secret place of the Most High God shall abide under the shadow of the Almighty. He shall cover us with His feathers, and under His wings shall we trust. His truth shall be our shield and buckler. Amen!

The Holy Spirit would like to draw your attention to Hannah in 1 Samuel chapter 1. This woman was barren, but she prayed and wept bitterly before God: "And she vowed a vow, and said, O Lord of hosts, if thou wilt indeed look on the affliction of thine handmaid, and remember me, and not forget thine handmaid, but wilt give unto thine handmaid a man child, then I will give him unto the Lord all the days of his life, and there shall no razor come upon his head" (v. 11 KJV).

Let your eyes be turned to the hills from where comes your help. Your help comes from the Lord. The One who made heaven is God, Abba, your Father. Hannah was misunderstood, but she humbled herself and spoke to Eli. She received her blessing and rose up early in the morning and worshipped before the Lord. Then she returned to Ramah and God remembered her.

This woman of God conceived, and when the appointed time had come, she gave birth to a son and named him Samuel, which means "asked of God." If God answered Hannah, His ears are not deaf so that He cannot hear you. His hand is not short so that He cannot save you. He has not changed! He is able to do it again and again!

Hannah promised the Lord that she would give her only child to serve the Lord all the days of his life. She was faithful; she said, "Oh my lord, as thy soul liveth, my lord, I am the woman that stood by thee here, praying unto the Lord. For this child I prayed; and the Lord hath given me my petition which I asked of him" (vv. 26-27 KJV).

Anna was a widow, but she served the Lord night and day in fasting and prayer. Anna was an instrument for God's glory! She was a prophetess in the Temple. She recognized that Jesus was the Messiah. Hannah was an unhappy married woman, but she rose up and went into the Temple and offered up her supplication unto the Lord. God heard her, and she conceived and gave birth to a son. God was faithful to these wonderful women of God; He will also be faithful to you as you present your body as an instrument of righteousness unto God.

Prayer: Lord God of Hosts, when we are pinned down by our rival or opponent, help us to arise and enter the house of prayer or Your secret place and pour out or spread out our letter to You. Our eyes fixed upon You will cause our barrenness to cease, and we will be impregnated and bear much fruit, in Jesus' precious name. Amen.

In you dwells the incorruptible Seed, the Word, to strengthen, comfort and edify. You have the gift of prophecy. Fan it aflame in the name of Jesus Christ of Nazareth. Trust me, there is somebody close to you who needs comfort, strength and building up, so rise up, prophetess, and do the work in the house of God. What is prophecy? It is to speak with forthrightness and insight, especially when enabled by the Spirit of God.

CHAPTER 14

FEAR

God's people are fearfully and wonderfully created to accomplish great things on the face of this earth. There are many individuals, however, who are destined for greatness but, without Christ, they may make an insignificant spiritual impact! They mostly leave no legacy that others can remember or by which they may be encouraged to fight the good fight of faith. Many have succumbed to the spirit of fear and have not fulfilled or accomplished the plan of God in their lives. We need to apply the Word of the Lord in our lives that the apostle Paul wrote to his spiritual son Timothy. This significant quotation can be found in 2 Timothy 1:7: "For God did not give us a spirit of timidity, but a spirit of power, of love and of self-discipline."

Fear has caused many to achieve less than they ought to attain for God. It has also caused many individuals to doubt themselves and as a result has lead to unrealized potential. Fear has crippled many, and so their minds are muddled and they cannot perceive what the Holy Spirit is telling them. As a result, they are in confusion and full of anxiety. They therefore need to turn to the One who is able to redirect and restore them. When you are redirected to Him, you will know that God has not given you the spirit of fear but the power to recover all and remain militant as a dressed-up soldier of the cross of Jesus.

The Hebrew word for fear is *yir-ah*, and the Greek word is *Phobos*. Fear has two principal meanings in English. The first meaning of fear is apprehension of evil, which normally leads one to flee or to fight.

It is therefore fair to say that fear could result in fight or flight. It is of great interest to know that the physiology of the body is affected when there is an alarm. When we are faced with physical danger or psychological stress, the adrenal gland responds by producing or secreting adrenaline. Adrenaline is a powerful hormone or heart stimulant which enters the bloodstream or circulatory system and in seconds causes dramatic action in the body. This process is known as fight-or-flight response since it prepares one either to physically encounter or to flee from an enemy.

Fear is awe and reverence, which a person senses or feels in the presence of God; fear is to serve or worship God. Fear is no respecter of persons; everyone has some kind of fear, especially during childhood days. The icy fingers of fear creep up the spines of amateurs and professionals alike. Some people have a dreaded social problem called *laliophobia*, a fear of speaking.

I do not believe that God desires for His children to be dominated by this type of fear. Throughout the Bible "fear not" is recorded ninety times, and is sometimes followed with the phrase "neither be dismayed." For instance, Isaiah 41:10 tells us, "So do not fear, for I am with you; do not be dismayed, for I am your God. I will strengthen you and help you; I will uphold you with my righteous right hand."

It is quite apparent that fear affects us at some point during our pilgrimage on this earth. The Bible informs us about a man who had a problem with timidity but was encouraged by the great herald of the Gospel. Accordingly the apostle Paul, the dynamic mentor, discerned that his spiritual son Timothy was fearful, so in 2 Timothy 1:7 scriptures reveal that Paul wrote a letter to encourage him. Here again is the quote in Paul's letter to his spiritual son: "For God did not give us a spirit of timidity, but a spirit of power, of love and of self-discipline."

Paul was concerned about Timothy's gentle nature and the danger that fright might cause him. That is, he might have been confounded and subdued by those who opposed the Gospel. Therefore Timothy needed to be encouraged to be bold and fearless in order to stand before those who might stand against him. This word of encouragement might be applicable in our lives. If so, we must lay hold of Paul's admonishment to Timothy until the word is woven into our minds and hearts.

As followers of Jesus Christ, we must have this awareness that opposition is inevitable, but the Word of God is available to help us overcome every opposition. 2 Timothy 3:16-17 states, "All Scripture is God-breathed and is useful for teaching, rebuking, correcting and training in righteousness, so that the man of God may be thoroughly equipped for every good work." Fear is a spirit, but be informed that it is not of God for us to fear. Scripture says in 1 John 4:18, "There is no fear in love. But perfect love drives out fear, because fear has to do with punishment. The one who fears is not made perfect in love." One of the devil's ploys is to cast the spirit of fear upon God's people.

If we are ignorant of this fact, fear will dominate our lives, crippling our abilities. Have you ever seen people who possess greatness or have potential, yet when they are called upon to show forth their treasure or their power, they begin to make excuses? We must purpose in our hearts to be steadfast in the Lord and turn to Him, because He is the one who gives gifts and abilities that can be used for glorification purposes. Ask Him therefore to fan aflame the treasure in your earthen vessel so that God's glory might be magnified in your life.

It is imperative that we know who we are in Christ Jesus. We are vessels of honor destined for greatness. We are possessed with wisdom and authority to declare to the spirit of fear, "Greater is He who is in us than he who is in the world." This may be the reality in your life; your knees may be shaking and buckling under you as though you are experiencing an earthquake, when, in reality, you are called upon to do something for the Lord. God's word to you is, be strong and be of good courage, and let your shaking knees kneel in prayer before the Almighty God and lay hold of His Word, which is able to give you the security you need in life.

God is able to bless you exceedingly and abundantly even more than you can ask or think because of the power that is at work in you. We are His children, and He has endowed us with godly potential to do all things through Jesus Christ. Fear must be conquered, and that can be done if we are found doing the things we fear, which will cement in us the assurance through which we know and believe that fear has loosened its power that binds or torments us. Fear can affect the mind and warp our thinking, but we must continue to look to God, submitting to Him, resisting the devil so he will flee from us.

We have also been informed that we have the mind of Christ, according to the Word of the Lord in Philippians 2:5: "Your attitude should be the same as that of Christ Jesus." Isaiah 26:3 says, "Thou wilt keep him in perfect peace, whose mind is stayed on thee." Here is a very important question: On what is your mind stayed?

Can you imagine all the things that could go wrong in your life if your mind is not stayed on God? Are you concerned about the instantaneous speech impediment or the tripping on the stage, choking on water or someone criticizing you? Instead of keeping our minds on negative issues, our minds are supposed to be reservoirs of the Word of God in order for us to be settled and to stop us from worrying and playing the "What if?" games which put us into utter despair. Worry is just another form of fear, which must be subjected to the active Word of God.

The Word of the Lord instructs us in Philippians 4:6-7 saying, "Do not be anxious about anything, but in everything, by prayer and petition, with thanksgiving, present your requests to God. And the peace of God, which transcends all understanding, will guard your hearts and your minds in Christ Jesus." For that matter, we need not entertain fear for anything or anyone. Rather, let's examine this spiritual nugget about King Zedekiah, who feared his opponents and suffered the consequences. King Zedekiah at one point was afraid of the Jews, so he consulted the prophet Jeremiah regarding the future. The prophet of God instructed him to surrender to his enemy, for God had mapped out a route for him, but because he was afraid of ridicule he decided not to listen to the instruction given by God. Therefore his children were killed before his very eyes, and then his eyes were plucked out of their sockets. He was bound in prison and died a blind man (2 Kings 25:7). There are enormous facts in this man's life we need to grasp, namely that through the name of Jesus Christ of Nazareth, we can cast out the fear that is holding us.

Fear must not be tolerated! It must flee from us. Here is a personal testimony about my experience with fear intended to edify, encourage and strengthen the body of Christ. The spirit of fear had me bound for a long time. I used to shake like a reed when called upon to do or say something. My knees buckled and my jaws jumped as if they literally had legs. This testimony has brought to my mind the story about the unschooled fishermen in the Bible.

They were very fearful, but when the Holy Ghost descended upon them, they were as bold as lions. They faced opposition, at times were thrown into jail, and were beaten for their faith in Christ, but they did not give up. These men gathered themselves together in their homes and turned their eyes toward heaven, and God moved on their behalf. Similarly, despite the fear that was holding me, I boldly entered the throne of grace or the presence of the Lord like the unschooled fishermen, and I prayed fervently to God. I said, Father, if they overcame fear, I can also be an overcomer in Jesus' name. Now look at me, I am preaching the Word to many, and the Lord is using me to write encouraging, inspirational books to build up the body of Christ.

Paul wrote to the Philippians, "I can do everything through him who gives me strength" (4:13). This word is for you and me. In real terms we can do anything, but do not fail because of fear. Therefore lay hold of the Word of God and you will be a fearless Christian soldier. Christian soldier, the war is on, but you cannot give up. You must fight the good fight of faith!

Prayer: Father, Your unconditional love enables us to stand boldly and fearlessly in overwhelming situations, and we want to thank You. Help us not to entertain the spirit of fear, for we will inhibit the greater works that You so desire to perform in us. We humble ourselves and submit to You, knowing that the devil is resisted and he will flee, in Jesus' precious name. Amen.

Fear has caused many to achieve less than they ought to attain for God. It has also caused many individuals to doubt themselves, and as a result has lead to unrealized potential. Fear has crippled many, and so their minds are muddled and they cannot perceive what the Holy Spirit is telling them. As a result, they are in confusion and full of anxiety. They therefore need to turn to the One who is able to redirect and restore them.

CHAPTER 15

JEHOVAH'S PRESENCE WITH POWER AND FIRE

How interesting it is that we figuratively see or rather encounter the fire of the Lord at Mount Horeb, the place Moses and Israel saw and encountered the Lord during their pilgrimage from Egypt to the Promised Land. When we are at this place, the Almighty God knows how to construct or train us for greater things. Here, it's absolutely important that we focus on Him and stay in God's holding pattern until we see the burning bush and experience His fiery presence. Only then will He give us clarity and direction to life, prosperity and salvation.

Read these scriptures: "For the Lord your God is a consuming fire, a jealous God" (Deuteronomy 4:24). "'Then you call on the name of your god, and I will call on the name of the Lord. The god who answers by fire—he is God.' Then all the people said, 'What you say is good.'" (1 Kings 18:24). Deuteronomy 4:24 and Hebrews 12:29 say that the God whom we serve is a consuming fire. The fire of God will consume everything that is not of faith in Christ and the Cross:

> By the grace God has given me, I laid a foundation as an expert builder, and someone else is building on it. But each one should be careful how he builds. For no one can lay any foundation other than the one already laid, which is Jesus Christ. If any man builds

on this foundation using gold, silver, costly stones, wood, hay or straw, his work will be shown for what it is, because the Day will bring it to light. It will be revealed with fire, and the fire will test the quality of each man's work. If what he has built survives, he will receive his reward. If it is burned up, he will suffer loss; he himself will be saved, but only as one escaping through the flames. Don't you know that you yourselves are God's temple and that God's Spirit lives in you? If anyone destroys God's temple, God will destroy him; for God's temple is sacred, and you are that temple (1 Corinthians 3:10-17).

The Greek word for fire is *puri* and speaks of the ability of Christ, who will be the Judge and who sees through everything we do (Revelation 2:18). He alone knows our motives! I believe it is worthwhile to look at this word in depth because fire is a very important commodity. According to one writer:

> Fire is an agent of purification, one of the so-called elements which burns, inflames, warms or heats: heat and light emanate visibly, perceptibly and simultaneously from anybody. The terrific energy of fire, the most important agent of civilization, the similarity of its effects with that of the sun, its intimate connection with light, its terrible and yet genial (cheerful) power, and the beauty of its changeful flame, easily account for the reverence in which fire was held in ancient days.

Can we survive without fire? Not in this life! One commentary states, "The universe is full of fire. The sun is a great globe of incandescence, every star shines by its own, and even the center of our planet is fire. Every volcano is a dynamic illustration of God's character." God is goodness, life and energy. God is a consuming fire! He is all-powerful! He is the omnipotent Father of mercy and grace. The Bible contains over five hundred references to fire, linking it with God ninety times. God in action is like a blazing fire.

The fire of Jehovah God has the same effect on all it touches. Fire is God's essential characteristic, "for the Lord is a consuming fire." The God whom we serve is like a forest fire, not an iceberg or icicles. Whatsoever Jehovah God does, He carries out with intense desire and blazing purposes. True partnership with Jehovah God means being on fire! Intimate relationship with God guarantees you being endowed with the Holy Ghost and with fire, for this God whom we serve has not changed; He is the same yesterday, today and forever. This God of fire whom we praise and worship has no fellowship with lukewarm or cold folks.

If there was ever a time when the twenty-first century church needed the fire of God, it is now! We need the burning which brings about purification. We need God's train again! We need His glory, His life, His presence. What has hindered us from seeing the fire, the power and the glory of God? Our ungodliness in the presence of a holy God has been the deterrent. Therefore it's imperative that we sanctify ourselves for God to come down and tabernacle with us. We must depart from evil and do good. We must turn to the God of fire, for certainly He knows how to answer us by fire.

The Word of the Lord was written for our learning, and if we take a look into the perfect law of liberty, we will all be saved. In the church under the cloud, God directed Moses to sanctify the people on the third day and He would come down on Mount Sinai. Moses was obedient, according to Exodus 19:14: "Moses went down from the mount unto the people, and sanctified the people; and they washed their clothes" (KJV). And on the third day, God came down in thunder and lightning and there was a thick cloud upon the mount, and the voice of the trumpet waxed very loud, so that the people in the camp trembled.

Then Moses led the people out of the camp to meet with God, and they stood at the foot of the mountain. Mount Sinai was covered with smoke because the Lord descended on it in fire. The smoke billowed up from it like from a furnace, the whole mountain trembled violently, and the sound of the trumpet grew louder and louder. Then Moses spoke and the voice of God answered. The Lord descended on the top of Mount Sinai and called Moses to the top of the mountain. So Moses went up and the Lord said to him, "Go down and warn the people so that they do not force their way through to see the Lord and many of them perish" (v. 21).

In order for God to come down and for us to be drawn close to Him, consecration must be our chief business. How is one consecrated? Being consecrated means being set apart for God's use. It involves oneself and one's clothing, symbolizing the need for purity before God. Jeremiah 33:3 says, "Call unto me, and I will show thee great and mighty things, which thou knowest not" (KJV). Hear this, we cannot take heed to this invitation if we are not living a holy life, for our God is a holy God.

Without holiness we will not be able to please Him, for they who come to Him must be holy. We, the blood-bought church of the living God, the righteousness of God through faith in Jesus Christ, should remain holy. We are a kingdom of priests, a royal priesthood that God made us through faith in Christ Jesus. The Bible refers to Jehovah God as a God of brimstone and fire and as a consuming fire. Because God's essential characteristic is fire, His desire is to connect or minister through us, his ministers of flame, to all peoples and nations.

Let me tell you why we can be referred to as ministers of flame. In Deuteronomy 30:14 and Romans 10:8 the Bible says, "'The word is near you; it is in your mouth and in your heart,' that is, the word of faith we are proclaiming." This word that is in your mouth is fire. Jeremiah, one of the Major Prophets, said in 23:29, "'Is not my word like fire,' declares the Lord, 'and like a hammer that breaks a rock in pieces?'" Also, listen to what my brother James says in 3:6: "The tongue also is a fire, a world of evil among the parts of the body. It corrupts the whole person, sets the whole course of his life on fire, and is itself set on fire by hell." Own this truth, that when the word is in your mouth, the tongue is consecrated, so your tongue will become fire that will cause a world of goodness, transformation, encouragement, life, healing, salvation and all things that bring life and godliness.

So the tongue among your members does not defile the whole body, but the whole body is infused with life and health to set you on fire, which is the course of nature. This is good! This is what we need in our lives and behind the four walls of the church—set the whole course of nature on Holy Ghost fire. Why are we considered ministers of flame? Is it not because you have the mind of Christ?

Paul wrote to the Philippians saying, "Let this mind be in you, which was also in Christ Jesus" (2:5 KJV). Therefore this mind of ours is supposed to be girded with truth! We are supposed to be thoroughly equipped to have an encounter with the heavenly light. Though God lives in unapproachable light, He is the consuming fire that is eternal, immortal, invisible, the only wise God who works in the affairs of His people.

The Word of the Lord tells us in James 5 that Elijah was a man subject to passion like us. This dynamic man of God prayed earnestly that it might not rain, and it rained not on the earth for three years and six months. And he prayed again, and the heavens gave rain, and earth brought forth her fruit. This is what is called the effectual prayer of a righteous man! Man's prayer—as well as woman's prayer—is powerful and effective. We need this *dunamis* power, we need the can-do power, for which cause I pray, *Lord send us more* Prophets like *Elijah to pray the power down! To heal the sick! To raise the dead! That the Lord would be glorified!* Let us pray for God to stir us to pray. If we just turn and never look back, we will find God. His Word says if you seek Him with all your heart, you will find Him.

Oh Lord, send us more Prophets like *Elijah to pray the power down!* Prayer is the most powerful force in the universe. James 5:16 states that the prayer of faith by the righteous man will cause God to answer by fire. Elijah, a dynamic vessel of honor, had an intimate relationship with Jehovah God. He was an anointed prophet with a double portion of anointing. Elijah presents us with a real challenge. He purposed in his heart to confront the wicked King Ahab, who was married to Jezebel.

Israel had abandoned the Lord's commandments and followed after Baal. Baal was the Canaanite fertility god believed to be responsible for germinating crops, increasing flocks, and adding children to the community. Baal was best known among the Canaanite gods. Ahab wanted Elijah to solve the problem of drought that was upon the land, but God had other plans for him. The name *Elijah* symbolized the message: "the Lord is my God!" This man of God was to call Israel back to their God. Elijah told Ahab to gather the people together from all over Israel to meet him on Mount Carmel.

This is something interesting and dynamic! For on this mountaintop came the fire. There won't be any real fire until we are set apart. We must be filled with the Holy Ghost. Elijah was a true prophet of God! He spoke on behalf of God. This anointed vessel of honor was not impressed with the four hundred and fifty prophets of Baal and the four hundred prophets of Asherah who ate at Jezebel's table. Elijah knew his God, and he had a desire to showcase the God who answers by fire. The prophet of God asked a very important question which is still applicable to our Christian life: How long will you waver between two opinions?

If God be God, follow Him, but if Baal is god, serve him. Turn from the false gods that do not have hands to save or ears to hear, but when you call upon Jehovah, He will hear you and by His hand that is not short and He will save you. Look at what Scripture says in Psalm 115:4-8: "But their idols are silver and gold, made by the hands of men. They have mouths, but cannot speak, eyes, but they cannot see; they have ears, but cannot hear, noses, but they cannot smell; they have hands, but cannot feel, feet, but they cannot walk; nor can they utter a sound with their throats. Those who make them will be like them, and so will all who trust in them."

The people were still; they did not mutter a word. Elijah knew that his God is the incomparable supernatural Being that had not failed and would never fail. Exodus 15:11 says, "Who among the gods is like you, O Lord? Who is like you—majestic in holiness, awesome in glory, working wonders?" Elijah was the only true prophet alive with a peculiar ministry, but Baal had four hundred and fifty prophets. Does it not seem at times that the devil and his cohorts outnumber the people of God? Joshua said that they that are with you are more than they that are against you.

Elijah knew this and was therefore ready to showcase his God! Are you ready to showcase your God? Are you ready to boast in your God? Elijah stated his requests! Bring two bulls! He would choose one and so would the worshippers of Baal. They were told to cut their bull in pieces and put it on the wood. Elijah told them not to set their sacrifice on fire. He then commanded them to call upon their God and he would also call upon his God, and the God who answered by fire, He is God. The Word of the Lord tells us that they called on the name of Baal from morning till noon. They moaned and groaned, saying, "O Baal, answer us." They shouted, for it seemed that their god was dead because he did not answer them by fire. They thought of appeasing him by dancing around the altar, but this gesture had no effect on their dead god. Elijah taunted them; he said to them, "Shout louder, for surely your god is real." We know about our God! He is real! Elijah said, "Maybe he is deep in thought or busy. Maybe he is traveling, or maybe he is sleeping and must be awakened."

So they were aroused, and they shouted louder and slashed themselves with swords and spears as was their custom, until blood gushed from morning till noon. They continued their frantic prophesying until the time for the evening sacrifice, but their god did not show up. They had a god who did not have ears to hear them, but we have a God whose ears are not deaf so that He cannot hear us. Their god had hands that were short, so it could not deliver, but we have a God whose hands are not short so that He cannot save us. Isaiah 59:1 says, "Surely the arm of the Lord is not too short to save, nor his ear too dull to hear." He will uphold us with the righteousness of His right hand.

Elijah had confidence in his God! He got the attention of the people. He had some very important things that he had to do! You have to prepare your sacrifice! "Lord, prepare us to be a sanctuary! Pure and holy, tried and true, with thanksgiving, we'll be a living sanctuary for You." Elijah prepared the altar of the Lord, which was in ruins. He took twelve stones for each of the tribes descended from Jacob, to whom the word of the Lord had come, saying, "Your name shall be Israel." Elijah used the stones to build the altar in the name of the Lord. He dug a trench around the altar to hold two seahs of seed. He arranged the wood, cut the bull in pieces and laid it on the altar. He then commanded them to fill four large jars with water and to pour it on the offering on the altar. He told them to pour the water three times. The water ran down around the altar and filled the trench. The number three in the Bible has great significance. The number three denotes favor, victory, healing, restoration, resurrection power and life.

Elijah was a man of prayer! If your desire is to see the power of God and the fire of God, you will have to be a man or woman of prayer. The God of our salvation is the God who answers by fire! His house is a house of prayer. Prayer is the match that will release the explosive power of the Holy Ghost in the affairs of God's people. Elijah stepped forward, turned his eyes toward heaven before offering up his sacrifice, and he prayed, "O Lord, God of Abraham, Isaac and Israel, let it be known today that you are God in Israel and that I am your servant and have done all these things at your command. Answer me, O Lord, answer me, so these people will know that you, O Lord, are God, and that you are turning their hearts back again" (1 Kings 18:36-37). Then the fire of the Lord fell and burned up the sacrifice, the wood, the stones and the soil, and licked up the water in the trench. I know about fire burning things that are combustible, like straw, trees, stubble and wood, but I have never seen stones burned up by fire. This fire is a different kind of fire! It is a strange fire! He is the God of brimstone and fire, that is why these stones were burned up by the consuming fire. The people were dumbstruck, they fell prostrate and cried, "The Lord is God! The Lord is God!"

When the fire of God falls, every knee shall bow and every tongue shall confess that Jesus Christ is Lord. The Spirit of the Lord is saying to the Church in a time such as this that God does not delight in Elijah's sacrifice because He sent His only Son to be the sacrifice. Jesus Christ was the perfect Lamb of God. He was manifested to be the perfect sacrifice so that you and I may present ourselves to Him as a living sacrifice, holy and acceptable. This is our reasonable service! Therefore you and I are supposed to be living sacrifices, consecrated so that the consuming fire will entrench us and burn us as ministers of flame until the fire is shut up in our bones. When we feel the fire in our innermost being, we will have to say like Jeremiah, "I feel like the fire is shut up in my bones!" We are living sacrifices!

We have tongues as of fire! The word, which is fire, is in our mouths, and it should indwell our hearts richly. You are a living sacrifice, the double-edged sword is in your hand and your feet are shod with the preparation of the Gospel of peace so that fire will burn, thus impacting others. Your fire and my fire join forces with the consuming fire, the Holy Ghost. The effect will be like that of Mount Sinai, Mount Carmel and the Upper Room. There will be cloven tongues like as of fire.

This is what the Spirit is saying to you and me about the living sacrifice Elijah offered. Fire gives warmth and light. One writer says, "Fire consumes what is combustible and tests that which is not so; it cleanses that which air nor water cannot cleanse. Its action is like giving life, just like the warmth of the mother bird while she broods upon her nest". Fire gives light and therefore indicates knowledge, the illumination the Holy Spirit imparts, that the eyes of your understanding would be enlightened (Ephesians 1:17-18; Hebrews 6:4). Fire gives heat and warms cold things and persons, which symbolizes the Spirit power that warms cold hearts (Romans 5:5).

Fire gives power and generates steam. It is a driving force, and so represents the energizing influence of the Spirit. When our souls are caught on fire, somebody is going to ask the question, "Why are you so ignited or empowered?" Then you can answer, "I am Holy Ghost filled. I am a vessel carrying the fire of God." We are possessed with that radiance and power to draw and impact those around us. Let us therefore go out into the world ignited by that fire, to save lives and build cities and nations for God.

Prayer: Almighty God, may You, the consuming fire, burn us so that we will have the discipline to maintain the fire of God in our bones, mind, mouth, hands and feet. Set us on fire so that we will run with the mandate or mission to impact Your people to catch the fire. Help us to be believers of flames ready and prepared to do the Master's perfect will, in Jesus' name. Amen.

If your desire is to see the power of God and the fire of God, you will have to be a man or woman of prayer. The God of our salvation is the God who answers by fire! His house is a house of prayer. Prayer is the match that will release the explosive power of the Holy Ghost in the affairs of God's people.

CHAPTER 16

PROCLAIMING THE POWER OF PENTECOST

If there was ever a time we needed to see the operation of the Holy Ghost in the life of the believer, it is now. The operation of the Holy Ghost in the Church has not changed; it is the believer who has fallen short. We are not seeing the evidences of miracles, signs and wonders as promised because we have turned away from God. We are either too busy running around doing our own thing, or we do not spend enough time in the presence of Almighty God seeking His face. Individually and collectively, we must make a turnaround and assemble ourselves in our upper room of prayer.

We must purpose in our hearts to spread out our letter before Almighty God, like Hezekiah, and put our head between our knees and turn our faces to the wall until heaven is unfolded and God descends to take a look into our life. Scripture says in Acts 1:8, "But you will receive power when the Holy Spirit comes on you; and you shall be my witnesses in Jerusalem, and in all Judea and Samaria, and to the ends of the earth." In *Merriam-Webster's Dictionary*, *power* is defined as "position of authority, ability to act, physical might, force or energy used to do work." The Greek word for power is *dunamis*—this means "dynamite," the "can-do power" in Christ Jesus.

The Church of the living God is known as the *Ecclesia*, or the body of Christ. Jesus Christ of Nazareth is the Head, and you and

I are the members. It is joy unspeakable and great glory when one understands that the church of the living God was purchased with Jesus' incorruptible blood. The Word of the Lord says in 1 Peter 1:18-19, "For you know that it was not with perishable things such as silver or gold that you were redeemed from the empty way of life handed down to you from your forefathers, but with the precious blood of Christ, a lamb without blemish or defect."

I would like you to bear in mind that the body of Christ is ordained and organized by a wise and all-powerful God. We are fearfully and wonderfully made to serve God so that He may glorify Himself in our bodies. Our bodies are the temple of the Holy Ghost. It is interesting to note that in the Old Testament period, the Spirit did not normally abide with or indwell mankind. He came upon people temporarily to inspire or enable them to do specific tasks. Pentecost marked the beginning of a new period in the Holy Spirit's relation with humanity when He came to possess believers. He came to inhabit the Church. Pentecost has been described as the birthday of the Holy Spirit, and the birthday of the Church on earth. The first-century church was Spirit-filled (Pentecostal). Speaking in tongues, prophecy, healing and miracles were a normal part of the life of the church. These manifestations continued to be the norm throughout the Greco-Roman world as the Gospel was carried beyond Jerusalem.

In the early church, leaders were endowed with spiritual gifts. They looked to and depended entirely upon the anointing and the presence of the Holy Spirit. There was no program or human agenda; it was all about Jesus, who was crucified, buried and resurrected. The expectation of the early church was a ministry filled with the supernatural based upon the very teaching of Jesus. Jesus told His disciples that when the Spirit came, believers would be enabled to do the same works that He had done, and even greater. John 14:12 says, "I tell you the truth, anyone who has faith in me will do what I have been doing. He will even do greater things than these, because I am going to the Father." Before He ascended, Jesus spoke to His disciples about the power and Holy Spirit they would receive. Again, Acts 1:8 tells us, "But you will receive power when the Holy Spirit comes on you; and you will be my witnesses in Jerusalem, and in all Judea and Samaria, and to the ends of the earth." The disciples depended entirely upon the anointing and presence of the Holy Spirit. In 10:19 of the same book, the Bible says, "While Peter was still thinking about the vision, the Spirit said to him, 'Simon, three men are looking for you.'" We must desire this operation of the Holy Ghost in our lives whereby we can hear and listen to His still small voice as He speaks, guides and directs our lives. Luke revealed in Acts 13:2, "While they were worshipping the Lord and fasting, the Holy Spirit, 'Set apart for me Barnabas and Saul for the work to which I have called them.'" The impression Jesus created in John 14:12 carried a strong meaning; He said, "The Spirit will come upon you, and you will be enabled to do the same works that I have done and even greater works."

Therefore it is not man's prerogative to tell us who we are. We are to do greater works because the Greater One and His anointing abide in us. We have the unction to function. This awesome anointing will enable us to do the good work we are called to do as we journey on this pilgrim pathway to our finish line. God, the all-powerful supernatural Being of mercy and grace, anointed Jesus of Nazareth with the Holy Ghost and power. He healed all those who were oppressed by the devil because His Father was with Him. God was with Jesus, and here is a great assurance: He is also with us.

Emmanuel is with us! The God of Hosts is with us! If there was ever a time when we needed the Holy Ghost and power, it is now. We need the Holy Ghost to preach the Word with the anointing and to do the greater works that we are told we are called to do. When we present ourselves, it must not be the Word only! There must be a demonstration of Spirit and power.

Paul's words to the Thessalonians are, "For our gospel came not unto you in word only, but also in power, and in the Holy Ghost, and in much assurance" (1 Thessalonians 1:5 KJV). In 1 Corinthians 2:4 he wrote, "My message and my preaching were not with wise and persuasive words, but with a demonstration of the Spirit's power." This anointed man of God wrote to the Romans saying, "I am not ashamed of the gospel, because it is the power of God for the salvation of everyone who believes: first for the Jew, then for the Gentile" (1:16). Jesus accomplished His earthly mission in the power of the Spirit. We must also carry out His mission in the same power of the

Spirit. God's strategy has not changed, and He will not change, for He is the same yesterday, today and forever.

So it is imperative that we take time out and think about our calling. The apostle Paul wrote in 1 Corinthians 1:26-28, "Brothers, think of what you were when you were called. Not many of you were wise by human standards; not many were influential; not many were of noble birth. But God chose the foolish things of the world to shame the wise; God chose the weak things of the world to shame the strong. He chose the lowly things of this world and the despised things—and the things that are not—to nullify the things that are."

The disciples heard about the promise of the Holy Ghost many times. In Acts 1:8, this is what we discover: "But you will receive power when the Holy Spirit comes on you; and you will be my witnesses in Jerusalem, and in all Judea and Samaria, and to the ends of the earth." They received the promise on the Day of Pentecost. They grew in the grace and knowledge of the Lord and Savior Jesus Christ. The disciples continued with one accord in prayer and supplication with the women, also with Mary the mother of Jesus as well as other brothers and sisters of the faith.

If there was ever a time when we needed unity and prayer in our life, it is now. Prayer must be our chief business! It is no secret what God can do when we offer our petitions to Him. When our life is saturated with prayer, praise and worship, we will experience the explosive power of the Holy Ghost.

The saints of the early church were people of prayer. Their chief business was prayer. They prayed from house to house! They were not anxious about anything, but in everything, by prayer and supplication, they made their requests known unto God. One writer says, "Prayer is the most powerful force in the universe and the greatest means of fulfilling the great commission." In the Book of Acts we are told that Peter and John were on their way to a prayer meeting when they had an encounter with a lame man. We are told that this man was born lame and he sat at the gate called Beautiful all the days of his life, begging for alms with the expectation to receive. Wherever there is spiritual power, greater works will be accomplished.

The time came for Peter and John to do the greater works. They were anointed and prepared to show forth power from God; they received power for service. We are possessed with the same power, even the power that raised Lazarus from the dead. The Holy Ghost abides in you and me. This is the Word of the Lord regarding the indwelling presence in our lives. John 14:16-17 says, "And I will ask the Father, and he will give you another Counselor to be with you forever—the Spirit of truth. The world cannot accept him, because it neither sees him nor knows him. But you know him, for he lives with you and will be in you."

Peter and John fastened their eyes upon the lame man and they said, "Look on us." The lame man was attentive; he asked and his expectation was to receive money, but the Greater One who indwelt Peter and John was to be displayed in the lives of these men. That day was the lame man's day of salvation and deliverance. There was going to be a demonstration of power and Spirit. Peter said, "Silver and gold I do not have, but what I am possessed with, today you are going to experience." It is imperative that we know what we are possessed with. What do we have to offer or give? Many are sitting at their gates of dormancy! There is no life! Many are not productive; you may have been barren for a long time. There is no growth! No fruit! You may have been a spiritual dwarf! What do we have to eradicate or pull down and loose that which is at work? What do we have to do to change the cycle, to renounce the spell or curse that binds and torments us?

We need a demonstration of power and Spirit! We need the operation of the Holy Ghost! We need the explosive power of the Holy Ghost in our lives. Peter said to the lame man, "In the name of Jesus Christ of Nazareth, rise up and walk." It is time for the Church to rise up in power and authority. The same Spirit which raised Lazarus from the dead lives in you and me. Romans 8:11 says, "And if the Spirit of him who raised Jesus from the dead is living in you, he who raised Christ from the dead will also give life to your mortal bodies through his Spirit, who lives in you." This is the church of the living God. Rise up and declare the glory of the Lord!

We did receive power against unclean spirits, to cast them out in the name of Jesus Christ of Nazareth. We received power to heal all manner of diseases! We received power and authority over scorpions and devils, and they shall not harm us. The body of Christ is armored and we do have our ammunitions, and we are dangerous. The blood of Jesus Christ of Nazareth is the life of the flesh in and all over us, and He is keeping us alive. Jesus is keeping us alive! Though the Death Angel may come, he cannot take our life before it is God's appointed time. We are aware of this truth: that it is appointed unto man once to die and then the judgment, but the devil's plan is to try to abort the plan of God in our lives.

John 10:10 says, "The thief comes only to steal and kill and destroy; I have come that they may have life, and have it to the full." Therefore we shall not die: we will live to declare the works of the Lord. When the Death Angel sees the blood of Jesus upon the blood-bought church of God, he will have to flee or pass over. Jesus said to Peter when he declared about His lordship or messiahship, "Upon this rock [or revelation] I will build my church; and the gates of hell shall not prevail against it" (Matthew 16:18 KJV).

We are therefore to continue to walk soberly, uprightly and godly, and the church will be armored and well dressed for the battle. We need the helmet of salvation on our head! The breastplate of righteousness! Truth girding our waist! Our feet shod with the Gospel of the preparation of peace. The shield of faith, the Word of God, must be used by the believer to undo, to cut, to smash, and to tear down strongholds in the name that is above every other name. In that Spirit, Peter took the lame man by the right hand and lifted him up, and immediately his feet and ankles received strength. And he leaped up, stood, walked, and entered the Temple with them, walking and leaping and praising God.

This was a remarkable miracle! Tendons, ligaments and muscles which had not contracted nor relaxed in this man's body were now functioning. Everything was lame, but when Jesus said, "It is finished," you must believe that it *is* finished, especially when He shows up. This manifestation of the power of God in the life of the lame man caused a great stir among the people. The people ran to them in Solomon's Porch, greatly wondering. Peter, the once-upon-a-time impulsive guy, the one who had betrayed Christ, stood boldly before the people and, endowed with the Holy Spirit, addressed the crowd:

Men of Israel, why does this surprise you? Why do you stare at us as if by our own power or godliness we had made this man walk? The God of Abraham, Isaac and Jacob, the God of our fathers, has glorified his servant Jesus. You handed him over to be killed, and you disowned him before Pilate, though he had decided to let him go. You disowned the Holy and Righteous One and asked that a murderer be released to you. You killed the author of life, but God raised him from the dead. We are witnesses of this. By faith in the name of Jesus, this man whom you see and know was made strong. It is Jesus' name and the faith that comes through him that has given this complete healing to him, as you can all see" (Acts 3:12-16).

There is power in the name of Jesus to heal humanity! There is strength in the name of the Lord; all that you need is in the name of Jesus. There is no other name given among men by which men can be saved. We shall have the victory in the name of Jesus! Miracles were commonplace in the synoptic Gospels and in the Book of Acts. There were many displays of power: "With great power the apostles gave witness to the resurrection of the Lord Jesus. And great grace was upon them all" (4:33 NKJV). They did not cease, even when they were told to stop teaching and preaching Jesus Christ in the Temple and from house to house.

Prayer is the engine or the fuse to magnify what you have already received. Prayer will cause the eyes of your understanding to be enlightened so that you may see Jesus better. Prayer will cause you and me to abound in wisdom and revelation. For the Church to be empowered, we will have to pray without ceasing. Jesus was anointed with the Holy Ghost and with power, but He withdrew from the crowd and prayed to His Father. Mark 1:35 says, "Very early in the morning, while it was still dark, Jesus got up, left the house and went off to a solitary place, where he prayed." Also, Hebrews 5:7 says, "During the days of Jesus' life on earth, he offered up prayers and petitions with loud cries and tears to the one who could save him from death, and he was heard because of his reverent submission."

For the explosive power of the Holy Ghost to be in our life, we will have to purpose in our hearts to cry out to God like the voice of the Messiah crying to His Father in Psalm 61 and Hebrews 5:7. There is mercy and help at the throne of grace in the time of trouble. We must have confidence on entering, for the Father is on the throne and Jesus is at His right hand making intercession for the saints. We need life in the body of Christ! The Holy Ghost and the implanted Word will cause marvelous things to happen among us when the life of Christ is embedded in us.

We must press toward touching the royal scepter that is in the hand of the King. In Acts 16, the Word of the Lord tells us that Paul and Silas were going to a prayer meeting when a girl possessed with a spirit of divination followed them declaring that these men were servants of the Most High God. What I would like you to bear in mind is the fact that when we begin to show forth the power of God, which is not of ourselves, there could be great afflictions, oppositions, and rejection.

The anointing will cause great suffering, but it is imperative that we carry our cross. No cross, no crown! No pain, no gain! It is God's plan that we run the race to the finish line. One day you and I will have to say, "It is finished," like Jesus. Also, like the apostle Paul, the great ambassador of the gospel of Jesus Christ, you and I will have to say one day, "We have fought a good fight! We have finished the course and we have kept the faith." When we are suffering or experiencing excruciating pain, the Word of the Lord says, "Be joyful in hope, patient in affliction, faithful in prayer" (Romans 12:12).

This demon-possessed girl followed Paul around for a few days, taunting them. Paul could not tolerate her taunting any longer. It was a great distraction! So Paul, being grieved, turned and said to the spirit, "I command you in the name of Jesus Christ to come out of her," and he came out that same hour. That was a demonstration of power and Spirit! Whenever there is a demonstration of power and Spirit, be very alert, for the devil is going to be very mad. You will be persecuted! The girl was now clothed and in her right mind, and her owners were very upset.

This girl's ability to foretell the future had caused her owners to gain much wealth. So they dragged Paul and Silas to the magistrate and accused them falsely. They said, "These men are Jews and they are causing great trouble for the city. They teach customs which are not lawful for us to receive, neither to observe, being Romans." The magistrate then commanded them to be stripped and whipped. Then they thrust them into the inner prison and fastened their feet in stocks. Had they not known that their moment of suffering was for the glory of God to be revealed?

Had they not known that being beaten, imprisoned and bound was for the salvation of a jailor and his family? They would have done something to disrupt God's divine plan for the situation. We tend to gripe and complain when we are facing our various temptations. Paul and Silas did not complain. They began to count it all joy! Brother James says, "Count it all joy when you suffer temptation, knowing that the trying of your faith works patience, but patience must have its complete work in you until we are complete, not lacking any thing" (see 1:2-4). We must be possessed with the joy of the Lord to make a joyful noise unto the Lord when we are imprisoned and bound. At midnight Paul and Silas began to pray and sing praises unto God, and the prisoners heard them. The Bible does not tell us what kind of songs they sang, but one thing I believe is that the Holy Ghost led them to sing praises to the King of kings, the Lord of lords, the conquering Lion of the tribe of Judah.

I do not know what you are going through, but take the time and praise God! The Bible says that suddenly there was a great earthquake and the foundation of the prison was shaken, and immediately the door was opened and everyone's bands were loosed. This was an awesome demonstration of power and Spirit.

If He be lifted up, He will draw all men unto Himself. When Jesus was lifted up, the jailor was drawn to Him. The keeper of the prison had just woken up and the prison door was opened. He panicked, knowing that if the prisoners had escaped, he would be executed. So he decided to commit suicide, but Jesus, by His Spirit, was at work, for that day was his day of salvation, not death or eternal damnation. Life eternal was to be his portion.

Paul said, "Don't harm yourself! We are all here! (Acts 16:28). They did not have to beg for anyone to accept the Lord as their personal Savior. The jailor fell down before Paul and Silas trembling, and he asked a very important question: "What must I do to be saved?" (v. 30). And they said, "Believe in the Lord Jesus, and you will be saved—you and your household" (v. 31). Later, they spoke the word of Jesus to all that were in his house.

Although you may not feel like it because of your diverse and adverse situations, somebody's salvation, victory, and deliverance are in your prayer and praise. God, the all-powerful, eternal, immortal, invisible, supernatural Being, is able to turn around those things. Those things need the finger of God. We desire spiritual power, therefore let us be in one accord in prayer and praise to the Almighty God. There is going to be a Holy Ghost tremor in our lives if we turn away from our wicked ways and look to the Lord. I believe it and I decree it, and it shall be so.

The Bible says if you decree a thing, it shall be established. Somebody's prison door is about to be opened! Somebody's shackles are about to be loosed in the name of Jesus. I have a feeling that everything is going to be all right. We desire Pentecostal fire! Let us take heed to the Word of the Lord that came to King Solomon after he had made an end to his prayer. The fire came down from heaven and consumed the burnt offering and sacrifices, and the glory of the Lord filled the house. The priest could not enter into the house of the Lord because the glory of the Lord had filled the Lord's house.

When all the people of Israel saw how the fire and the glory of the Lord came down upon the house, they bowed themselves with their faces to the ground, praising the Lord saying, "He is good! For his mercy endures forever!" This is the same song they sang in 2 Chronicles 20:21 when Jehoshaphat consulted with the people. He appointed singers unto the Lord who should praise the beauty of His holiness. Therefore they went before the army and said, "Praise the Lord; for his mercy endureth forever!" Even so today, His grace and mercy have brought us through!

We are living this moment because of Him. Would you also find a reason to thank and praise Him for His grace and mercy which has brought you through? Turn your beautiful eyes upon your God who is looking down on you with hand extended reaching out to the oppressed. He desires to put His hand in your situation and turn it around. Late in the midnight hour, God is going to turn it around. I feel His anointing so rich that even as I pen this for your eyes only, God is going to do it for you.

Prayer: Lord of all, we desire Holy Ghost power and fire to demonstrate in us so that others may know and be blessed. Thank You for the unction to function in Your great name. Help us that we will lay hold of the Word of God that says there is a greater power residing in us to accomplish Your will, in Jesus name. Amen.

> We are either too busy running around doing our own thing, or we do not spend enough time in the presence of Almighty God seeking His face. Individually and collectively, we must make a turnaround and assemble ourselves in our upper room of prayer. We must endeavor to spread out our letter, put our head between our knees, and turn our faces to the wall until heaven is unfolded and God descends to take a look into our life.

CHAPTER 17

A FRESH ANOINTING IS FLOWING OUR WAY

Once upon a time, believers in Christ did not have the indwelling Holy Ghost. God's people were anointed only at certain times when they needed to perform a task. However, when Jesus Christ of Nazareth was manifested, He mentioned several times about the promised Holy Spirit, particularly during His ascension. Therefore the disciples turned their eyes toward heaven while He was taken up. As part of their expectation, they later gathered in the Upper Room where they all received the endowment of the Spirit.

We have also turned to God and His Word, believing that the promised Comforter has come. Because we believed, His presence came upon us and has always stayed with us. John 14:16-17 says, "I will ask the Father, and he will give you another Counselor to be with you forever—the Spirit of truth. The world cannot accept him, because it neither sees him nor knows him. But you know him, for he lives with you and will be in you."

Scripture informs us that in the believer dwells Jesus and His anointing. If the Greater One and His anointing indwell you and me, it is appropriate to say a fresh anointing is flowing our way. This anointing is a burden bearer and a yoke destroyer. Isaiah 10:27 says, "And it shall come to pass in that day, that his burden shall be taken away from off thy shoulder, and the yolk from off thy neck, and the yolk shall be destroyed because of the anointing." Also, in

1 John 2:20 we are told, "But you have an anointing from the Holy One, and all of you know the truth." Verse 27 says, "As for you, the anointing you received from him remains in you, and you do not need anyone to teach you. But as his anointing teaches you about all things and as that anointing is real, not counterfeit—just as it has taught you, remain in him."

While we take a critical look at the word *unction*, bear in mind that the Greek word is *charisma*. This word refers literally to the "oil" with which a person has been anointed. In the Old Testament, kings were anointed as part of the inaugural ceremony (1 Samuel 16:6-13); it involved simply pouring oil on the head of the chosen person. The chosen person who had the "oil" on him was called the "anointed" (Hebrew, *meshiach*; Greek *Christos*). Thus, throughout the New Testament God's chosen King, the Messiah, is designated the Christ, which when translated means "the Anointed One" or the One who had the oil.

When John uses the word *unction* (Greek, *charisma*), as it occurs twice in verse 27, it means that all believers have the Holy Ghost, so we can declare with confidence that fresh anointing is flowing our way. The same Spirit, the Holy Ghost who raised up Jesus from the dead, is flowing our way. Let's take a look at another term: the *Anointed One*, Jesus Christ of Nazareth, which from a biblical perspective is significant to our discussion. According to Luke 4:16-22, the Anointed One walked into the synagogue and the priests handed Him the scroll. He opened Isaiah 61 and declared His mission statement. The Anointed One read out loud:

> "The Spirit of the Lord is on me, because he has anointed me to preach good news to the poor. He has sent me to proclaim freedom for the prisoners and recovery of sight for the blind, to release the oppressed, to proclaim the year of the Lord's favor." Then he rolled up the scroll, gave it back to the attendant and sat down. The eyes of everyone in the synagogue were fastened on him, and he began by saying to them, "Today this scripture is fulfilled in your hearing." All spoke well of him and were amazed at the gracious words that came from his lips. "Isn't this Joseph's son?" they asked (vv. 18-22).

It is very important for us to know what our mission is, for the anointing that is upon your life is for that purpose. You did not receive the anointing to sit down, but the anointing is to do the work of God. It is not given to us to turn away from the path of righteousness, but for us to do the greater works of Jesus Christ. Jesus Christ, the Anointed, was the Word made flesh in the womb of a woman who was highly favored by God (What will the Word become inside of you?). The Bible tells us that Jesus is grace and truth; He was possessed with the Word of God and He is the Word. John 1:1 says, "In the beginning was the Word, and the Word was with God, and the Word was God."

The Anointed One received the word from the Father to impart to all His disciples. In John 17:8 the Word of the Lord declares, "For I gave them the words you gave me and they accepted them. They knew with certainty that I came from you, and they believed that you sent me." Verse 14 says, "I have given them your word and the world has hated them, for they are not of the world any more than I am of the world." John 6:58 says, "[The Anointed One] is the bread that came down from heaven. Your forefathers ate manna and died, but he who feeds on this bread will live forever." Jesus is the true Bread of Life who gives eternal life. We must accept Jesus for who He is and what He has done, and the work He began will continue in us. In accordance to the Scriptures, we are anointed too; we are possessed with oil, which enables us to function in the body of Christ.

The centurion with that faith and understanding beseeched the Anointed One saying, "Lord, my servant lieth at home sick of the palsy, grievously tormented" (Matthew 8:6 KJV). Then the Anointed One said unto him, "I will come and heal him" (v.7 KJV), but the centurion replied, "Lord, I am not worthy that thou shouldest come under my roof: but speak the word only, and my servant shall be healed" (v. 8 KJV). Just speak the Word and healing will take place! Psalm 107:19-20 says, "Then they cried to the Lord in their trouble, and he saved them from their distress. He sent forth his word and healed them; he rescued them from the grave." You do not have to work it up, for the Word is already alive. It's also spirit, life and light. You can command the Word of God! You can use the double-edged sword.

Everywhere Jesus went, the anointing was flowing! They who were vexed with unclean spirits were healed, the whole multitude sought to touch Him and virtues went out of Him, and He healed them all. The folks in those days knew that Jesus was their source, and they brought everyone who needed Him and they looked at Him intently for answers. If what they did worked for them, we must follow suit and turn to Jesus with all our troubles and we will also receive answers to our troubles.

When the anointing is flowing, signs and wonders will follow: we shall speak with new tongues, cast out devils, and eat any deadly thing and it shall not harm us. We shall lay hands on the sick and they shall recover as testified by Mark in chapter 16 of his Gospel. The anointing flows to affect, to impact or influence, to pull down strongholds, to raise the dead and set the captive free. It was God who anointed Jesus with the Holy Ghost and power; He went about doing good, healing all those who were oppressed of the devil, for God was with Him.

As the Anointed One went about doing good, His fame went abroad and great multitudes came to hear Him and to be healed by Him of their infirmities. We need the Holy Ghost and power—the same Holy Ghost and power that overshadowed the Virgin Mary! We need the same Holy Ghost and power that raised Lazarus from the dead. We need that unction to function while it is day, for the night is coming when no man can work.

There was something remarkable about the Anointed One. According to Luke 4:32, 36, 40, the multitudes "were astonished at his doctrine: for his word was with power. . . . And they were all amazed, and spake among themselves, saying, what a word is this! For with authority and power he commandeth the unclean spirits, and they came out. . . . Now when the sun was setting, all they that had any sick with diverse diseases brought them unto him; and he laid his hands on every one of them, and healed them" (KJV). The Anointed One was manifesting everywhere He trotted, and the onlookers, scribes and Pharisees were amazed.

Mark 1:22, 27 says, "They were astonished at his doctrine: for he taught them as one that had authority, and not as the scribes. . . . And they were all amazed, insomuch that they questioned among themselves, saying, what is this? What new doctrine is this? For with authority commandeth he even the unclean spirits, and they do obey him" (KJV). There is fresh anointing flowing; the same anointing that raised the dead is accessible to you. Romans 8:11 says, "But if the Spirit of him that raised up Jesus from the dead dwell in you, he that raised up Christ from the dead shall also quicken your mortal bodies by his Spirit that dwelleth in you" (KJV).

It is time for the church of the living God to show forth the power and Spirit of God, and not of anything else. The Church must do greater works, and if Jesus said it, we must believe it in His name. Rise up, Church, with faith in your hearts. Rise up and be healed in the name of Jesus. Jesus will cleanse you and make you whole, but you must believe. You must turn away from unbelief and things that so easily beset you by turning your eyes upon Him. The anointing is flowing our way! As a matter of fact, we are the carriers or conveyers of the anointing. Is there a life-and-death situation in your life? Grace and truth is here! The anointing is flowing your way. It was grace and truth who stood at Lazarus' grave and called him to come forth from the dead.

The Word has power to change corruption to incorruption. The Word has power to resurrect the dead to life. The word has power to call some things that are not as though they were. The Word has power to defeat the devil and his cohorts. It is written! It is written! It is written! The Anointed One stood at Lazarus' grave and commanded the onlookers to take away the stone from the place where the dead was laid.

There is a fresh anointing flowing right now, but the reality is this: some of us are dead in many areas of our lives. There is unbelief, doubt, envy, jealousy, contention, gossiping, and diverse desires of the flesh. All these stones have to be rolled away so that God may do the unpredictable and the impossible. He will do what no other power can do! "Jesus lifted up his eyes, and said, Father, I thank thee that thou hast heard me. And I knew that thou hearest me always: but because of the people which stand by I said it, that they may believe that thou hast sent me. And when he thus had spoken, he cried with a loud voice, Lazarus, come forth. And he that was dead came forth, bound hand and foot with grave clothes: and his face was bound about with a napkin. Jesus saith unto them, Loose him, and let him go" (John 11:41-44 KJV).

Church of the living God, if the anointing indwells you and me, the anointing is flowing our way. The call is for the Church to come forth in the name of Jesus. Some of us are bound hand and foot, and our eyes are blinded by the lust of our eyes. It will take nothing but the anointing to loose the Church in the name of Jesus.

When the anointing is flowing, there will be great criticism and attacks! For everywhere the Anointed One went and did good, they debated and opposed Him. They wanted an opportunity to trap Him. They even tried to kill Him, but His time had not yet come. If you have an issue, the anointing is here to lift the burden and destroy the yoke. You will have to purpose in your heart to press on. It's hard to share the pain of your affliction! But you are the one, who has been bleeding for a long time, and at this time, you probably have lost a lot of blood and you are depleted of energy.

You can barely make it! You have had it! You have gone to see the palmist, the evangelist, the family doctor and the specialist only to find out that your diagnosis is grave. There is no cure and it seems that God is not answering you by fire. Nevertheless, there is a balm in Gilead! Jeremiah 8:22 says, "Is there no balm in Gilead? Is there no physician there? Why then is there no healing for the wound of my people?"

You will have to purpose in your heart that if I perish, I perish, but I am not going to sit back and die. There is no zest, no energy, no life! There seems to be no hope, but I am going to press on. The Anointed One is with you, but words are important in the healing process. The woman with the issue of blood was saying few words as she pressed toward the Anointed One. She said, "If I could but touch the hem of His garment, I know I shall be made whole." She said, "I know! I know! I know!" Do you know? This is faith in God, for this is the confidence I have in him: If we shall ask anything according to His will, He hears us. And if we know that He hears us, then we should believe that whatever thing we ask of Him, He will grant it unto us.

The woman pressed until she touched the hem of Jesus' garment. It was just the hem of His garment, but this was the Anointed One!

This was grace and truth! This was the One whom God anointed with the Holy Ghost and power. The anointing was reaching out to this woman, but she had to touch the Anointed One by faith. Therefore Jesus asked the question, "Who touched my clothes?" Later He said, "Virtue has left Me." Our garment must be anointed! The anointing must be bone-deep. The anointing must affect our tripartite being—spirit, soul and body. When the anointing affects the epidermis, dermis cells, connective tissues, muscles, organs and systems of the body, and I mean the skeletal system, we have what is known as bone-deep anointing.

Bone-deep anointing will heal the sick, set the captives free, break the bands of wickedness, break down prison doors and raise the physically and spiritually dead. In times like these we need bone-deep anointing to do the works of the ministry and to defeat the devil and his cohorts. The Holy Spirit impressed upon my spirit a powerful verse of Scripture from 2 Kings 13:20-21. This is an example of bone-deep anointing! The Bible says that Elisha died, and they buried him. And the bands of the Moabites invaded the land at the coming of the year. And it came to pass, as they were burying a man, that, behold, they spied a band of men; and they cast the man [the corpse] into the sepulcher of Elisha: and when the man was let down, and touched the bones of Elisha, he revived, and stood up on his feet (KJV).

This is the kind of anointing we need in the body of Christ! When I am dead in any area of my life or I am under the shadow of premature death and I come into contact with the anointing, whether it be bone, handkerchief, the hem of somebody's garment, or another encounter with the shadow of the anointing, I shall be revived! I feel like shouting! I must live because of the anointing. I would like you to know that this is the final miracle attributed to Elisha, even though he was now dead: this last miracle fulfilled the promise of God in that his ministry numbered twice as many miracles as Elijah's and some were twice as great. So the double portion held true, even to the very end.

The Church needs bone-deep anointing! The Church needs double-portion anointing! We will have to desire it and lay claim to this kind of anointing. Take heed, church of the living God, Elisha received a double portion of the anointing upon Elijah. He witnessed the miracles and he desired nothing less. Elijah asked him, "What can I do for you before I am taken from you?" And Elisha said, "Let me inherit a double portion of your spirit" (2 Kings 2:9).

Elijah said, "You have asked a hard thing" (v. 10 NKJV). The use of the word *hard* in Hebrew actually means "you have made a great claim." It is time for the twenty-first century church to stake a great claim. We the believers, the blood-bought church of God, must know in whom we have believed. We serve a great, big and wonderful God. Therefore, let us stake a great claim! We need bone-deep, double-portion anointing. Elijah said, "Nevertheless, if you see me when I am taken from you, it shall be so for you: but if not, it shall not be so" (v. 10 NKJV). What do you see? I will tell you what I see! I see the miracle-working power of God working in us that which is pleasing to him. So do not deviate! Do not be distracted! Turn around from whatever situations you are in to Jesus and see what He can do for you. His anointing is with you, and it will be with you to the very end.

Prayer: My God, my Father, to You be all praise and worship for Your awesome presence that is with us. We are blessed to be conveyors or carriers of Your Spirit, which enables us to be and do what You have called us for. Help us to empty ourselves of carnal weakness and to cast all our cares upon You, for truly Your anointing is flowing our way. Amen.

It is very important for us to know what our mission is, for the anointing that is upon your life is for that purpose. You did not receive the anointing to sit down, but the anointing is to do the work of God. It is not given to us to turn away from the path of righteousness, but rather, the anointing is given for us to do the greater works of Jesus Christ.

CHAPTER 18

JESUS' BLOOD IS ON OUR SOULS

There is a strong urge within me to commence this chapter with this intriguing question: How can we ever turn away from the profound message of the Cross? For in the beginning of time when God looked on the sins of humankind, a provision for life was made for us. Someone's life was poured out on our behalf to make us righteous, and the cross was the means and Jesus was the source. Ironically, the devil's plan was intended to make Jesus forsake His suffering, even the suffering of the cross. Nevertheless, the heart of Jesus was pulsating with blood to be poured out for the sins of humanity. Now that He has given us life, it is our duty to cling to the old rugged cross by faith. Remember, His life was poured out on the cross, giving us life more abundantly.

What is hindering us to turn around and see Him, that we may know who He is? I beseech you therefore to find the hindrances and overcome them so that you may turn to the God of your salvation with all of your strength, heart and soul, for therein lies abundant blessings and prosperity. In the following scriptures you may discover a few refreshing thoughts on the blood of Jesus. Here is what Leviticus 17:11 says: "For the life of a creature is in the blood, and I have given it to you to make atonement for yourselves on the altar; it is the blood that makes atonement for one's life."

1 Peter 1:18-19 reads, "For you know that it was not with perishable things such as silver or gold that you were redeemed from the empty way of life handed down to you from your

forefathers, but with the precious blood of Christ, as of a lamb without blemish or defect."

The word *blood* occurs over four hundred times in the Scriptures and is frequently used in the Book of Leviticus, which deals with Hebrew worship and the way to holiness. Blood contains the vital principle or the essence of animal and human life. There is absolutely no way an animal or human being can survive without blood. If one loses blood profusely, transfusion of blood must take place right away.

It is absolutely necessary that blood is restored to the body, and that the person who receives the blood receives the right blood type. Despite the fact that everyone's blood is red and looks the same, there are many different blood types. Type A blood cannot be given to someone requiring type O blood. Coagulation of blood will take place, which will eventually lead to death. I thank God for the blood of His cross; it is neither A, B, AB nor O. Jesus' blood is one for all. The blood of Jesus is pure and it is poured out on our souls, according to God's Word in Leviticus 17:11. It is also important to know that in our bodies are two types of blood: the pure blood and the impure blood.

The pure or oxygenated blood leaves the left side of the heart with oxygen to distribute to the entire body, then takes back impure or deoxygenated blood with carbon dioxide and waste products and brings it to the right side of the heart to be eliminated. Though the Lamb of God was made flesh and blood and He dwelt among men, it was pure or efficacious blood and not impure blood which flowed through His body. (I am not suggesting that Jesus had a pure body before His resurrection—His blood was pure).

Blood has had great significance from the beginning of time as evident in the Scriptures! When mankind disobeyed the Lord, as told in the Book of Genesis, God showed us that blood had to be poured out to cover man's sin. The Bible tells us that when Adam and Eve sinned, they found themselves naked; therefore they made fig leaves and covered up. It's quite interesting that they were still naked despite their cover-up, for blood was not the fluid flowing through the veins of the fig leaves.

God therefore killed an animal, and this was the first shedding of blood in the Bible. The animal blood was poured out, giving life, and God used the coat of the animal to clothe Adam and Eve. There is no remission of sin without the shedding of blood. Hebrews 9:22 states, "The law requires that nearly everything be cleansed with blood, and without the shedding of blood there is no forgiveness." Bear in mind that the animals' lives poured out were types of Christ.

In this sacrifice was laid the foundation of the entire plan of God with regards to redemption. It was God who furnished coats for Adam and Eve, showing us that salvation is of God and not of man or of our own accord. The Word of the Lord declares that it is by grace through faith that we are saved, which is not the will of man, lest any man should boast (Ephesians 2:8-10). The sacrificial system in the Old Testament was very elaborate, but it was not perfect! The blood of the animal was a foreshadowing of the more perfect sacrifice which was to come. God would become flesh and blood in the womb of a woman, and one day His flesh would be broken, pierced and bruised, and his blood would be poured out to redeem the people of the world.

Before we delve into the efficacious blood of the Paschal Lamb, it is necessary for us to grasp information about the unblemished Lamb in the Book of Exodus and the elaborate sacrificial system. Exodus 12 is a perfect picture of Christ, the true Paschal Lamb. God instructed Moses and Aaron to tell the people of Israel to take an unblemished lamb, every man according to his household. They were told to kill it in the evening. Bear in mind that in the evening was about three o'clock local time, the exact time that the holy Lamb of God died on the old rugged cross (Matthew 27:46).

They were told to take the blood and to strike it upon the lintels and the two side posts of their houses. This blood represented the shed blood of Jesus Christ of Nazareth. Please bear in mind that the blood was applied to the header (lintel) and the two side posts. This header and the two side posts were a picture of the cross of Jesus. Jesus was the Sin-Bearer just as the sin-bearer was the scapegoat in the Old Testament. He did not bear our sin in the manger! He did not bear our sin in the wilderness! Jesus did not bear our sin in the Garden! Jesus bore our sin on a tree, the cross, the header and the two side posts.

1 Peter 2:24 says, "He himself bore our sins in his body on the tree, so that we might die to sins and live for righteousness; by his wounds you have been healed." God's chosen people placed the blood upon the lintels of their houses, for this was to be a sign to the Death Angel that when he passed through he would have to pass over.

The word of the Lord says in Exodus 12 that the blood was a token—meaning a symbol—upon the houses where they were. The blood was a symbol of the One who was to come, Jesus, who would redeem mankind by the shedding of His blood. Jesus was the sin offering! Jesus was the perfect Lamb of God! The lamb chosen in the Old Testament had to be one without blemish. John the Baptist perceived Jesus to be the perfect Lamb of God. He said, "Behold the Lamb of God, which taketh away the sin of the world" (John 1:29 KJV).

The offering up of the lamb in the Old Testament was a type of Christ and what He would do on the old rugged cross for all the people of the world. The lamb represented innocence and gentleness. The lamb was an important symbol! The lamb was a worthy symbol of our Savior, who in innocence patiently endured the cross, despising the shame. Jesus humbled Himself to death, even the death of the cross. In his writing to the Philippians, Paul gave a graphic description of Christ suffering on the cross: "And being found in appearance as a man, he humbled himself and became obedient to death—even death on a cross!" (2:8). As the blood on the header (lintel) and the side posts was a sign to the Death Angel, so also the blood on Jesus' cross is upon God's chosen people. Exodus 12:13 says, "The blood will be a sign for you on the houses where you are; and when I see the blood, I will pass over you. No destructive plague will touch you when I strike Egypt." This speaks of the saving blood of Jesus Christ of Nazareth. He was a perfect sacrifice, for Jesus was the perfect Lamb of God.

It is evident in the Old Testament that once a year Aaron, after detailed preparation, entered the Holy of Holies with the atoning blood. On the Day of Atonement everything was sprinkled with blood and cleansed. The Holy Place was sprinkled seven times, even the mercy seat in the Holy of Holies. The priests, the garments, the holy vessel, everything was cleansed by blood.

According to Rev. Alex W. Ness, blood was sprinkled on the horn of the altar. There was a bullock for a sin offering, a ram for a burnt offering, and a goat for a sin offering. These were several sacrifices, and each presented some aspect of the sacrifice of Christ. Thank God that we don't have to depend on the elaborate sacrificial system for the atonement of our sin.

We cannot forget Gethsemane, lest we forget the agony of Jesus which led Him to Calvary! Jesus paid the price for our redemption. We cannot forget the scourging, the spitting and the mockery. The old sacrificial system was not perfect. The Day of Atonement only covered up sin, but it was a foreshadow of that which was to come.

If the old sacrificial system would have been perfect, there would not have been the need to repeat it annually. I thank God that Jesus was the Passover Lamb. The Word of the Lord says in Hebrews 9:14-15, "How much more, then, will the blood of Christ, who through the eternal Spirit offered himself unblemished to God, cleanse our consciences from acts that lead to death, so that we may serve the living God! For this reason Christ is the mediator of a new covenant, that those who are called may receive the promised eternal inheritance—now that he has died as a ransom to set them free from the sins committed under the first covenant."

Lest we forget Gethsemane! For if the blood of bulls and of goats, and the ashes of an heifer sprinkling the unclean, sanctifieth to the purifying of the flesh; how much more shall the blood of Christ, who through the eternal Spirit offered himself without spot [unblemished] to God, purge your conscience from dead works to serve the living God?" (vv. 13-14 KJV).

Lest we forget Gethsemane! I thank God that Jesus received the fatal blow. It pleased God to bruise Him. It was necessary for Him to be stricken, smitten and afflicted, for our salvation depended upon the shedding of His blood. In Isaiah 53, the prophet saw Jesus stretched naked. He was hanged on a wooden cross and bled like a slaughtered animal. He was despised of men, "a man of sorrows and acquainted with grief: and we hid as it were our faces from him; he was despised, and we esteemed him not" (v. 3 KJV).

Lest we forget Gethsemane! May we always remember the header and the two side posts. "Surely he took up our infirmities and carried our sorrows, yet we considered him stricken by God, smitten by him, and afflicted. But he was pierced for our transgressions, he was crushed for our iniquities; the punishment that brought us peace was upon him, and by his wounds we are healed" (vv. 4-5).

There is healing in the Atonement! Healing is the children's bread. The fullness of time had come for the Son of Man to offer up His life for His friends. For without the shedding of His blood, there would have been no remission of our sin. Remember now that He became flesh and blood and was born a man. His flesh had to be bruised! His blood had to be offered to redeem us. The pathway to His death was a gruesome one. He had to endure the scourging! He had to endure the wooden cross, the nails and the spear.

Let's look at scourging. Scourging is an excruciating and brutal experience. To scourge means to whip. This whip had sharp metal tongs situated at the tip, so that when it cuts into the flesh it causes severe lacerations. Whipping was a public spectacle for the culprit or the condemned. Forty strokes were given to the prostrate victim. Jesus was the prostrate victim! His back was turned to the tormentors, and God turned his back on Him. Jesus endured the suffering all by Himself. I believe He was weak and fainting, but they placed the header and the two side posts upon Him. He struggled with the old rugged cross. Blood flowed down His face and His back.

A trail of blood was printed on the ground as He struggled to the finish line. Without the shedding of His blood we would have had no hope, no life, no forgiveness. The nails penetrated his hands, but thank God He was reaching out to humanity. His hands reached down into the pits of hell, and He took the keys from Satan.

He released those who were held captive and he gave gifts to man. Now that His blood was shed for us, our names are written on the palms of His hands. The nails penetrated His feet, but I thank God that the head of Satan is bruised and now Jesus is Head of the Church! He is Head of all principalities and powers of darkness, and we are complete in Him. Colossians 2:10 declares, "And you have been given fullness in Christ, who is the head over every power and authority." The blood of Jesus covers our souls! This is why we can say with confidence that we are the blood-bought church of God. The blood of Jesus is upon the *Ecclesia*, the body of Christ, you and me.

The blood is keeping us alive; Jesus is keeping us alive. Are you sin-sick and heavy laden? There is power in the blood of Jesus for you.

What can wash away our sins? Nothing but the blood of Jesus! What can make us whole again? Nothing but the blood of Jesus. We, the blood-bought church of God, know what the blood is. We know it is the blood of Jesus that saves us.

Once upon a time when we were lost, Jesus died upon the cross for us. We know it is the blood that saves us. For it reaches to the highest mountain and flows to the lowest valley! The blood that gives us strength will never, never lose its power! We rest securely in His love, for Jesus' blood is on our souls. It is over the church of the redeemed!

Let the Death Angel come! Let the darts and weapons come. When they see the efficacious blood of Jesus, they will have to pass over. They will have to flee, for the blood of Jesus is a sign, a symbol, a token that we are the redeemed bought with a price. The death of Jesus was not an assassination or execution. This man Jesus willingly laid down His life for His friends. They raised Him on the cross, the header (lintel) and the two side posts. They gave Him vinegar to drink and they mocked Him, but all this suffering was for man's redemption. He opened His mouth and said, "It is finished."

It is finished, and Jesus' blood is the antidote, the remedy for this sin-sick world. In our blood is the white blood cell that kills bacteria or pathogen, and the process is known as phagocytosis; but Jesus' pure blood was the antidote to wash away our guilty stain, and the process was the Crucifixion. It's by the blood of Jesus we now obtain redemption, salvation, righteousness, justification and sanctification. There is wonder-working power in the blood of Jesus!

The Bible says that Joseph of Arimathea and Nicodemus asked Pilate if they could bury the body of Jesus. They took His bloody, bruised and pierced body down. They wrapped Him in linen and placed Him in a new sepulcher. Joseph and Nicodemus were careful to place a huge stone upon the mouth of the tomb, and guards were assigned to keep watch. Jesus told His disciples that wicked men would kill Him, but that He would rise on the third day.

This was the will of God! On the third day, God raised Jesus from the dead! The veil in the temple rent in two, the wall of partition was removed, so now Jesus is the Way and the Door to the Father. Jesus is now our Second Adam! Jesus is the Almighty King! Jesus is the Anointed One. Jesus is the beginning and the end of the creation of God.

Jesus is the Bread of Life! He is Emmanuel! Jesus is the Good Shepherd. Jesus is the Head of the Church. Jesus is life! Jesus is light! Jesus is the sweet Nazarene! He is the Great Physician, and He is coming again as the King of kings, the Lord of lords, and the conquering Lion of the tribe of Judah. Your Jesus, my Jesus, is the eternal King. He was born a King, died a King, and proved His sovereignty in the Resurrection.

In heaven Jesus rules as the King for the glory of God and for the fulfillment of His purposes (Matthew 28:18; Hebrews 1:3). What a glorious coronation it will be, when the sky shall unfold and we behold His face! What a glorious time it will be when His kingdom comes and He reigns supreme over the earth. The great awe is that we will reign with Him and dwell with Him forever, and ever.

The great sacrifice of Jesus should quicken or convict us so that with all of our beings we will purpose in our hearts to turn away from the things that hinder our progress in the Lord and turn to God. Are we willing to turn? Are we willing to take up the cross and run to the finish line to declare what He had declared? It is finished, and my eyes have beheld the finished work of Jesus, and for that matter I cannot look back. God bless you as you hear His voice and turn around to see Him.

Prayer: Our Father who is in heaven, Your eyes were on fallen humanity from the very beginning of time, and You do not desire the sacrifice of the scapegoat anymore. You desired a perfect sacrifice, and thank You for the gift of salvation You sent us. May we always turn our eyes upon You because You have given us access to the way, the truth and the life. Amen.

> It is finished, and Jesus' blood is the antidote, the remedy for this sin-sick world. In our blood is the white blood cell that kills bacteria or pathogen, and the process is known as phagocytosis; but Jesus' pure blood was the antidote to wash away our guilty stain, and the process was the Crucifixion.

CHAPTER 19

THE POWER OF PRAYER

It's incomprehensible that even though there are many intelligent people and geniuses, they do not always have answers to the many diverse situations that challenge us. Even so, looking up to others does not always solve our problems; but there is One, even Jesus, who is faithful and who bids or pleads with us to turn to Him in prayer and talk about the things that easily beset us.

Prayer is the gateway to the throne of grace. James 5:16 says, "The prayer of a righteous man is powerful and effective." As you may now know, "power" in Greek is *dunamis*! This is dynamite, the can-do power—supernatural strength or ability. Also, as you know, prayer is talking to God. It is asking, seeking and knocking! Matthew 7:7-11 says the following:

> Ask and it will be given to you; seek and you will find; knock and the door will be opened to you. For everyone who asks receives; he who seeks finds; and to him who knocks, the door will be opened. Which of you, if his son asks for bread, will give him a stone? Or if he asks for a fish, will give him a snake? If you, then, though you are evil, know how to give good gifts to your children, how much more will your Father in heaven give good gifts to those who ask him!

I believe it is appropriate to mention that Jesus told His disciples in Acts 1:8 that they would receive power after the Holy Ghost had come upon them and they would be His witnesses throughout Judea, Jerusalem, and Samaria and unto the uttermost parts of the world. These mere fishermen were in the Upper Room waiting for the promise with great expectancy. They were not anxious about anything; rather, they were in prayer, and suddenly the Holy Ghost and power descended upon them. The atmosphere was electrifying! There were tremendous signs and wonders!

These folks received power and they became as bold as a lion. They should be as bold as a lion because the Lion of the tribe of Judah had given them the Holy Ghost and power. In that boldness they faced the members of the Sanhedrin, fearlessly expounding the Word. These uneducated folks were transformed into spiritual stalwarts by the power of the Holy Ghost. Their prayer shook buildings! Their prayer caused earthquakes in the prisons where they were bound. They turned everything upside down because they made prayer their chief business (Acts 17:6 KJV). They prayed in season and out of season.

The Bible tells us that when Peter was thrown in jail for defending the Gospel, the disciples gathered in a house and they began to pray. God listens to the prayer of a righteous man. Heaven was drawn nigh to earth! God is interested in every little detail of our life. That is why it is important to offer our prayers to Him. Let's forget about our intelligence and eloquence and tell it to Jesus according to the ability we have received.

Know that prayer caused God to send an angel to release Peter! Are you in bondage? You just have to purpose in your heart to enter the throne of grace and tell your Father about it. We do have the tendency to pray only when we are in crisis. That is all right, but do not take God for granted! We must always be in prayer so that in the midst of trouble we will manifest His virtues and glory.

We do not have to be panic-stricken, for Daniel's God surely delivers. He will do it again! Peter, James and John were well "prayed up" before they set out to that prayer meeting! Prayer was their chief business! The man at the gate Beautiful begged for money and expected nothing but some coins. Peter said to the man, "Silver and gold I do not have, but what I do have I give you: In the name of Jesus Christ of Nazareth, rise up and walk" (Acts 3:6 NKJV).

What did they have? They were possessed with the Word and they had the Holy Ghost and power. So it is with Joy Vassal. I wish I had enough money with me to give away, nonetheless I encourage you to rise up in the name of Jesus and let your prayer move God. Turn your entire complex situation around by letting your prayer move the Lord your God. If you would only turn and offer your prayers, it is no secret that your heavenly Father is going to look down and say, "I am going to see why I am moved!" When the children of Israel cried to God because they were afflicted by their taskmasters, He decided to come down and take a look at their situation. He showed up with the answer: "Moses, you must turn toward Egypt and deliver My people from their bondage" (see Exodus 3:3-33).

This is awesome, but sometimes we pray and our prayers only bat the air. God has not been impressed and sometimes does not cultivate any intention to move on our behalf. On the contrary, He is always waiting for someone who will turn around and believe Him for who He is. The prayer of God's righteous saints is powerful.

The onlookers at the Beautiful gate knew that these men had been with Jesus. Satan is also knowledgeable! He knows about your prayer life. We must be at that place in God where the Enemy is afraid to approach. We must be energized, saturated, ignited and empowered by the habit of prayer so that others may know and be inspired or motivated to launch out in faith and do what God has called them to do. We must purpose in our heart to move God with our prayer.

John Nichols, a great evangelist, said that truth will move men but prayer will move God, and we need a move of God. Spirit-authored prayer springs from the mind of Christ and touches the heart of God. Prayer is supposed to be a joyful experience. There is a sense of sweetness when the saints in Christ approach the throne of grace.

One songwriter wrote, "Sweet hour of prayer that calls me from a world of care, and bids me at my Father's throne make all my wants and wishes known.... And since He bids me seek His face, believe His Word and trust His grace, I'll cast on Him my every care, and wait for thee, sweet hour of prayer!"

Joy Dawson, an anointed vessel of honor says, "If you have ever attended a dead prayer meeting where God's presence was not there, there is nothing as dull as that. There is nothing that fulfills God's will in such a situation until we pray and hear His voice speaking to us and telling us to come to Him". Thus, do not turn to the left or right; just take heed and look steadfastly to Him.

God is the most exciting being in the universe. He will answer us by fire if we believe and call on His name. He will send an earthquake to shake the prison door open and loose the shackles if we learn to trust Him when we pray. The Word of the Lord says in 1 John 5:14-15, "This is the confidence we have in approaching God: that if we ask anything according to his will, he hears us. And if we know that he hears us—whatever we ask—we know that we have what we asked of him." Our "Lazarus" will come forth alive as we remove the stones of unbelief, doubt, fear, jealousy and all the fleshly desires in our lives.

God's desire is to communicate with us, so communicating with Him should be part of our normal relationship with Him. He frequently speaks to His children who dilligently seek him. In Jeremiah 33:3 His Word declares, "Call to me and I will answer you and tell you great and unsearchable things you do not know." Hebrews 4:16 says, "Let us then approach the throne of grace with confidence, so that we may receive mercy and find grace to help us in our time of need."

Donald S. Whitley says that "Prayer expresses the largest and most comprehensive approach unto God. It gives prominence to the elements of devotion. It is communion and intimacy with God. Prayer is enjoying God. Prayer is having access to God. However, supplication, a form of prayer, is more restricted and more intense. It's accompanied by a sense of personal need, limited to the seeking of an urgent manner of a supply for pressing needs." Supplication is the very soul of prayer; it's an act of pleading for someone or something greatly needed. It's said with the attitude that will cause the need to be intensely felt.

Hannah's prayer in 1 Samuel is an example of a prayer of supplication. When we come to God in supplication, we can rest assured that He will move on our behalf just as He did for patriarchs, prophets, judges, kings and others. Do you have a situation facing you? Turn around and see God! Hezekiah had to turn to God when King Sennacherib sent Rabshakeh with the threatening words "Don't think that your God will deliver you. You might have heard that I have defeated nations. I am the great king of Assyria. And I now come up without the Lord against this place to destroy it" (see 2 Kings 18 and 19).

Rabshakeh boasted and insulted God. Hezekiah heard about the king's threatening words and he sought the Lord. He rent his clothes and covered himself in sackcloth and went into the house of the Lord. The word *sackcloth* refers to the humbling of oneself in the sight of God. The house of the Lord refers to the Temple, where God dwelt in the Holy of Holies between the mercy seat and the cherubim.

The only help for Judah was God! Likewise, the only help for the Church is God! We will have to look to heaven, His dwelling place. Are you looking to the hills from whence comes our help? It comes from the Lord, who made heaven and earth! He will not suffer our foot to be moved. He who keeps Israel shall never slumber nor sleep. He is a shade at our right hand. The sun will not smite us by day nor the moon by night. He will protect us. God will take care of us!

Hezekiah sent word to the prophet Isaiah saying, "This day is a day of trouble, and of rebuke, and blasphemy; for the children are come to the birth, and there is not strength to bring forth" (19:3 KJV). Judah had no strength! They must look to God. Isaiah had a word for the king. He said, "Thus saith the Lord, Be not afraid of the words which thou hast heard, with which the servants of the king of Assyria have blasphemed me. Behold, I will send a blast upon him, and he shall hear a rumor and shall return to his own land; and I will cause him to fall by the sword in his own land" (vv. 6-7 KJV). The king sent to Hezekiah, saying, "Let it be known to you that all of the other gods of these nations I have destroyed, and shall you be delivered? (See v. 11). Hezekiah knew in whom he believed. He read the letter the great king of Assyria sent to him, but he went up into the house of the Lord and he spread out the letter before the Lord. He said:

> O Lord God of Israel, which dwellest between the cherubims, thou art the God, even thou alone, of all the kingdoms of the earth; thou hast made heaven and earth. Lord, bow down thine ear, and hear: open, Lord, thine eyes, and see: and hear the words of Sennacherib, which hath sent him to reproach the living God. Of a truth, Lord, the kings of Assyria have destroyed the nations and their lands, and have cast their gods into the fire: for they were no gods, but the work of men's hands, wood and stone: therefore they have destroyed them. Now therefore, O Lord our God, I beseech thee, save thou us out of his hand, that all the kingdoms of the earth may know that thou art the Lord God, even thou only (vv. 15-19 KJV).

God heard the cry of the king and sent Isaiah to prophesy deliverance. He said, "Thus saith the Lord concerning the king of Assyria, He shall not come into this city, nor shoot an arrow there, nor come before it with a shield, nor cast a bank against it. By the way that he came, by the same shall he return, and shall not come into this city, saith the Lord. For I will defend this city, to save it, for mine own sake, and for my servant David's sake" (vv. 32-34 KJV).

Turn around and take your situation to the Lord in prayer. Vengeance is God's! He will repay. It came to pass that night that the angel of the Lord went out and smote a hundred and eighty-five thousand in the camp of the Assyrians. When they arose early in the morning, behold, they were all dead corpses. The great king fled and went to Nineveh, and it came to pass, as he was worshipping in the house of Nisrock, his god, that Adrammelech and Sharezer, his sons, smote him with the sword. They then escaped and his youngest son, Esarhaddon, reigned in his stead. The devil does not give up easily! He will continue to buffet and challenge the saints of the living God with intensity. What are you going to do? Are you going to shrink and back up and let him destroy you? Are you going to throw in the towel? Are you going to roll over and give him a foothold to come in and dominate your life? Are you going to have a pity party and let the devil have a field day? You cannot give him any grounds, absolutely no grounds! You will have to say, "I am giving you no chance whatsoever; I am giving up no grounds!"

What do you do when you are found in a life-or-death situation? When the doctor says, "There is nothing I can do for you," whom do you turn to? King Hezekiah had great enemies and God killed them, but now he was faced with death. The prophet said to him, "Thus says the Lord: 'Set your house in order, for you shall die, and not live'" (20:1 NKJV).

The Word of the Lord says in 2 Kings 20:2 that Hezekiah turned his face to the wall. I do not know what you are facing right now, but it is imperative that you turn your face to the wall. We must enter the throne of grace radically and with intensity, and spread out our petitions to God! The problems are more diverse and intense, therefore we have to be fired up in prayer. The monarch turned his face from all the riches, glory and grandeur of Judah and Jerusalem. He saw himself as undone, helpless and totally dependent on the mercy of God. He said, "I beseech thee, O Lord, remember now how I have walked before thee in truth and with a perfect heart, and have done that which is good in thy sight" (v. 3 KJV). The king wept sorely.

I have been weeping before God like Hezekiah for some time now. I said, "God, you are not dead. The Church that you sent your only Son to die for is dead." The Church is bound by the spirit of lethargy, stagnancy, dormancy. There is no life, and the blood-bought saints of the living God seem to be living under the influence of a Zombie spirit. This is a spirit of slumber! I asked where the fire is! Why are there no signs and wonders? Why is the Church afraid of speaking in tongues when the Spirit of the Lord gives them utterance? I do not want to hear any foolishness that miracles ceased when Jesus ascended to His Father and His disciples died. That's a lie from the pit of the devil! Greater works shall we do because He is gone to the Father and we did receive the promise of the Holy Ghost and power.

I prayed, "Abba, I need to see signs and wonders! We need the Shekinah glory! We need God's train in the house! We need the fire of God!" If God is a God of fire, then we are ministers of fire. The Church was born in prayer, therefore the Church must not be anxious about anything but must be in prayer and supplication. "Let your requests be made known to God; and the peace of God, which surpasses all understanding, will guard your hearts and minds through Christ Jesus" (Philippians 4:6-7 NKJV).

God heard Hezekiah's prayer! He will always respond to a broken heart. God spoke to Isaiah before he was gone into the middle court, saying, "Turn again, and tell Hezekiah the captain of my people, Thus saith the Lord, the God of David thy father, I have heard thy prayer, I have seen thy tears: behold, I will heal thee: on the third day thou shalt go up unto the house of the Lord. And I will add unto thy days fifteen years; and I will deliver thee and this city out of the hand of the king of Assyria; and I will defend this city for mine own sake, and for my servant David's sake" (2 Kings 20:5-6 KJV). And Isaiah said, "Take a lump of figs," and they laid it upon the boil and he recovered (v. 7 KJV). God is able to turn around an extremely ugly situation. What he did for the monarch, He will do for you and me. It is time to weep bitterly before God for the situation that is facing us and for the Church. Oh, that our prayers would move God to come down and take a look at our situation.

Darkness will be dispelled, and the plots of the Enemy will be demolished. Do not be dismayed! Just turn your eyes to God and speak His word over that stinking situation you are facing. His word is spirit and life! Resurrection power and life will saturate that situation. Then all people will have to give God the glory, honor and praise. He has never failed us yet! Everywhere I go, it's my hope that the world will know that the God of yesterday, today and forever has no failure in Him. He turned bitter water into sweet, opened up a pathway in the Red Sea, and destroyed nations upon nations for His chosen people.

He fed His people when there was no food! He gave them water when they were thirsty. He is God all by Himself, but do we believe? Are we living by faith? Are we calling some things that are not to be so? I believe God for a breakout and breakthroughs! I believe God wants to save His people, but before we hear the Word, it is too late . . . too late and mercy is gone! Too late and judgment comes! Let's believe God for revival, restoration, healing and miracles in the lives of His people. While He was on earth the prayers of Jesus were personal, familiar and paternal. Strong, touching and tearful were His prayers.

In Hebrews 5:7 the Word of the Lord states, "During the days of Jesus' life on earth, he offered up prayers and petitions with loud cries and tears to the one who could save him from death, and he was heard because of his reverent submission." You and I have access to the throne of Grace to offer prayers and supplications with strong crying and tears. God is attentive to the cry of His children, and His desire is to move on our behalf. According to the Word of God in Psalm 34:6, "This poor man called, and the Lord heard him; he saved him out of all his troubles." David cried out to God in Psalm 61:1-3: "Hear my cry, O God; listen to my prayer. From the ends of the earth I call to you, I call as my heart grows faint; lead me to the rock that is higher than I. For you have been my refuge, a strong tower against the foe." This Rock is Jesus, and He is at the right hand of the Father, still praying for you and me. Keep your eyes on Him, and He will transform you from glory to glory.

Prayer: God of heaven and earth, we love You and appreciate You more and more every day. When we grasp the great sacrifice of the perfect Lamb of God and the access it gives us to the throne of grace, we can't help but turn to You, lifting our hands to glorify You. For You have done well to call us to come to You when we are weary and heavy laden, and we will find rest for our souls. Amen.

I do not know what you are facing right now, but it is imperative that you turn your face to the wall. We must enter the throne of grace radically and with intensity, and spread out our letter to God! The problems are more diverse and intense, therefore we have to be fired up in prayer. The monarch turned his face from all the riches, glory and grandeur of Judah and Jerusalem. He saw himself as undone, helpless and totally dependent on God.

CHAPTER 20

THE PRODIGAL SON

Once upon a time, Jesus told His followers a very interesting story. What was this interesting story about? It was a story about a son who approached his father and asked for his inheritance because he felt it was time for him to leave home. The father, who reluctantly allowed the son to leave home, hoped and waited for the day when the son would return. A few years later after the son had left, he was faced with hardship. He had spent all his money lavishly, then he was left stranded with no one to help him.

When he could bear no more, he turned around and decided to return to his father. His father, as we know, welcomed him with open arms (Luke 15:11-32). Whether God, our heavenly Father, chooses to pursue or not to pursue us, His goal is the same; His unconditional love which emanates firmly and lovingly reaches out to those who even run away from Him. There are varied devices and pleasures of this world that have caused many people in Christendom to run away from the plan and purposes of God in their life. In Luke 15:11-32 the son asked for his portion of the inheritance. He knew that a certain amount of the heritage of his father belonged to each son by law.

He figured more or less that because he had a right to his portion it was time for him to take his and leave the house. He thought of going into a very far land; therefore, after getting his inheritance he set out on the journey. He thought not about the wonderful privileges he had in his father's house in that all of his needs were met.

He had not thought about the protection he had because he was with his father.

In a country far away from home, he wasted all that he had and there was no one to help him, so he had to look for a job. There was no lucrative position for him, so his last resort was to settle for the most menial of jobs, even the rearing of pigs. Caring for pigs, according to Jewish tradition, was a dirty and profane job because according to the Mosaic Law pigs are unclean animals.

This enterprise was the most degrading occupation a Jew could ever have. Can you imagine falling from a very lofty position and hitting rock bottom? This was the plight of the runaway son, but sin can as well strip us of our integrity and sanity and put us into a grave and miserable situation. He did not have anything to eat, so he shared the pig's pods. This must have tasted insipid, but he had to eat it for it was his only way of survival. The surroundings of a pig will always be filthy. They defecate, vomit, wallow and eat all in the same place. Animals do not have the instinct or ability like human beings to keep their surroundings immaculately clean.

The atmosphere must have been stagnant, certainly not good for respiration. In his father's house, the atmosphere was that of perfumes and highly scented spices. However, at a certain point in his calamity, he came to his senses. He thought about his father's hired servants, how they were cared and provided for, but now he was starving. Therefore he said, "I will arise and go to my father" (v. 18 KJV). He came to the realization that he had sinned against his father, and the first step toward reconciliation was to turn around and go back to his father. He thought of saying to his father, "I have done you wrong and have also sinned against my heavenly Father."

He did not put the blame on anyone! He blamed himself. He thought of himself being unworthy and just wanted his father to take him as one of his hired servants. He was desperate and wanted a way out! He knew his position with his father's hired servants would be far more prestigious than being with pigs.

In verse 20 the Word of the Lord says he arose and came to his father! It will take a person who is in a rut or who has hit rock bottom to muster up strength or faith to get up and move toward forgiveness, life, restoration, healing, victory and deliverance.

TURN AROUND AND SEE THE LORD

The father was looking for his son to turn around and come home. He could have gone to look for him, but he allowed him to choose whom he would serve. Would this prodigal son choose to stay in the pigsty and tolerate the stench, or would he prefer to sit at his father's table and feast with his family? The Bible says that on his return, when he was yet a great way off, his father saw him and ran to welcome him home. This is wonderful; one can see quite vividly that his father was watching out for him and had compassion for him, and he ran and fell on his neck and kissed him. This is the only occasion where it is written in the Bible that God ran typologically to welcome a lost son. He has not changed; He is still looking out and is more than ready to run and welcome you if you will come to your senses and arise and take your journey back home.

The son was penitent! He said, "Father, I have sinned against heaven and against you. I am no longer worthy to be called your son" (v. 21). The father loved his son regardless of his mistakes or imperfections. Grace and mercy embraced him in his tattered clothes, and he was clothed in the garment of the new man. The father had no time to dwell on his son's past. He said to his servants, "Bring the best robe and put it on him. Put a ring on his finger" (v. 22). The ring addressed here was a seal or signet ring, which was much the same as a modern credit card; the ring bore the crest of his father's house. They were told to put shoes on his feet! This is very important, as it shows ownership, for slaves were not allowed to wear shoes. He was greatly provided for; he was a son again and not a servant.

The servants were told to bring forth the fattened calf to kill it for them to eat and to make merry. This merrymaking signifies that the son had now returned to a covenant or relationship with his father. The father declared, this son of mine was dead and is alive again; he was lost and is found" (v. 24).

This story of the Prodigal Son is exactly what happens in our lives at times because of our fleshly desires. We turn our backs on God and do our own thing, causing us to be dead in our trespasses and sin. Moreover, we have lost our way and have fallen into utter darkness. It is when we repent and confess our sins that we live again and set our feet on the new path of righteousness. The Word of the Lord says that when a sinner receives the Lord as Savior, there is rejoicing in heaven. Jesus rejoices when a lost soul comes home.

And so they feasted. While they were feasting, the elder son was in the field. We do not know why he was not summoned. Maybe the father knew he might be very jealous and ask many questions. He heard the music and all the folks around were dancing, so he inquired of the servant what the meaning of this celebration was.

The servant told him that his lost brother had been found and their father joyfully received him and killed the fattened calf for him, for he had come home safe and sound. I would have imagined that his brother would have been happy to see his younger brother, but instead he was very angry and decided not to participate in the celebration. Even so, some people look dissatisfied when others are delivered from their pit of destruction. They would rather prefer the sinner to stay in sin and suffer, but I thank God for who He is! You can stay where you are if you choose to, but if you pull up your socks and make a decision to rise up and turn to God, there is nothing He will allow to hinder you from coming to Him.

The father knew that the elder son was upset, so he went outside and entreated him, but the son needed an explanation for his father's actions. He said to his father, "These many years I have been serving you; I never transgressed your commandment at any time; and yet you never gave me a young goat, that I might make merry with my friends" (v. 29 NKJV).

His heart was not right as a son; he was just as lost as his younger brother. He said, "As soon as this son of yours came, who has devoured your livelihood with harlots, you killed the fatted calf for him" (v. 30 KJV). It is quite evident that he disowned his brother. The elder son figured more or less that his younger brother should be punished, but instead he was showed love.

We all should have been punished because of our fallen foreparents, but God showed us love in the sacrifice of His only Son, Jesus Christ of Nazareth. John 3:16 says, "For God so loved the world that he gave his one and only Son, that whoever believes in him shall not perish but have eternal life."

The father said unto the eldest son, "Thou art ever with me, and all that I have is thine" (Luke 15:31 KJV). Salvation is free! You do not have to work to earn it. It is a free gift to humankind. The father said, "It was right that we should make merry and be glad, for your brother was dead and is alive again, and was lost and is found" (v. 32 NKJV).

Ephesians 2:1 says, "As for you, you were dead in your transgressions and sins," and when we came to our senses, we arose and came to Christ. Thus, we lived again and also found salvation. The death of the sinless calf was a necessity for the feast! It was necessary because without the shedding of blood there is no remission of sin.

It was a time of rejoicing, and the Prodigal Son accepted the new raiment; he humbly accepted his new place at his father's table. It would be inappropriate for him to sit at the table in his filthy garments when the father had just stretched forth his hand and embraced him with love. Besides, the Prodigal Son was truly repentant, as demonstrated in his conversation with his father. When we also truly repent and confess Jesus as Lord and Savior, He redecorates our lives and gives us a new place in heaven, our Father's house.

We, the believers of God the Omnipotent, are blessed to have a heavenly Father who is touched with the very feelings of our infirmities. He knows about our limitations and shortcomings, but He will never turn away from us. He is giving us time to return to our first love. His desire is for us to realize that His love is unconditional and we do not have to earn it. He gives it to us freely.

Our Father is watching and waiting for us to come home, but we have a significant part to play! Get up! Rise up! And run to Him, for He is forgiving and is ready to summon the messengers of heaven to their various assignments for our sake. The banqueting hall in no time will be decorated and the caterers will be summoned to prepare the delicious delicacies you have enjoyed; even that which you have not imagined will be added, for He loves us so much.

However, we must admit that we have sinned and that we are not worthy to be called His sons and daughters. Nevertheless, the blood of His Son has cleansed us from all impurities. Through Him we can turn away from our waywardness and find His bowels of compassion.

Prayer: Rock of Ages, we gracefully have access to Your throne of grace, even when we have fallen short. When we wallow in our pigsty and the stench of sin has overshadowed us, we thank You that when we come to our senses and rise up and run to You, Your arm is outstretched with forgiveness. Thank You, Lord. Amen.

> Even so, some people look dissatisfied when others are delivered from their pit of destruction. They would rather prefer the sinner to stay in sin and suffer, but I thank God for who He is! You can stay where you are if you choose to, but if you pull up your socks and make a decision to rise up and turn to God, there is nothing He will allow to hinder you from coming to Him.

CHAPTER 21

THE SEED OF SARAH

What the Almighty God has said, He will do, and what He has spoken, He will bring to pass. The things God desires to achieve through us may not be presented clearly, and it may be difficult to hold on at times to things not seen. Yes, it is during such muddled situations when one listens to other voices or succumbs to the dictates of the flesh. But if God says, "You shall bring forth your seed in due season," look intently to Him and say, "And so it shall be!"

The Hebrew word for "seed" is *zera*, and the Greek word is *sperma*. According to Zondervan's Pictorial Bible Dictionary, "There is a threefold usage of this word in Scripture: agricultural, pertaining to the farmer and his seed; physiological, pertaining to seed of copulation (emission of semen), which is a frequent expression in the Mosaic Law of uncleanness; and spiritual, pertaining to the New Testament's referring to Christians as having been begotten by God "of incorruptible seed." Seed can be a figurative expression. Here, seed means descendants (Genesis 13:16) or genealogy or a class of people. Paul's usage of seed in Galatians 3:16 portrays or shows proof that the promises of God to Abraham are realized in Jesus Christ. God was interested in the seed of men from the very beginning, and He still has interest in the seed of His Word, which must dwell richly in our minds and hearts.

Genesis 13:16 states, "And I will make thy seed as the dust of the earth: so that if a man can number the dust of the earth, then shall thy seed also be numbered" (KJV). Genesis 17:15-16 says, "God also said to Abraham, 'As for Sarai your wife, you are no longer to call her Sarai; her name will be Sarah. I will bless her and will surely give you a son by her. I will bless her so that she will be the mother of nations; kings of peoples will come from her." Yet this faithful woman of God remained barren for a long time. God appeared to Abram and Sarai to reassure them that He had not forgotten His promise.

Genesis 18:9-15 states thus:

> "Where is your wife Sarah?" they asked him. "There, in the tent," he said. Then the Lord said, "I will surely return to you about this time next year, and Sarah your wife will have a son." Now Sarah was listening at the entrance to the tent, which was behind him. Abraham and Sarah were already old and well advanced in years, and Sarah was past the age of childbearing. So Sarah laughed to herself as she thought, "After I am worn out and my master is old, will I now have this pleasure?" Then the Lord said to Abraham, "Why did Sarah laugh and say, 'Will I really have a child, now that I am old?' Is anything too hard for the Lord? I will return to you at the appointed time next year and Sarah will have a son." Sarah was afraid, so she lied and said, "I did not laugh." But he said, "Yes, you did laugh."

Sarai was a beauty to behold, but she struggled with barrenness and unbelief. Let's see what happened in the beginning of time. Genesis 1:2 says that "the earth was without form, and void; and darkness was upon the face of the deep. And the Spirit of God [the Holy Spirit] moved upon the face of the waters. And God said, Let there be light: and there was light [and firmament, creeping organisms, grass, herbs yielding seed, trees yielding fruit, fowls of the air and fish of the sea]" (KJV).

Colossians 1:16-17 says, "For by him all things were created: things in heaven and on earth, visible and invisible, whether thrones or powers or rulers or authorities; all things were created by him and for him. He is before all things, and in him all things hold together." John 1:1-3 says, "In the beginning was the Word, and the Word was with God, and the Word was God. He was with God in the beginning.

Through him all things were made; without him nothing was made that has been made."

God said, "Let there be," and there was, and when God looked at what was brought into existence, he saw that it was all good. God said, "Let us make man in our image" (Genesis 1:26). In chapter 2:7 of the same book, we read: "God formed man of the dust of the ground, and breathed into his nostrils the breath of life; and man became a living soul" (KJV). Man was then placed in the Garden of Eden to dress and keep the Garden. Satan made an attempt to corrupt the lineage of God's creation so that the promised Seed of Genesis 3:15 would not come to pass.

In (v.18) the Lord God said, "It is not good for the man to be alone. I will make a helper suitable for him." Verses 21-22 say, "The Lord God caused the man to fall into a deep sleep; and while he was sleeping, he took one of the man's ribs and closed up the place with flesh. Then the Lord God made a woman from the rib he had taken out of the man, and he brought her to the man." This woman was Eve, and her seed was Cain, Abel and Seth. In the Book of Genesis, it is quite vivid that this generation of people multiplied until the birth of Enoch.

According to Genesis 5:30-31, Noah descended from the lineage of Adam. He gave birth to Shem, Ham and Japheth, and it is interesting to note that every person who ever lived since then is a descendent of Shem, Ham and Japheth. God had given his instruction to our fore-parents.

They were not to eat of the Tree of the Knowledge of Good and Evil, but they broke the divine commandment and sin infiltrated the human race. Mankind since then has fallen short of God's glory, and, according to Genesis 6, the wickedness of man increased. But God was still interested to redeem mankind from the curse of sin at the very beginning of Creation; that is why this wonderful promise was given in Genesis 3:15: The seed of the woman shall bruise the head of the Serpent (Satan).

In Genesis 6:1-2 the Word of the Lord says that when men began to increase in number on the earth and daughters were born to them, the sons of God saw that the daughters of men were beautiful, and they married any of them they chose. The sons of God portrayed here refer to fallen angels who were thrown down in their lot with Lucifer, the archangel who led a revolution against God sometime in eternity past. This old Dragon made an attempt to corrupt the lineage of God's creation so that the promised Seed would not come to pass. He intended to spoil the human lineage through which the Messiah would ultimately come.

Satan worked relentlessly to stop the plan of God. He kept the human race steeped in sin. Genesis 6:5-7 states that "The Lord saw how great man's wickedness on the earth had become, and that every inclination of the thoughts of his heart was only evil all the time. The Lord was grieved that he had made man on the earth, and his heart was filled with pain. So the Lord said, 'I will wipe mankind, whom I have created, from the face of the earth—men and animals, and creatures that move along the ground, and birds of the air—for I am grieved that I have made them.'" However, Noah found favor with God; he was a righteous man, and God used him to preserve His lineage because of the promised Seed, the Messiah, who would come to pass at the appointed time. The preservation of the promised Seed is quite interesting when you read about the life of Noah, the structure of the ark, and the instructions that were given to him regarding the animals that were sent into the ark along with Noah's family.

Although God destroyed everything He created, He remembered Noah and all that was in the ark. God blessed Noah and his family and said to them, "Be fruitful, and multiply, and replenish the earth" (9:1 KJV). You may discover as you read about the generation of Noah in Genesis 10 that from the lineage of Shem came the descendant of Terah, and Terah's sons were Abram, Nahor and Haran. There was nothing Satan could do to hinder the plan of God to bring forth this promised Seed when the fullness of time had come. He caused the first woman to break the divine commandment, also the other women who were corrupted having been born through the lineage of the first woman; nevertheless, God was in control.

He called Abram, the moon worshipper, out of Ur of the Chaldees. He commanded him to get out of his country (separation), from his kindred (separation) and from his father's house (separation), and unto a land He would show him. God told Abram in Genesis 12:3 that

He would bless them who blessed him and curse those who cursed him, and in him would all the families of the earth be blessed.

In verse 7, the Lord appeared unto Abram and said to him, "Thy seed will I give this land" (KJV). Abram's wife was Sarai. She was a beautiful woman, and God had it in His plan for them to bring forth a seed into the world through whom ultimately His beloved Son would come, the Messiah, the Redeemer of the world.

Satan had a plan, and this plan could only be accomplished through the weakness of Abram. Abram had a plan also, but this was a plan of deception, which God could not and would not honor. What we ought to grasp from the Word of God is that God wants us to turn to Him at all times. Our eyes must be fixed on Him only. In Proverbs 3:5-6 the Word of the Lord says, "Trust in the Lord with all your heart, and lean not on your own understanding; in all your ways acknowledge Him, and He shall direct your paths" (NKJV). But Abram was not trusting God with all of his heart. He thought of his wife's beauty and he lied to Pharaoh about her being his sister, fearing for his life. Sarai was taken into Pharaoh's house in order that she might become the mother of a child by the Egyptian king, thus defeating the Messianic promise made to Abram.

God did not allow Satan to defeat His plan, so He plagued Pharaoh and his house with great plagues because of Sarai, Abram's wife. What we need to grasp from this account of Abram's life is the fact that unlike Abram being a blessing to Canaan, Egypt nearly became a curse. God's children are also a blessing when we walk in the path of righteousness; when we turn away from Him and do our own thing, we often get into trouble. Now Pharaoh, seeing the power of God and witnessing that the hand of God was with Abram, swiftly sent him away despite the fact that Abram was to be blamed. God used His sovereignty to protect Abram because the delivery of His Seed was for the world's salvation. God was dramatically involved in the protection and ultimate manifestation of this promise.

According to Genesis 13:14-16, "The Lord said to Abram after Lot had parted from him, 'Lift up your eyes from where you are and look north and south, east and west. All the land that you see I will give to you and your offspring forever. I will make your offspring like the dust of the earth, so that if anyone could count the dust, then your offspring could be counted.'" This was an awesome reminder of God's promise, for He intended to help Abraham's faith to remain anchored in Him even though during that period the womb of his wife Sarah, which would deliver the promise, was closed. Nevertheless, Abraham questioned the promise, because in situations such as this and during waiting periods, there is a human tendency to question God. But man's expectation and timing are at times most contrary to that of God. To demonstrate the never-ending nature of God's comfort to His children, the angel declared to them, "Nothing is too hard for God."

Luke 1:37 says it this way: "What is impossible with men is possible with God." The same sentiment is amplified in Jeremiah 32:17, which states, "Ah, Sovereign Lord, you have made the heavens and the earth by your great power and outstretched arm. Nothing is too hard for you." And in verse 27 God says, "I am the Lord, the God of all mankind. Is anything too hard for me?" Since both Abraham and Sarah were stricken in age, his loins and her womb being worn out, Abraham was concerned, as any human being would be. They thought this promised Seed seemed impossible. Patience was not their interest anymore, and eventually what happened is depicted in the Bible. Prior to that, in Genesis 15:1, we learn that God's Word came to Abram as follows: "Do not be afraid, Abram. I am your shield, your very great reward." This word came to Abram because at this point in time it was quite apparent that Abram's eyes shifted to the promise instead of the Giver of the promise.

It's interesting to note, however, this truth about God's promises: what God promises, He is always faithful to bring to pass. Regardless of that, Abraham was anxious about his seed, so he questioned God. He asked him, "O Sovereign Lord, what can you give me since I remain childless and the one who will inherit my estate is Eliezer of Damascus?" (v. 2). Further, Abraham said, "You have given me no children; so a servant in my household will be my heir" (v. 3). Then the word of the Lord came to him: "'This man will not be your heir, but a son coming from your own body will be your heir.' God took him outside and said, 'Look up at the heavens and count the stars—if indeed you can count them.' Then he said to him, 'So shall your offspring be'" (vv. 4-5).

Anyone in such a position would be facing a test of faith. Perhaps they considered adopting a baby, or maybe having a child from one of their family members. Nevertheless, God continued to appear to Abraham, and He spoke to him, saying, "To your descendants I give this land, from the river of Egypt to the great river, the Euphrates" (Genesis 15:18). But Sarah had waited a long time and did not have patience to wait much longer for the promise to be fulfilled.

Every living organism that God makes on the face of this earth has a set time for conception and delivery. It may be a few weeks for the smaller organisms, but bigger animals such as the elephant take twenty-two months. During our waiting period God does not want us to turn to our own understanding; we must look intently to Him at all times. "Sarai said unto Abram, Behold now, the Lord hath restrained me from bearing: I pray thee, go in unto my maid; it may be that I may obtain children by her. And Abram hearkened to the voice of Sarai [instead of God]" (16:2 KJV).

This handmaid, whose name was Hagar, conceived and bore a son, but this plan turned out to be a thorn in their life. Hagar began to act unkindly toward Sarah. According to Genesis 16:5, Sarah discovered that she had done wrong. Then Sarah said to Abraham, "You are responsible for the wrong I am suffering. I put my servant in your arms, and now that she knows she is pregnant, she despises me. May the Lord judge between you and me." Anything accomplished by the dictates of the flesh will cause trouble and dissension. The name of this woman's seed was Ishmael. Sarah dealt harshly with Hagar, and Hagar fled from her presence. Later, according to the angel of the Lord, Ishmael would be a wild man; his seed would be against every man, and every man's hand against him. And he would dwell in the presence of all his brethren.

Abram was eighty-six years old when Ishmael was born. He had to wait for another fourteen years before the promise of a son would be fulfilled, receiving assurances from God about His promise, as shown in Genesis 17:7. Verse 15 states that God changed Sarai's name to Sarah, meaning "princess." Figuratively, she was no more Abraham's princess, but generally a princess or mother of the Church. She had been through her moments and experienced the attitude of not being willing to wait upon the Lord. But despite her anxiety, the angels of the Lord appeared to Abraham in Genesis 18 and they asked for Sarah. Abraham answered, "There, in the tent" (v. 9). Then the Lord said, "I will surely return to you about this time next year, and Sarah your wife will have a son" (v. 10).

At this time of the conversation Sarah was behind the tent door and heard what the angel said about her. She thought it was one of the funniest things she had ever heard, therefore she laughed. This was laughter of unbelief. Naturally, she was old, so unbelievingly she repeated what the angel had said: "I am going to have pleasure with my husband who is also old?" (See v. 12). Sarah's anatomy at such an age would not permit her to have child. Her womb was dead, but it was Jehovah who promised, and nothing is too hard for Him. He knows how to restore, repair and make new dead and worn-out cells.

God said, "I am going to bless you, Sarah. You will be a mother of many nations, and kings of many people shall be of you." Abraham thought this was funny, so he fell on his face and also laughed, saying in his heart, "Shall a child be born unto me who is one hundred years old and Sarah who is ninety years old? (See 17:16-17). Unlike Sarah's, Abraham's laughter was one of joy. I believe it was for this reason they gave the name Isaac to their son, which means "laughter." Isaac's name was of great significance, for many would laugh through faith in the Son of God, even Jesus, Isaac's typology. God told Abraham that He would establish His covenant with him for an everlasting covenant.

God told Sarah that a year after he appeared to Abraham she would deliver, and she laughed. God questioned Sarah's laughter and we know that she did not believe, but may God's name be praised for the son she brought forth, which meant "laughter." Therefore, the puzzle inherent in the question "Is there anything too hard for the Lord?" is resolved. He who promised was faithful to His friend, and He is still faithful to those who call upon His name. They were indeed His friends. It took twenty-five years for Abraham to receive the promise, but God's word came to pass. Satan tried to intercept God's plan, but God would not allow the lineage of Sarah to be corrupted.

Because Sarah was a beautiful woman, men of caliber desired her, including King Abimelech. He sent for Sarah, but he could not have her because God appeared to him in a vision saying, "The woman you have in your palace is another man's wife, and if you touch her you are going to be a dead man" (see 20:3). God told the king to return Abraham's wife, for he was about to destroy all his people and everything he possessed. What we have to bear in mind is that this man was innocent, since Abraham and Sarah had lied to him, but God said, "I have kept you from sinning against me" (v. 6).

The king was told that Abraham would have to pray for him. God had closed up the womb of Abimelech's people, and this happened because Abraham abandoned the plan of faith. As long as he failed to walk in faith, there were no children born to Abimelech and his household. This physical fact illustrates a spiritual reality in the believer's life. The birth of spiritual children through the Gospel is hindered or delayed by our inconsistent conduct or unbelief. But after they had waited and the fullness of time came, the Lord visited Sarah and did for her what He had spoken or promised. She conceived and bore a son, and Abraham named him Isaac. Despite all of Satan's interferences, Isaac, the progenitor and type of the Messiah, was born. His name meant "laughter"! Laughter speaks of blessing, increase, healing, life and well-being.

Millions have laughed for joy because of an experience of Jesus Christ in their lives. Psalm 126:2 says, "Our mouths were filled with laughter, our tongues with songs of joy. Then it was said among the nations, The Lord has done great things for them.'" It is time for someone with the incorruptible seed in him or her to have a mind made up to impact homes, societies, churches and the world at large, that someone would open the mouths of many and make them laugh with unspeakable joy. It is laughing time in Zion, and today is the appointed time to conceive, deliver and let someone laugh in the name of Jesus Christ of Nazareth.

Prayer: Heavenly Father, thank You that You created us to conceive and give birth at Your appointed time. May we endeavor to be pregnant with Your Word so that, as we manifest, someone will receive You and laugh with joy forevermore, in Jesus' name. Amen.

> It is time for someone with the incorruptible seed in him or her to have a mind made up to impact homes, societies, churches and the world at large, that someone would open the mouths of many and make them laugh with unspeakable joy. It is laughing time in Zion, and today is the appointed time to conceive, deliver and let someone laugh in the name of Jesus Christ of Nazareth.

CHAPTER 22

THE TRANSFORMING POWER OF GOD

The word *transform* means "to change form, nature, or disposition." It will most definitely take the power of God to come upon us and overshadow us for that change to be wrought in our lives. If there was ever a time when the church of the living God (you and I) needed the transforming power of God, it's now! It really seems as if the gates of hell are unleashed against the Church and we are not prevailing. But I hear the Word of the Lord through the Spirit saying, "Greater is He that is in us than he that is in the world" (see 1 John 4:4).

Scripture says in Acts 1:8, "But you will receive power [miracle-working power] when the Holy Spirit comes on you; and you will be my witnesses in Jerusalem, and in all Judea and Samaria, and to the ends of the earth." We did receive power after the Holy Ghost came upon us. This power is the Holy Spirit of God. As you may now know, "power" in Greek is *dunamis*; this is supernatural power, ability and strength. *Dunamis* can be referred to as the can-do power of the Spirit of God. If Jesus was anointed with the Holy Ghost and power and He was the perfect Holy Lamb of God, then we need this miracle-working power more than ever.

Acts 10:38 describes how "God anointed Jesus of Nazareth with the Holy Spirit and power, and how he went around doing good and healing all who were under the power of the devil, because God was with him." But it seems as if darkness is overshadowing the church of the living God in these last days. There are many oppressed, depressed, rejected, despondent, discouraged folks roaming to and fro, and it seems as if God has given up on them. Actually, it is not God who has given up on them; they have failed to appropriate the Word of God in their lives. They have failed to walk by faith. We do have the Holy Ghost and power to do good because God is with us. Emmanuel is with us! The God of our forefathers is with us. Malachi 3:6 says that God has not changed, therefore what he did in the days of old he is able to do exceedingly abundantly today, more than we can ask or think, simply because of the power that is at work in you and me.

There is no excuse for the Church to lack the transforming power of God! There is no excuse for the Church to be lukewarm; however, if we are ignorant about the transforming power of God and we are steeped in sin, we won't experience this power. We won't see the manifestation of the power of God in our lives. First John 2:20, 27 says, "But ye have an unction from the Holy One and ye know all things. . . . But the anointing which ye have received of him abideth in you" (KJV). Every believer has the anointing of the Holy Ghost. We are possessed with the Spirit of God, who causes transformation.

The transforming power of God was evident in the lives of the disciples in the Book of Acts. But what must we do to work the works of God? The transforming power of God healed those who were at their gates of physical maladies. The transforming power of God caused prison doors to open, and confession of Jesus Christ of Nazareth was made without an altar call.

This power caused conversion, blind eyes popped open, the lame walked, and many who were dead experienced the resurrection power. I don't know which area in your life needs the finger and the hand of God, but one thing I do know is that the can-do power, the miracle- working power, the King Eternal, the immortal, invisible, only wise God knows all about our situations.

And He is well able to work on your behalf. Ezekiel 12:25 says, "But I the Lord will speak what I will, and it shall be fulfilled without delay. For in your days, you rebellious house, I will fulfill whatever I say, declares the Sovereign Lord." Numbers 23:19 says, "God is not a man, that he should lie, nor a son of man, that he should change his mind. Does he speak and then not act? Does he promise and not fulfill?" The Church was not born weak; it was not born anemic; it was not born spiritless. It was born in power. There was a mark on it, or signs and wonders! There were flames of fire! There were other tongues. There were miracles. The Church is not a recreation center. It is not a place of merchandise. It is not a social club. It is the body of Christ. It is the lifeline of Christ. It is the healing center of Jesus Christ to set mankind free from their burden of sin and sufferings.

The Church of God must work the works of Him who called us out of darkness while it is now day, for the night is coming and we will not be able to work. Somebody said the kingdom of God is within us and we know no defeat, only victory. The transforming power abides in us. Yes! It is so, I know it is so! Romans 8:11 says, "And if the Spirit of him who raised Jesus from the dead is living in you, he who raised Christ from the dead will also give life to your mortal bodies through his Spirit, who lives in you." Do you not know that Jesus purchased His church—you and me—with His precious incorruptible blood, and then He went to be with His Father and He sent us the Holy Ghost and power?

In the name of Jesus we have the power that raised Christ from the dead, and it's available to us only on the premises of the Cross and our faith in the sacrifice. Jesus, our example and our reason for living, worked the works of His Father when He was on earth. One of His works was to destroy the works of the devil. John 3:8 says, "The reason the Son of God appeared was to destroy the devil's work." One of the works of the devil is sickness, but thank God Jesus came to heal the sick and the afflicted.

In Mark 6:56 we learn how "wherever he went—into villages, towns or countryside—they placed the sick in the marketplaces." They begged Him to let them touch even the edge of His cloak, and all who touched Him were healed. There is power in the Word to heal: the Word of the Lord declares in Psalm 107:19-20, "Then they cried to the Lord in their trouble, and he saved them from their distress. He sent forth his word and healed them; he rescued them from the grave."

In Proverbs 4 we are told, "Let [the words] not depart from thine eyes; keep them in the midst of thine heart. For they are life unto those that find them, and health to all their flesh" (vv. 21-22 KJV). According to Mark the gospel writer, healing can take place by the laying on of hands. He says in 16:18, "They shall lay hands on the sick, and they shall recover" (KJV).

The prayer of faith, according to James 5, will cause the sick to be healed. The change, the transformation, the miracle-working power, the resurrection power, must be our portion and we must work the works of God on this side of the grave. Is there drought in our lives individually and collectively? Is there deadness in our life which stinks? Jesus is here, and by faith we must come forth in the name of Jesus. By faith we will rise up in the name of Jesus! There is no power or entity on earth that can keep the body of Christ down. Jesus died and was resurrected for the Church so that we too may be empowered to show forth His power, which is not of ourselves but of God.

Nothing is impossible with Jesus! Once upon a time Jesus heard that a friend of His was sick, but He delayed going to heal His friend just because He was on a mission when He received the information. Meanwhile, when He heard about the sickness, He said, "This sickness is not unto death, but for the glory of God, that the Son of God might be glorified thereby" (John 11:4 KJV). Bear this in mind: God does not receive glory from sin and sickness, but His glory is made evident in delivering men from sin and healing the sick. Later, Jesus' friend Lazarus died and was buried, and folks gathered around the sisters of Lazarus, Mary and Martha, to pay their condolences.

They wept with them, but Jesus, the One God anointed with the Holy Ghost, knew that He had the life which takes preeminence over death. Even though Jesus delayed His going to Lazarus' sickbed, it was never too late for the One who has the answer to all problems. This happened for no other reason but for men to glorify God. When the time finally arrived for Him to attend to His friend, He said to His disciples, "Let us go and wake up Lazarus, for he is asleep." The disciples misunderstood Him, thus using plainness of speech He said to them, "Lazarus is dead" (see vv. 11-14). All this time they had no understanding of the resurrection power!

They needed to know about the coming resurrection power and life. They needed a demonstration of the resurrection power to believe that Jesus Christ was Lord. Jesus arrived and Martha began to complain. She said, "If You had been here when we needed You the most this would not have happened, but I know that even now, whatsoever You will ask of God, He will give it to You." Up to this point it was unclear to Martha who Jesus was. Jesus said to Martha, "Your brother shall rise again," but Martha was in doubt, so she misunderstood what Jesus said to her. She said, "I know that he will rise in the resurrection at the last day." Jesus answered her and said, "I am the resurrection and the life; he who believes in Me, though he was dead, yet shall he live" (see vv. 21-25).

Jesus was saying to Martha, "Look at Me and believe. I am the resurrection and the life!" We did receive this power, the power to speak in new tongues and to cast out devils! Eat any deadly thing and it shall not harm us; lay hands on the sick and they shall recover in the name of Jesus. We do not have to seek any deliverance services of the elites! We are possessed with the Holy Ghost. I know what the Bible says in James 5:14-16: "Is any one of you sick? He should call the elders [the pastors] of the church to pray over him and anoint him with oil in the name of the Lord. And the prayer offered in faith will make the sick person well; the Lord will raise him up. If he has sinned, he will be forgiven. Therefore confess your sins to each other and pray for each other so that you may be healed. The prayer of a righteous man is powerful and effective." There are times when we need to take a personal step of faith to release God's blessings into our life. There are times when we need to use boldness to release the transforming power in us in order to establish God's providence in our life.

Jesus asked Martha a question: "Do you believe?" (John 11:26). She answered, "Yes Lord, I believe that you are the Christ, the Son of God, who was come into the world" (v. 27). She saw Jesus in a different light than she had known Him previously! She now believed that Jesus was God. Mary now had heard that Jesus was present, and she hastily went out to meet Him. She fell at His feet saying, "Lord, if you had been here, my brother would not have died" (v. 32). Jesus had compassion when He saw everyone weeping. He groaned in the Spirit and was troubled! Then He said, "Where have you laid him?" (v. 34). They led Him to the tomb and He wept. When He approached the grave, He groaned in the Spirit again.

There stood in front of Him the grave with a stone upon it. He therefore instructed the people to take away the stone, but Martha was concerned. She said, "My brother died four days ago, and by now he stinks" (see v. 39). This is what happens to a dead body when it's buried; it decays and there is an obnoxious odor or stench! But this stench was about to be transformed into the sweet aroma of life!

Turn to your heavenly Father and pray to Him just as Jesus turned to Him prior to the resurrection of Lazarus from the dead. Give God your stench! It may be stinky to man, but it's no secret what God can do with your stench! What He did for Lazarus He is well able to do for you. Jesus is the resurrection and the life! He said to Mary, "Did I not tell you that if you believe, you would see the glory of God?" (v. 40).

Oh how we want to see the glory of God in another dimension in the Church again! Oh how we need to get beyond the fruit of the blessing and speaking in tongues and believe God for the transforming power of God which is no respecter of persons. Just take heed and remove the stones no matter what they represent in your life.

They took away the stone and Jesus lifted up His eyes and said, "Father, I thank you that you have heard me. I knew that you always hear me, but I said this for the benefit of the people standing here, that they may believe that you sent me" (vv. 41-42). Jesus had a relationship with His Father! The people heard Him pray to His Father and now the Father must answer His prayer, and surely He did. I know that when we also come to Him in prayer, He is not going to let us down. He is bidding us to come when we are weary and heavy laden.

The invitation is open to all who will heed His voice. There is grace and help in the time of trouble. Come and spread out your hands and lift up your eyes to Him, like King Jehoshaphat in the Old Testament. The Word says that Jesus cried with a loud voice, "Lazarus, come forth" (v. 43 KJV). This was a command from the Creator of all ages, the One who is the resurrection and the life, the God of the living and the dead. This loud voice, the voice of God, echoed beyond putrefaction and called Lazarus by name. The words were "Come forth!" This was the Word sending the double-edged sword into dead flesh and blood imparting resurrection power and life.

If Lazarus had not been called by name, that voice of power and authority would have awakened all the saints who were dead. This voice is calling us by name! The voice is the Word of God! It was this voice that was in the very beginning, whose Spirit moved upon the face of the earth and pierced the void and the darkness on the surface of the deep and said, "Let there be," and there was. This voice is still calling, "Come forth," whatsoever your name is. He says, "I know you by name and by number, and your names are written on the palms of My hands." Verse 44 says, "He that was dead came forth, bound hand and foot with grave clothes: and his face was bound about with a napkin. Jesus saith unto them, loose him, and let him go!" (KJV).

We may be going through some stuff which may seem like a dead situation. Do not throw a pity party! Jesus can fix it for you! He has delayed His coming and our situations are dormant. He knows how to set out late, but He always arrives on time. There is stagnancy, complacency, drought, infertility, lethargy, you name it. It's been a long time now, but He is going to show up at the appointed time. We must therefore turn our eyes upon Him, knowing that He who has delayed His coming is an on-time God.

Lay hold of His Word taken from 2 Corinthians 1:3-10:

> Praise be to the God and Father of our Lord Jesus Christ, the Father of compassion and the God of all comfort, who comforts us in all our troubles, so that we can comfort those in any trouble with the comfort we ourselves have received from God. For just as the sufferings of Christ flow over into our lives, so also through Christ our comfort overflows. If we are distressed, it is for your comfort and salvation; if we are comforted, it is for your comfort, which produces in you patient endurance of the same sufferings we suffer. And our hope for you is firm, because we know that just as you share in our sufferings, so also you share in our comfort. We do not want you to be uninformed, brothers, about the hardships we suffered in the province of Asia. We were under great

pressure, far beyond our ability to endure, so that we despaired even of life. Indeed, in our hearts we felt the sentence of death. But this happened that we might not rely on ourselves but on God, who raises the dead. He has delivered us from such a deadly peril, and he will deliver us. On him we have set our hope that he will continue to deliver us.

You did receive power after the Holy Ghost came upon you. It is time to manifest in the name of Jesus! Signs and wonders must follow the believer! We must believe that all things are possible with God.

Prayer: Father, You promised that You will not leave us comfortless but You would send the Comforter to guide us into all truth. We thank You for the power to transform our lives. We rely on You to do the greater work in us so that others may be influenced or motivated to do all the good they can for Your sake. Amen.

Turn to your heavenly Father and pray to Him just as Jesus turned to Him prior to the resurrection of Lazarus from the dead. Give God your stench! It may be stinky to man, but it's no secret what God can do with your stench! What He did for Lazarus He is well able to do for you. Jesus is the resurrection and the life! He said to Mary, "Did I not tell you that if you believe, you would see the glory of God?" (John 11:40).

CHAPTER 23

THERE IS A RIVER OF LIFE FLOWING IN THE HOUSE OF GOD (EZEKIEL 47:1-12)

The Word of the Lord says in John 7:38, "Whoever believes in me, as the scripture has said, streams of living water will flow from his innermost being." The word *river* is mentioned in the Bible for the first time in Genesis 2:10: "And a river went out of Eden to water the garden." This river branched into four rivers that watered the Garden and the earth. In the latter part of this chapter, we will talk about a river in a wilderness, and what you should bear in mind is that this wilderness is also a supernatural one.

Rev. Alex W. Ness states, that the purpose of the river in Genesis 2:10 was not only to water the Garden of Eden but to make it productive as well. The river was to supply drinking water to beast, fowl and fish, for the water was life to them. As mentioned elsewhere, the river was to supply water to the earth. But significantly, life flowed from God to His creation by His continuous loving provision. This God whom we serve has limitless supply of that which He initiates! There is no shortage with Him.

It is quite vivid that Genesis 2:10 says that the river became rivers. The Creator's purpose for patterning the river with the Spirit is to magnify the supply of water and reproduction of life with the coming of the Holy Ghost, the river of God. Therefore the living water, the greater One that is in you, has what it takes to cause you to do greater works and to affect any form of physical and spiritual growth in you. The river mentioned above is the physical type of the Holy Ghost flowing through us.

According to Ness, the Holy Spirit would flow or proceed as one river from the throne of God, and the river or the Spirit would come upon the Son of God, even Jesus Christ. Thereafter, He would proceed from the Son of God, the source, to the Church. Thence, out of the innermost being of the Church shall He also flow to the inhabitants of the earth.

Now, according to the Word of God in Ezekiel 47:1, the phrase "from under the threshold of the house eastward" (KJV) shows that the waters shall not flow of themselves. The prophet was not referring to a literal river, but a symbolic one. As in nature, there would be no access from other streams. This is quite interesting and can be considered supernatural, since Ezekiel's vision was a mysterious and spiritual revelation. Again, the supernaturalism of the river was portrayed in this chapter because the river was brought into the Temple without pipes for the washing of sacrifices or the cleansing of the Temple furniture! Let us be realistic and imaginative about the water in the Temple; the carrying of other waters to this pleasant river would contaminate it. This was indeed supernatural!

John the Revelator also saw a vision of a pure river of the water of life in Revelation 22:1-2, which to me is the river of Eden. It's unfortunate, however, that the river of Eden, which was intended to flow continuously, has ceased to flow because of the upheaval of sin. Relatively, if your living-water river that should spring up continuously ceases to flow, then it's imperative that you find out why it's not flowing continuously. What is it that has caused it to dry up? For the river in the Book of Revelation does not dry up! It is flowing and bearing fruit continuously. God's Word is calling us to come to Him! He desires for us to join to Him so that our rivers will keep on flowing. Here the river is not symbolic, but rather a spiritual one. It is the living water in you and me.

The preceding paragraphs have taught us that the river in us is the Holy Ghost: "On the last and greatest day of the Feast, Jesus stood and said in a loud voice, 'If a man is thirsty, let him come to me and drink. Whoever believes in me, as the scripture has said, streams of living water shall flow from within him.' By this he meant the Spirit, whom those who believed in him were later to receive. Up to that time the Spirit had not been given, since Jesus had not yet been glorified" (John 7:37-39).

It is meant not for the Spirit to be trapped in a vessel or a temple. Jesus said the Spirit will flow like rivers of living water. Literally speaking, one cannot stop a river from flowing! Rivers generally carve their own course. On the contrary, we have allowed sin, the cares of life, to hinder the free-flowing Holy Spirit in our life. If we will let Him flow from out of us unto others, oh how we are going to see humanity drinking, quenching their thirst through us. If we will only yield and live holy lives, the Holy Spirit will flow out of you and me.

According to *Matthew Henry's Commentary*, the river does not flow through corroded pipelines as a drop or trickle. It flows out of your temple, your body, as a river that is ever deepened and ever widening. This is what is clearly portrayed about this supernatural, free- flowing river in Ezekiel's vision. Christ's body is the temple! He is also the door; from His pierced side flow living waters. The living water that flows from Him will make any person who drinks it spring up into everlasting life. John 4:14 says, "But whoever drinks the water I give him will never thirst. Indeed, the water I give him will become in him a spring of water welling up to eternal life." The good news is that if we are dried up and our fountain ceases to flow, we can spring up again. No one can hinder you from springing up again, for this river flows from God. The Bible says that this river sprang up from under the threshold! This is described by the prophet and is kind of difficult to grasp. But so it is with the believer's life in Christ; it is a mystery! The Word of the Lord says in Colossians 3:3, "For you died, and your life is now hidden with Christ in God."

It's significant to note that water flowed from the side of Jesus when He was pierced on the cross! For in Ezekiel's vision, water came from the side of the altar, like the water that flowed from the side of Christ. It is in and by Jesus Christ, the great Altar, that God blesses us with spiritual blessings in heavenly places. Psalm 46:4 says, "There is a river whose streams make glad the city of God, the holy place where the Most High dwells." The river Ezekiel saw flowed out of the house of God. The Holy Ghost flowed out of Jesus

Christ. We have become His temple. First Corinthians 3:16-17 says that we are the temple of God. 1 Corinthians 6:19 says that our bodies are the temple of the Holy Ghost. Springs of living water must flow out of us.

In Ezekiel 47 the Word of the Lord tells us that Ezekiel is a guide. And like Christ, who is also a guide, the waters which ran down from the holy mountain followed Ezekiel, and when they followed him it came to about 1,000 cubits. He went over it and tried the depth of it, and it was to the ankle. At this stage it was about 1,500 feet wide, and it was very shallow! It was to the ankle. This immediately suggests walking in the Spirit. The ankle represents the entrance of the river, portraying salvation. Some of us have entered this first stage and we have not moved on. The water is ankle-deep, but we need to lift our feet out of shallow water and swim into the river of life. We received salvation but we have not grown. We have been drinking milk for a long time now, but there comes a time when a baby has to grow up and eat pabulum and baby cereal, then porridge and mashed potatoes, and then after a few years, he or she is able to consume any kind of solid substances.

Hebrews 5:12-14 says, "In fact, though by this time you ought to be teachers, you need someone to teach you the elementary truths of God's word all over again. You need milk, not solid food! Anyone who lives on milk, being still an infant, is not acquainted with the teaching about righteousness. But solid food is for the mature, who by constant use have trained themselves to distinguish good from evil." In Hebrews 6:1-2 comes the challenge: "Therefore let us leave the elementary teachings about Christ and go on to maturity, not laying again the foundation of repentance from acts that lead to death, and of faith in God, instruction about baptisms, the laying on of hands, the resurrection of the dead, and eternal judgment."

Rivers of living water flowing from our innermost being will enable us to walk in the Spirit, like Jesus. Galatians 5:16 says, "So I say, live by the Spirit, and you will not gratify the desires of the sinful nature." Verse 25 says, "Since we live by the Spirit, let us keep in step with the Spirit." Ephesians 2:10 states, "For we are God's workmanship, created in Christ Jesus to do good works, which God prepared in advance for us to do."

Now, it would be interesting to delve into the second measurement in the Book of Ezekiel. They walked along the bank of the river on the other side, 1,000 cubits more, and then tried the depth of it. They went through it a second time and it was up to the knee. "Knee" signifies prayer and total dependence upon the Lord. The things concerning the kingdom of God are of power and are operated by the Spirit and not by the flesh. Also, knees portray the baptism of the Holy Spirit! The born-again Christian must be found bowing his or her knees before God, saying, "Let Your will be done on earth as it is in heaven." Let us lift up our ankle and walk from shallow water to the knee level and kneel before the Almighty God to pray for the baptism of the Holy Ghost.

Those who call upon the name of the Lord shall be saved! They who call upon the name of the Lord shall be enriched. Also, they who hunger and thirst for righteousness shall be filled. They who will bow their knees before God in humility and in submission will have springs of living water flowing from deep within. Kneel in prayer! It will release the living water. First Kings 18:41-42 tells us that the prophet Elijah put his head between his knees and prayed, and God sent rain. Ezra 9:5 tells us that Ezra knelt in prayer for the nation. He confessed and interceded for the land, and the Lord answered. Jesus, the One who said, "The Spirit of the Lord God is on me" (Luke 4:18). Jesus kneeled in the Garden of Gethsemane and prayed until His tears were like drops of blood. To enter the river in the deepest dimension, you have to move from the shallow waters. You've got to kneel in prayer while launching out into deeper waters.

Ezekiel had now passed through the river at the knee, but there was yet deeper water to measure. They walked by the river 1,000 cubits more the third time, and then they were in the middle. The waters were up to the waist. "Loins" in the Scriptures has two meanings. One refers to progeny. Genesis 35:11 says, "Kings shall come out of thy loins" (KJV). But in Exodus 1:5, Acts 2:30, and Hebrews 7:5, the loins represent the procreative part of man, which points to the miracle-working power that should indwell all Spirit-baptized believers. The Bible says we shall receive power, miracle power, after the Holy Ghost has come upon us.

Why is it that the living water is not flowing through us? Is it because of sin or unbelief? Have we believed a lie? Do we not understand the Word of God? Or is it the little faith that we have? How can we make a difference in these last days? The Word of the Lord says that faith comes by hearing the Word of God. Some of us have remained in shallow water for too long, dictating to and limiting God. We give credence to Jesus, Elijah, Elisha, and the disciples and other great elites of the gospel of Jesus Christ. We have come to the conclusion that these people are the only ones with the living water.

There are those who are baptized with the Holy Ghost who should be seen and heard speaking in tongues. We need to remember where we have fallen from and turn to the Lord, for He is more than willing to revive us and save us from our spiritual wilderness, knowing that we are also temples of the Holy Ghost.

There is a river of life flowing out of us! It causes the lame to walk and the blind to see! It opens prison doors and sets the captives free! There is a river of life flowing out of us. This living water will cause those who are bent over to be straightened up in the name of Jesus. Jesus said to the woman, "Thou art loosed" (Luke 13:12 KJV). Those who have an issue shall be made whole, for you know who the source of that living water is. Those who are blind and demented shall see physically and spiritually. Your mind shall be made whole, because your mind belongs to Christ. If you are demon-subjected and demon-possessed, you shall be delivered in the all-powerful name of Jesus. Here comes the last measurement, and this is where the challenge is!

This is what we call deep water—deep calling unto deep. Ezekiel walked 1,000 cubits further and attempted to pass, but the water had risen so much that no man could pass over safely to swim through it. This is beyond the capacity of man. Indeed, so much water to swim in makes it impossible for man to pass over. The author says that the river represents the last progression. Its open end symbolizes the whole Gospel for the whole man. In another sense, the river is a physical type of the Holy Ghost and His works within our lives.

Let us therefore get a thorough grip of this vision! The waters of the sanctuary are running waters, as those of a river. It's not standing water! It's not water in a pond or lake! Standing water tends to stagnate! Standing water collects all kinds of slime or grime, which settle to the bottom of the water where there is no filtration or sterilization. Also, it's not running into other waters! Why are you not experiencing the Living Water in all His measures? Why are you standing in one place for so long? Listen, if you do not have living and free-flowing water, you are like the pond! You need to walk and kneel and pray to the Guide.

Walk from the surface or shallow water and dive deeper into the things concerning the kingdom of God. It's high time for us to leave the surface water level and say as a mature Christian, "I am crucified with Christ: nevertheless I live; yet not I, but Christ liveth in me: and the life which I now live in the flesh I live by the faith of the Son of God" (Galatians 2:20 KJV). This is thrusting out into deep waters because it is not about us; it is about the enabling power of God.

God is calling His children: "Come unto Me and you shall thirst no more! Come and do deep swimming, and while you are doing so I will do the multiplication. I shall do a work in you. I will hasten and watch over My word to perform it." The Word dwelling in us and the Holy Ghost flowing through us is the powerhouse in our lives. The apostle Paul said, "I did not come to you in word only, but in power and in the Holy Ghost with great assurance" (see 1 Thessalonians 1:5).

Ezekiel 47:6-9, says thus:

[The guide] said unto me, Son of man, hast thou seen this?' Then he brought me, and caused me to return to the brink of the river. Now when I had returned, behold, at the bank of the river were many trees on the one side and on the other. Then said he unto me, These waters issue out toward the east country, and go down into the desert, and go into the sea: which being brought forth into the sea, the waters shall be healed. And it came to pass, that everything that liveth, which moveth, whithersoever the rivers shall come, shall live: and there shall be a very great multitude of fish, because these waters shall come thither: for they shall be healed; and every thing shall live whither the river cometh (KJV).

The guide turned Ezekiel's attention to the force of the river. The source is the sanctuary. The waters of the sanctuary flow with a free course and with restorative power. The Word is like the salt Elisha cast into the spring of water in Jericho (2 Kings 2:20-21). Furthermore, Christ is the Truth, the Word, the Wellspring of water; He says, "Come unto Me and let Me water you." Wherever the river goes, dead sinners are made alive and God's people are made lively stones.

There is remedy for humanity in the Word. Revelation 22:1, 17 says, "Then the angel showed me the river of the water of life, as clear as crystal, flowing from the throne of God and of the Lamb. . . . The Spirit and the bride say, 'Come!' And let him who hears say, 'Come!' Whoever is thirsty, let him come; and whoever wishes, let him take the free gift of the water of life."

Remember Ezekiel 47:7, "Now when I returned, behold, at the bank of the river were many trees on the one side and on the other" (KJV). Note this: the many trees signify the bearing of much fruit. God said to the prophet, "These waters issue out toward the east country, and go down into the desert, and go into the sea; which being brought forth into the sea, the waters shall be healed" (v. 8 KJV).

The purpose of the river is to bring life to the desert. The desert is a place that is dry and nonproductive! It needs water to make the environment supple and moist for plowing, planting, and germination to take place. The Holy Ghost is the living water that can bring life to the unregenerate man who is dead in his sins. It shows how the Holy Ghost flowing through us will bring life and water to our dead situation and make it come alive.

This Scripture speaks of the Dead Sea, which contains no life whatsoever but is healed symbolically to magnify what the Lord can do through the Holy Spirit in a person's life. The mysterious river the prophet of God saw ultimately emptied itself into the sea. I believe the Lord God of Hosts desires to carry us by His free-flowing Spirit into the deeper waters. He desires for us to swim and dive deep, carried by the current of His mighty wind. As we swim into the deep things of God, the living water will be poured out into other people's lives as we come into contact with them.

We will become trees of righteousness standing on the brink of the river, ready and prepared to do works of ministry. It will not be our own doings or abilities, but God's empowerment. When we are drenched in the Spirit and are saturated and engulfed by this river, we will be His vessel conveying healing power to the nations. Ezekiel's river brought healing to the sea. There is a river of life flowing out of us!

But spiritual wilderness is associated with barrenness, lukewarmness, all carnality and sin in the body of Christ or the Church. When the Church fails to live in righteousness and holiness, we will not see a flow of signs and wonders. But according to Isaiah 43:18-19 God says, "Forget the former things; do not dwell on the past. See, I am doing a new thing! Now it springs up; do you not perceive it? I am making a way in the desert and streams in the wasteland."

Until the Church swims into revival, she will not experience this remarkable promise of God. Therefore, people of all nations, tongues and races, let us turn to our Guide and lift our ankles out of shallow water and kneel before Almighty God until the living water is released and we are engulfed by the current of the deep sea of God. Then and only then will we be carried by its waves into the deeper things of God.

Prayer: Jesus, You are at the right hand of the Father praying for us. Thank you. You offered the woman at the well living water that springs up into eternal life, and she received You. May we hunger and thirst for the living water so that our thirst will be quenched and our life here on earth will magnify You. Amen.

Kneel in prayer! It will release the living water. First Kings 18:41 tells us that the prophet Elijah put his head between his knees and prayed, and God sent rain. Jesus, the One who said, "The Spirit of the Lord God is on me" (Luke 4:18), kneeled in the Garden of Gethsemane and prayed until His tears were like drops of blood. To enter the river in the deepest dimension, you have to move from the shallow waters. You've got to kneel in prayer while launching out into deeper waters.

CHAPTER 24

THOUGH WE ARE SOMETIMES DEAD AND DRY, WE CAN BE RESUSCITATED BY THE WORD OF GOD (EZEKIEL 37)

When we have erred against the Almighty God because of sin, sometimes the valley engulfs us. This condition often saps us of our anointing and we are left dry and dead. This is when God will have to turn His attention to us and send someone to prophesy over our lives. God intentionally turns to His people and revitalizes them because He desires for them to show forth His glory. According to *Webster's Dictionary*, *revival* means "to come back to life; to awaken; to resuscitate; to recover from neglect; to refresh or restore." One writer says, "Revival is God greatly stirring, shaking and changing His people from apathy or selfishness, stagnancy, complacency, dormancy, or spiritual dwarfism to a repentant and humble, fervently praying and praising people." Prayer and hearing the Word of God are two spiritual weapons that will cause the people of God to experience God's stirring and a shaking in their lives.

Ezekiel, one of the Major Prophets, brought revival to an army of God's people who found themselves in the valley of dead and dry bones because of their rebellion and disobedience. Ezekiel is known as the most eccentric of the Old Testament prophets. This man of God had an odd or strange personality. One author states, "His writing is the strangest of the Old Testament prophets' because of his use of imagery, symbolism, parables, and apocalyptic signs. He was very dramatic in the proclamation of his message to God's people".

According to Homer G. Rhea, "Ezekiel spoke to the people of God that faith is a matter of the heart and of an individual's relationship with God. This prophet was carried off into exile by the Babylonians in the Second Deportation in 597 BC. During that time he was a young priest in Jerusalem, according to the Word of the Lord in Ezekiel 1:3. God's hand was upon him in an unusual way. Ezekiel was ordained and called to be prophet and preached to encourage the people of God to walk worthy of their calling even in the land of captivity. His mission lasted for twenty- two years as a prophet in exile. His ministry took place in Babylon, the place of captivity. This man of God had three fundamental or paramount qualities in his life that give us a vivid understanding of the kind of person he was. He had a fervent zeal for God; he was passionate about his ministry; and his earnest desire was to encourage the people of God with the word that if they live by faith, God will deliver them".

The Bible is clear that Ezekiel was very dogmatic or opinioned about his belief and conviction, which was very much evident in his ministry. This prophet of God had a twofold theme: judgment and hope. Despite the judgment the Israelites faced as a result of their sin, God had sent them a message of hope that they would come out of captivity. Ezekiel was to reassure them with that hope. He taught the people of God that even though they were bound in Babylon, God was with them. He taught them the meaning of being the chosen people of God. He transformed their whole concept of corporate religion to a one-on-one relationship with God. To fulfill his mission, this strange prophet of God received a fascinating vision from the Lord.

He had visions of the sovereign God (chs. 1-3), the vision of God's glory departing from the Temple (chs. 8-11), the vision of the valley of dry bones (ch. 37), and the vision of the new Temple and the glory of God returning (chs. 40-48). Most people are familiar with chapter 37 of Ezekiel, and the Holy Ghost has impressed upon my spirit to treat this chapter here. The subject in this treatment is intended to bring to your attention that even though Israel had been destroyed by the Babylonians, Ezekiel saw that Israel was going to live again. Although the body of Christ may appear dead as a result of the consequence of sin so that we are found in a state of dormancy, complacency and stagnancy, we can live again. There can be a resurrection of souls from the valley of death and sin to a life of righteousness—to holy, lively stones empowered by God.

The apostle Peter says that we are living stones. First Peter 2:5 states, "You also, like living stones, are being built into a spiritual house to be a holy priesthood, offering spiritual sacrifices acceptable to God through Jesus Christ." The resurrection of the church of the living God, or any part of it, from an afflicted condition is tied to the hearkening of the Word of God. The Word of the Lord is sharp, alive and active. It has power to cut asunder soul and spirit, and it discerns the intent of the heart. This Word can cut into dead bodies and dry bones and there will be life! According to Jeremiah 23:29, "Is not my word like fire,' declares the Lord, 'and like a hammer that breaks a rock in pieces?"

There will be a stir! There will be a noise! There will be a shaking! But what effect does the Word have on you? If you do not feel the quickening power of the Word, if you do not feel the Word cutting or piercing you, if the Word does not affect you, then you are dead and need to be awakened. We need to be resuscitated! We need to be refreshed and restored by the Word of prophecy and prayer. What has caused you to lose your sinews and muscle? What has caused you to lose your important organs so that you can't function as an organism anymore in the body of Christ?

The Church is a living organism kept alive by the Spirit of the living God. What has caused you to be barren for so long? Why have you not reproduced or borne fruit? You have remained a spiritual dwarf and have not allowed your light to shine so that men may see and glorify God. Our bodies, our dead dry bones, have not laid hold of the Word of God. The Word of the Lord says in John 15:5, 7-8, "I am the vine; you are the branches. If a man remains in me and I in him, he will bear much fruit; apart from me you can do nothing. . . . If you remain in me and my words remain in you, ask whatever you wish, and it will be given you. This is to my Father's glory, that you bear much fruit, showing yourselves to be my disciples."

We cannot affect our families, schools and surroundings because we are held captive in our spiritual Babylon. When the prophet Jeremiah experienced the word, the fire of God, in his innermost being, he said, "I feel like the fire is shut up in my bones" (see Jeremiah 20:9). I read about God's people who were once upon a time in spiritual bondage in Egypt, but they cried out to God and He sent them a deliverer. If we cry out to God, He will deliver us. It is time to cry out to God to deliver you from the devil, your spiritual taskmaster who appears to have successfully mutilated the Church. He has taken off your covering, and so your bodies are left exposed to the elements of destruction. The Church is left exposed to the powers of darkness which have sapped its vitality or life, and all that remains are corpses. All that remains are dead and dry bones!

There is not much life! There is not much demonstration of power and Spirit! There are no signs and wonders, but Ezekiel's God is faithful. He promises restoration and life again! You will live. Live, because the Word is going to wake you up! Live, because He is going to breathe on you. The occupants of the house of the Lord are living, breathing organisms!

The Word of the Lord says in Joshua 1:8, "Do not let this Book of the Law depart from your mouth . . . be careful to do everything written in it." Therefore let us carefully observe Ezekiel 37. Let us look at the deplorable condition of these bones as the prophet of God was commanded. It is believed that it was by prophetic impulse and divine power that in the vision the man of God was carried out and set in the midst of the valley of dry bones and God talked to him. God is in the midst of the Church, and she shall not move! This valley was full of bones! They were dead men's bones. These bones were not piled up as a heap, but were scattered upon the ground!

It seemed as if some bloodthirsty man had pursued them and slain them with the sword. There were many slain, left for the vultures of the air to feed upon their flesh. The sun and the wind helped in the putrefaction of their bodies, and their bones were left bare and disjointed from one another. They were dispersed! Isn't it quite evident how the body of Christ is fragmented? Isn't it evident how we are dead, scattered and disjointed, and we do not function as members of the body of Christ? One is the ear and the other the eye, one the head or the feet and the other the hands. When we all come together by the Word of God and the breath of His Holy Spirit permeates us, there is going to be a stir, a shake and a noise! There is going to be an earthquake experience for us to come together again.

Ezekiel, the eccentric man of God passed by the bones and observed that they were not only many, but they were very dry. They had been long exposed to the hot sun and the elements of the wind. Job 21:24-26 says that the bones that died long ago have lost all their moisture and they are dry as dust.

There are many of us in spiritual Babylon as a result of our sin. The deadly venom of sin has destroyed us! Its potency has infiltrated the whole body, and it saps or drains us of the anointing. When we are drained we become dead and dry, but thank God that the Word of God has the potency to raise or resurrect us.

The Jews, God's chosen people, were like those dead and dry bones, unlikely to ever come together again even as a skeleton, less likely to form a living body. But with God all things are possible! The God who used dust and made man into a living soul, the God who fearfully and wonderfully made man and breathed the breath of life into man and man became a living soul, is ever close to us to help and redeem us should we turn to Him.

He is able to breathe into the dead and dry bones of our bodies so that we will and can become a living sacrifice, holy and acceptable unto Him, which is our reasonable service. We will live to glorify God in our bodies, not dead or dry but wet and moist in the anointing! There will be oil, enough moisture in our lives.

The Jews were unburied in the open valley, but the eyes of God were upon them to restore them. He leads me beside still water, somewhere in the valley below. In the valley, He restores my soul. Even though I walk through the valley of the shadow of death, I will fear no evil, for He is with me. His rod and staff comfort me. In the valley the rod is the word of Christ. The question was asked, "Son of Man, can these bones live?" The prophet answered, "I do not know how that could be possible, but You are God! You know all things!" (See Ezekiel 37:3). What would it take to bring back the dispersed bones from a dead and dry condition to a living, breathing organism?

At this juncture let us be careful to observe the Word of God. The man of God was commanded to prophesy to the dead bones. He was to prophesy to the wind. He was to preach the Word to the dead and dry bones for them to awake. He was to pray, and the dead scattered bodies would come back to life as an answer to prayer. The Word coupled with prayer will raise the dead! We must be earnest in our prayers, always appropriating the Word of God until the breath or life of God comes into our bodies and raises us up from death because He is the life-giver. God says, "Prophesy," and if you prophesy as you are commanded, despite your condition or situation, God is going to bring to pass what He has spoken and what He has said He will do.

The prophet said, "Ye dry bones, hear the word of the Lord" (v. 4 KJV). As he prophesied, the dispersed valley of dead, dry bones found their individual person and became human beings. As he prophesied there was a noise, a shaking, and a commotion. The bones began to move. There was a noise, a shaking, when David heard the sound on top of the mulberry trees (2 Samuel 5:24). The Bible says he bestirred himself, and then there was a shaking.

When my favorite apostle, Paul, heard the voice of Jesus saying, "Why are you persecuting Me?" Behold, a shaking of the dry, unanointed bones began to tremble. He fell to the ground shaking and asking, "What would You have me do?"

When the Word was spoken by the prophet of God, something began to happen in the valley. The bones came together bone by bone! Though there are more than two hundred bones in the body of a human being, all the bones found their location and connected themselves to the right bones or joints. Not one bone was misplaced; they found their right positions, and then sinews and flesh came upon the bones and skin covered them again.

Man was lifeless until God blew the breath of life into him and he became a living soul. The army of God stood up, but there was no breath of life in them. The prophet of God prophesied to the wind or the breath or Spirit of God. He said, "Come . . . O breath, and breathe upon these slain" (Ezekiel 37:9 KJV). Immediately breath came into them, and there stood up on their feet an exceedingly great army, a resurrected, living, breathing army of the Lord.

God is not the God of the dead! He is the God of the living. Talk to Him now; ask Him to breathe upon you so that you may live now. You shall live! The answer was quick, so as you obey God and prophesy, your answer will also be quick! For with God all things are possible. He knows how to raise stones to do His work! He knows how to raise stones to praise and worship Him. He knows how to restore the army of God, but it takes us to open up our mouth and prophesy over our lives. It's God's time now! You shall all be restored. His hand is not short so that He will not deliver! His ears are not deaf so that He will not hear you!

Prophesy in the name of Jesus. God said, "I will open your graves! You shall be restored, even those of you who are unburied but dead, as well as those who are buried." Even though it seems like the power of darkness, the spirit of Babylon, or captivity has you bound, you shall be restored. You shall all break loose in the name of Jesus. The whole army in the valley of death and dry bones stood up when the Word was spoken over them.

You shall stand up in the name of Jesus. And having done all to stand, stand up as the living army of the living God. God is going to bring His people up from the depth of the earth (Psalm 71:20). You shall be brought into your own land! You shall live and not die! You shall fulfill your destiny. God said to His people, "I will bring you into your land, Israel, and place you there, and I will put My Spirit in you and you shall live." Let Him breathe on you! Let Him breathe on you! Let the breath of God now breathe on you. Breathe into us, Lord, and let us rise up as a living, breathing army suitable for the work of God, ready and prepared to do Your bidding!

When His life is invested in us, we will not be dead, dry and scattered, but we will be in unison. The Word of Christ that indwells the believer has the power to affect spirit, soul and body. He will use His finger to write His Word on the fleshly part of our hearts. When the Holy Spirit descended on the people of God, the Word of the Lord says there was a noise, an earthquake! There was commotion! There was a shaking, and the people felt the effect. They believed

God and did great and wondrous things for Him. When there is a shaking, the prison bars will be opened!

When there is a shaking, the breath of God will cause your chains, your shackles, to be loosed. Whatsoever thing that is loosed on earth is loosed in heaven. Whenever there is a shaking, those who are bound by the Enemy will be released by angels. Whenever there is a shaking and a noise and you have taken heed to the Word of God and do what is commanded, march around the fortified walls of your Jericho, for it shall come down in the name of Jesus.

When you prophesy to the dead, the dry and cracked earthen vessel will respond to the fire of the Word. It will tolerate the refiner's fire until it comes forth as pure gold. God sits as a refiner and purifier of silver. Does He sit there the whole time the silver is being refined? No! God does not sit there only holding the silver, but His eyes are on the silver the entire time it is in the fire. So His eyes are on you in the valley until your hand bone connects to the elbow bone and the elbow bone connects to the shoulder bone and the shoulder bone connects to the head bone, until all the bones of the body are connected! Yes, dead and dry bones, hear the Word of the Lord!

Everything in you shall obey the Word of God until you stand up, head bones above your shoulder bones, until you are resurrected, restored, awakened, quickened, stirred, pierced, resuscitated, revived and ready to do His work and will on earth as it is in heaven. We need a revival in our souls! It is time to praise the King of Glory, the King eternal, immortal, invincible, the only wise God! Praise should be the firstfruits of our lips, giving thanks unto His name. Praise is what we ought to do; let's lift up our praise to Him.

What is the highest praise? It is the double-edged sword in your mouth to utter, to prophesy, until you are loosed and set free . . . until you are consumed and caught on fire . . . until you are permeated with the Spirit and are wet and moist, wet and supple, pliable to the hand of the Almighty God, the all-sufficient God of yesterday, today and forever. Begin to prophesy and be in prayer, and watch God perform His Word over your life. That which He has spoken regarding your life shall surely come to pass!

Prayer: Father, we need the fire in our bones until it is impossible to be dry and dead in our Christian life. Even though some of us are in the valley because of diverse reasons, send Your Word to revive and quicken us again so that we may rise up as a living, breathing army dressed to do the works of ministry. Amen.

> The resurrection of the church of the living God, or any part of it, from an afflicted condition is tied to the hearkening of the Word of God. The Word of the Lord is sharp, alive and active. It has power to cut asunder soul and spirit, and it discerns the intent of the heart. This Word can cut into dead bodies and dry bones and there will be life!

CHAPTER 25

DEMONS ARE REAL

The Word of the Lord tells us that the heart of man is deceitfully wicked, and who can understand it? (See Jeremiah 17:9). Man is always in pursuit of secret knowledge of the demonic realm. People have turned to sorcery and divination rather than succumbing to the Omnipotent Father who is of absolute knowledge, wisdom and understanding. The Bible speaks about these demonic forces and how evil spirits fight against us. We need to submit to the Higher power and resist the devil and he will flee from us.

Demons are real and are very much rampant in the affairs of men, but the comforting word for the born-again Christian is this: "Greater is he that is in you, than he that is in the world" (1 John 4:4 KJV). As we fix our eyes on God, this greater power inside us will give us authority over demonic forces. Ephesians 6:12 states, "For our struggle is not against flesh and blood, but against the rulers, against the authorities, against the powers of this dark world and against the spiritual forces of evil in the heavenly realms." The word *wrestle* means "to throw or to swing." It is a contest between two opponents that continues until one becomes the victor.

We are not engaged in a human physical war, therefore we should not be found fighting our sisters and brothers. The word *wrestle* presents the idea of a personal, face-to-face and hand-to-hand conflict to the finish. It is a life-or-death struggle. Here, Paul is not describing a merrymaking event. He is referring to the kingdom of darkness, the spirit world that is well organized. We are contending with principalities, a high-ranking hierarchy of demonic authority, but we must also be confident of who we are in Christ Jesus. We should also remember that we are the righteousness of God in Christ Jesus, and as His saints we are complete in Him, who is the Head of all principality and power.

Power means having control over the authorities or rulers of the world who revolt against God. These authorities or world rulers are limited to the darkness here on earth. But spiritual wickedness is the army of invisible evil spirits in high places or heavenly realms. The sphere of this conflict is in the heavens, where Christ dwells with His Father, our Lord and God.

The Church should not be ignorant of spiritual warfare, but we must have the awareness that the Church has spiritual authority in the unseen or heavenly realms. It is lethal when there is a force or entity that is at work against us and we are ignorant of the fact. The Word of the Lord says in Hosea 4:6, "My people are destroyed from lack of knowledge."

The Bible explicitly states that demons or evil spirits exist. From the beginning of time they have existed, and they still exist. Demons or evil spirits are indestructible. The existence of evil spirits or devils pervades the Bible from the Old Testament to the New Testament. The word *demon* itself is not found in the Bible. What is found in the Bible are references to evil spirits or devils. *Demon* comes from the Latin word *daemon*, meaning "evil spirit," and the Greek word is *daimon*, meaning "a divinity." Demons are disembodied spirits which cannot be seen with the naked eye or with the aid of a microscope. They must be spiritually discerned.

There are many people who do not believe that evil spirits exist, and it is sad that many are destroyed, deceived and bound by them. Satan's ploy has been his successful deluding of humankind that he and his cohorts do not exist. There are three sources of power common to human understanding: the divine power that proceeds from the omnipotence of God; the satanic power that comes from the devil, the fallen archangel; and the human power, or the power of man, which is a force that can be directed by either the heavenly or the demonic power.

Demons or devils were rampant during Jesus' earthly ministry. They are knowledgeable! They knew that their time was at hand, therefore they were uneasy wherever Jesus went. Evil spirits proclaimed who Jesus was, and He cast out and silenced many. Although evil spirits are knowledgeable, they are not omniscient. Matthew 8:29 states, "'What do you want with us, Son of God?' they shouted. 'Have you come here to torture us before the appointed time?'" Luke 4:33-37 tells us thus:

> In the synagogue there was a man possessed by a demon, an evil spirit. He cried out at the top of his voice, "Ha! What do you want with us, Jesus of Nazareth? Have you come to destroy us? I know who you are—the Holy One of God!" "Be quiet!" Jesus said sternly. "Come out of him!" Then the demon threw the man down before them all and came out without injuring him. All the people were amazed and said to each other, "What is this teaching? With authority and power he gives orders to evil spirits and they come out!" And the news about him spread throughout the surrounding area.

The girl with the spirit of divination knew who Paul and Silas were. Acts 19:13-16 states that the evil spirits declared that Jesus they knew and Paul they knew, but they questioned the sons of Sceva, asking who they were. Evil spirits are powerful but not all-powerful (Acts 19:16; Mark 5:1-18). Evil spirits or demons cause vexation, suicide and lunacy.

Evil spirits can oppress, be jealous, tell fortunes, and imitate the departed or the dead. The Word of the Lord says, "But the Spirit of the Lord departed from Saul, and an evil spirit from the Lord troubled him" (1 Samuel 16:14-15 KJV). Evil spirits or demons cause error, deception, lying, witchcraft, heresies and false prophecies; they wage war on saints, influence men, deceive even a believer to be in league with them, and inflict physical maladies on those they possess. In 1 Timothy 4:1-2 the Word tells us, "The Spirit clearly says that in later times some will abandon the faith and follow deceiving spirits and things taught by demons. Such teachings come through hypocritical liars, whose consciences have been seared as with a hot iron." First

John 4:1-3 says, "Beloved, believe not every spirit, but try the spirits whether they are of God: because many false prophets are gone out into the world. Hereby know you the Spirit of God: every spirit that confesses that Jesus Christ is come in the flesh is of God: and every spirit that confesses not that Jesus Christ is come in the flesh is not of God: and this is that spirit of antichrist" (KJV). It is time for the Church of today to rise up and take authority over demons in the name of Jesus. It is time for the Church to take authority and put to death ignorance, doubt, fear and all the things that so easily beset us, and the devil and his cohorts will flee. In Psalm 60:12 the Word of the Lord says, "With God we will gain the victory, and he will trample down our enemies."

The gates of hell shall not prevail against the church of the living God. This Church is built upon the revelation Peter received, that Jesus is the Christ, the Son of the living God. This same Jesus, by His Spirit, is abiding in you and me, therefore we can say to the Enemy with confidence, "The blood of Jesus and the fire of God is against you!" As we submit to God and resist the devil, he will have to flee. The Church must come to the realization that Satan's coven is growing rapidly, and it is doing so with power and unity. Although it seems as if the devil is prevailing against the church of the living God, this is a lie from the pit of hell.

The Church is no doubt divided to the core, but God is in the midst of her, and she shall not be moved. We need cooperation and unity in the body of Christ, knowing that every kingdom divided against itself will be ruined and every city or house divided against itself will not stand. The Word of the Lord tells us that the Church must be in unity till we all come in the unity of the faith. The Word of the Lord says, "Oh that God's people will dwell together in unity" (see Psalm 133:1). If the Church will not come together, then we need to take a good look at Satan and his ministering angels.

I have discovered through research that Satan and his workers have to be strong to survive in the coven. Weaklings do not survive in Satan's coven. There is order in their service. Here is an illustration of unity and order in their gathering: Thirteen witches gathered together in a circle to worship their master. They dressed identically in long white robes with attached cowl-like hoods over their heads.

They each sat cross-legged on the highly polished wooden floor, backs straight, arms folded across their breasts. Staring with absolute concentration into the candles in front of them, these witches did not wear jewelry or ornament of any sort. There was no movement by any of them except for their continuous low-voiced chanting or humming as they offered their prayer to Satan.

In her book *He Came to Set the Captives Free* (a story about Elaine, a powerful witch delivered), Dr. Rebecca Brown states that she was told that if she wanted anything, all she needed to do was to light a candle and put every prayer request underneath it. She was made to believe that she could pray for another person's success or downfall through such practices. Some have even prayed for fame and for power to destroy the Church. You see, one of the devil's ploys is to destroy the prayer base of every church. Jesus said, "My house is a house of prayer," but Satan does not delight in seeing God's people praying.

Prayer releases the explosive power of the Holy Ghost in the affairs of God's people. All the recorded revivals in the Old and New Testaments were dependent upon prayer. It seems to me that the witches' prayers were answered because the church of the living God is fragmented and every kind of foul spirit is rampant in the body of Christ.

Satan's church is in unison, order and understanding! We need unity, order and understanding in the body of Christ! We must not be ignorant of who we are and whom we are up against. God is not the author of confusion! God is not at fault! The Church is at fault! We have fallen short of the glory of God, and we have given the Enemy a foothold in our lives. We have opened different doors for him to walk in and take up residence in our lives, thus wreaking havoc in our affairs.

The Church needs the cord of love to bind everyone together. The Church must rise up and be the Church so the glory of God the Father, the Son, and the Holy Ghost will be imminent in the Body. When God's glory overshadows the Church, the Prince of darkness and his cohorts, witches and wizards will not be able to resist the awesome presence of the Almighty God. You must come to the realization that wizards and witches chant or utter evil incantations against the body of Christ. Their utterances seem very effective, and therefore the prayer base in most spiritless churches is destroyed. Flesh and blood are fighting against flesh and blood; pastors against congregations and congregations against pastors.

There is gossiping, malice, lies, fraction, witchcraft, sexual immorality, physical maladies, grave misfortune, financial problems, accidents, lethargy and great distraction. It seems as if the devil is winning, and we often hear most believers quoting this scripture: "The gates of hell shall not prevail against the church of the living God" (see Matthew 16:18), but to no avail. Let us not fool ourselves; the gates of hell will prevail if we are found sleeping.

Arise, all you church-sleepers, in the name of Jesus Christ of Nazareth, for those who are of the day cannot sleep. There is a spirit of Zombie or lethargy that has overshadowed many individuals! You just cannot sleep, but you must rise up and take authority in the name of Jesus. Know when you are tired and sleep, but when you are not, rise and loose yourself and bind these entities in the name of Jesus.

The Church must be found praying without ceasing. Pastors, lay ministers and the congregation must be found praying. It is the Church's chief business to supplicate, pray, intercede and give thanks, for this is the will of God in Christ Jesus. It is time to pray fervently and persistently until the glory of God radiates in our midst. The Enemy must be resisted, and he must back off and flee in the name of Jesus. God will give His angels charge over us, lest we dash our foot against a stone. Psalm 91:13 says, "You will tread upon the lion and the cobra; you will trample the great lion and the serpent." It is a perilous time we are living in; let us come together in unity and prayer. Be alert and vigilant, for the Adversary is like a roaring lion seeking whom he may devour.

John 10:10 says the devil comes to steal, kill and destroy, but Jesus was manifested to destroy the work of the devil. Prayer and fasting are two weapons to destroy, tear down, and smash to pieces the stronghold of the devil. The Bible says that some of these things do not come except through prayer and fasting. Fasting will break the bands of wickedness, undo the heavy burden, and break the fetters. There is also power and authority in the name of Jesus to resist the devil. Besides the name of Jesus there is no other name by which man can be saved. The Church is complete in Jesus Christ and has been made the head of all principalities and powers of darkness. Evil spirits, principalities, rulers of darkness and spiritual wickedness in high places must bow and be rendered ineffective in the presence of the Omnipotent God.

Philippians 2:10-11 declares that every knee shall bow and every tongue shall confess that Jesus Christ is Lord. According to the Scriptures, Jesus was raised from the dead and He is Lord. We are possessed with power and authority over scorpions and serpents and all the powers of Satan. We are to dress in our spiritual armor from the crown of our head to the soles of our feet, as pictured or described in Ephesians 6.

We need the spirit of discernment in the body of Christ. The word *discern* means "to distinguish clearly, to behold as separate." Discerning of spirits is the ability the Holy Spirit gives to some Christians to discern between those who speak by the Spirit of God and those who are moved by false spirits. The discerning of spirits shows which of the gifts of the Holy Spirit are operating in a service. Some Christians, through discernment, are able to distinguish how God is working and how the evil spirits are working. It is imperative, however, that we allow the gift to operate so that the body of Christ can gain power and authority over demonic spirits. The phrase "discerning of spirits" occurs in 1 Corinthians 12:10: "To another [is given] the working of miracles; to another prophecy; to another discerning of spirits" (KJV).

We can rest assured that we are victors in Christ Jesus because of what Jesus wrought on the cross. We are the righteousness of God in Christ Jesus. Jesus' blood is incorruptible blood, and it was poured out on the altar for our sins. Leviticus 17:11 says, "The life of the flesh is in the blood" (KJV). The holy saving blood of Jesus is an expression of our faith in prayer when we plead the blood of Jesus. Pleading the blood of Jesus over attacks or diverse situations is not really scriptural, but it is accepted in Zion as an expression of faith in Jesus Christ. We are pleading with Jesus to assist us or interfere in all of our situations in His power, glory and authority.

If the blood of a one-year-old lamb prevented the Death Angel from destroying the firstborn of the children of Israel, what about the saving blood of Jesus Christ of Nazareth? There is protection in the blood of Jesus! Let us apply the blood by faith to our hearts. We must not be troubled; we must lay hold of the Word of God as Jesus did and defeat the devil. Jesus said, "It is written." Let us lift up our feeble hands in the name of Jesus and take up the sword of the Holy Spirit against the devil and his cohorts in the name of Jesus Christ. The Word is alive and active! It is sharp and will cut down, destroy, root up and pull down every stronghold of the devil.

For the Church to triumph over the devil and his cohorts, we must believe and know that our blessed Savior, Jesus, defeated the devil on the cross two thousand years ago. Through Him, our lives are hidden in Him and His Word abides in us. If His Word is not dwelling in us richly with the Holy Ghost's abiding presence, we will not be able to contend and bind the devil and his cohorts. Jesus, our great example, cast out many evil spirits with His finger or word. So with all of our getting, desire possession of the unadulterated Word of God which saves us. How can the Church defeat the Evil One? We must be found fasting and praying! For Jesus himself said to the disciples, "This kind of demon will come out only through prayer and fasting" (see Mark 9:29). Fasting, prayer and the Word are weapons to pull down, break and destroy the strongholds, thus sending the Evil One and his cohorts on a running spree. He must flee in the name of Jesus. Knowing who we are in Jesus Christ give us confidence and boldness in the spiritual armor we are supposed to dress in. Every soldier of Jesus Christ must be found wearing this armor.

Here it is, my brothers and sisters:

> Finally, be strong in the Lord and in his mighty power. Put on the full armor of God so that you can take your stand against the devil's schemes. For our struggle is not against flesh and blood, but against the rulers, against the authorities, against the powers of this dark world and against the spiritual forces of evil in the heavenly realms. Therefore put on the full armor of God, so that when the day of evil comes, you may be able to stand your ground, and after you have done everything, to stand. Stand firm then, with

the belt of truth buckled around your waist, with the breastplate of righteousness in place, and with your feet fitted with the readiness that comes from the gospel of peace. In addition to all this, take up the shield of faith, with which you can extinguish all the flaming arrows of the evil one. Take the helmet of salvation and the sword of the Spirit, which is the word of God. And pray in the Spirit on all occasions with all kinds of prayers and requests. With this in mind, be alert and always keep on praying for all the saints (Ephesians 6:10-18).

Second Corinthians 10:4-5 says, "The weapons we fight with are not the weapons of the world. On the contrary, they have divine power to demolish strongholds. We demolish arguments and every pretension that sets itself up against the knowledge of God, and we take captive every thought to make it obedient to Christ." God's Word is infallible and eternal! His Word stands firm in the heavens! May God's people have a relish for His Word.

Let it not depart from our mouths! Let it dwell in the midst of our hearts, for it is life unto those who find it, and health unto our flesh. Let the Word of Christ dwell richly in you in all wisdom, so that in the time of trouble the Holy Spirit will use the Word to raise a standard against the devil, the Enemy, when he comes in as a flood. Confess this loudly: There is victory in the name of Jesus! You are empowered and blessed by this confession.

Prayer: God, thank You that we are aware that there are evil spirits fighting against Your people, but thank You also that You have made provision for us. You sent Jesus to destroy the works of the devil so that we may be victorious in our Christian walk. We are blessed to have the words to say with great confidence, "It is written." Amen.

> The Church should not be ignorant of spiritual warfare, but we must have this awareness that the Church has spiritual authority in the unseen or heavenly realms. It is lethal when there is a force or entity that is at work against us and we are ignorant of the fact. The Word of the Lord says in Hosea 4:6, "My people are destroyed from lack of knowledge."

CHAPTER 26

IT IS FINISHED

According to the Scriptures, when Jesus had received the vinegar He said, "It is finished," and He bowed His head and gave up the ghost (John 19:30). Jesus left the splendor of heaven knowing His destiny. He knew that He had to lay down His life for His friends, and nothing could hinder Him from death on the cross. His eyes were on sinful humanity despite the many distractions and oppositions by His disciples and the Pharisees. The disciples did not believe that Jesus came to die for the world, and the Pharisees wanted to kill Him before His appointed time. Now that He has given His life to redeem us, we must look to Him by faith for life and prosperity. Jesus offered the perfect sacrifice for humanity. When He suffered for us, there was neither form nor comeliness about Him; there was no beauty about Him that we should desire Him. He opened His mouth and declared, "It is finished."

I have read this verse of Scripture over and over again. I have turned it over in my mind and turned to God in prayer. "It is finished" are three very important words that every individual needs to meditate on. For one to truthfully say "It is finished" means the life or mission or race that he or she began at one point in time has been accomplished. When you have started a race, you are expected to finish it, so that you can also say with joy and confidence that it is finished when you have done your good works and accomplished the race or mission you began. This is a perfect example of what Jesus displayed on the cross before He gave up the ghost and died.

Now that the profession of Christ on the cross has made us a royal priesthood, it's expected that we accomplish the journey to our destiny so that we might say as Christ did, "It is finished." It's quite interesting that for several years many prophets prophesied about the coming Jesus. Even Moses the great prophet testified about Him. The devil wanted to kill this prophet, but God's hand was on him. He was Israel's deliverer; he freed them from bondage in Egypt. He also stood as a marked example of Jesus, who would deliver God's people from their sins. Moses did signs and wonders. He spoke to God face to face in a profoundly direct and personal way. God spoke to him on Mount Horeb in smoke, fire, lightning and thunder.

Mount Horeb quaked and shook by the awesome presence of the Almighty God. The people who gathered at the foot of Mount Horeb were terrified at the fiery presence of Jehovah so they cried out to Moses, saying, "Do not let God speak to us again." They said, "Speak to Him on our behalf and we will listen." Now when the time came for Moses to go between or mediate between God and His people, the Lord promised that He would raise up a Prophet like Moses among them, and He would put His words in His mouth and they were supposed to listen to Him.

God was not slack concerning the promised Prophet of the seed of the woman. The Word of the Lord declares in Galatians 4:4 that when "the fullness of the time was come, God sent forth his Son, made of a woman, made under the law [Jesus, the Son of Man]" (KJV). Why did Jesus have to become like us? He became human, not just to die for our sins, but also to be our High Priest to fully communicate God's salvation to us and identify with our needs.

Jesus' ministry was a threefold one: prophet, priest and king. The news about the kingship ministry of the Son of Man got to the ears of the reigning king, Herod. He became jealous, full of rage, and intimidated by this new King. Therefore the devil, that old Dragon, the destroyer, the accuser, influenced Herod to beguile the wise men to search for King Jesus in order that he might kill Him. But God, the Omniscient One who knows the secrets and intents of one's heart, saw Herod's subtlety and craftiness and forewarned Jesus' earthly father, Joseph, in a vision to flee to Egypt until it was safe to return with his family to Israel.

Thus, Satan couldn't destroy Jesus, the One who created him. The time had not yet arrived for the Son of Man to die and to redeem mankind from sin, even though that was the purpose for Jesus' becoming flesh. Satan's desire, however, was not only to destroy Christ, but believers in Christ as well because they are a people of destiny. In fact, Satan's desire is to steal, kill and destroy us before we make it to the finish line and declare, "It is finished." The Word of the Lord declares in John 10:10 that Satan comes to steal, kill and destroy; nevertheless, he cannot touch you if God does not give him the permission.

This is what God's Word says, "It is appointed unto men once to die, but after this the judgment (Hebrews 9:27 KJV), but you shall not die now. You shall live to declare the works of the Lord, and you shall declare, "It is finished." Jesus was the perfect Lamb who journeyed, suffered and struggled to the finish line to declare, "It is finished." Jesus' life was one of ridicule, rejection, shame, scorn and name-calling. His journey was one of great humiliation to exaltation. Jesus' brothers, His own flesh and blood, did not believe in Him. They taunted Him, saying, "Why are You doing all these things in secret? Go out and show Yourself to the public," but He did not consider their taunting, for His time had not yet come (see John 7:3-9). Eventually when the time came for Jesus to be revealed, the Word of the Lord tells us in Luke 4:16-22 that He went into the synagogue and there He saw the book of the prophet Isaiah. He opened it to a familiar passage and He read about Himself:

> "The Spirit of the Lord is on me, because he has anointed me to preach good news to the poor. He has sent me to proclaim freedom for the prisoners and recovery of sight for the blind, to release the oppressed, to proclaim the year of the Lord's favor." Then he rolled up the scroll, gave it back to the attendant and sat down. The eyes of everyone in the synagogue were fastened on him, and he began by saying to them, "Today this scripture is fulfilled in your hearing." All spoke well of him and were amazed at the gracious words that came from his lips.

I would like you to bear in mind that Jesus is the embodiment of the Word of God. More so, the truth in God's Word was in His mouth, which, when uttered, gripped and pricked the hearts of sinful men. Many who heard cried out, saying, "What must we do to be saved?" Those who repented were freed from their sins. Also, many were healed of various sicknesses and diseases.

The Word was alive, sharp, active, penetrating, cutting into their devious hearts, exposing their evil deeds. Many of His opponents were jealous and angry with Him and they desired to kill Him instantly, but His time had not yet come. They questioned Jesus' genealogy: "Is this not Joseph's son? Where has He gained such knowledge and authority?" (See Luke 22). From that moment they looked for an opportunity to kill Him. When the appointed time had come for Him to lay down His life for His friends, the life in His blood was pulsating to be released for sinful mankind. Hence, the devil entered the heart of Judas, who decided to betray Jesus. He therefore went hastily to the temple officials, chief priests, and elders and told them his plan.

He then led a detachment of soldiers to seize Jesus. They led Him to Caiaphas, the high priest and then to Pilate. Pilate had Jesus on trial and found Him to be innocent of the charge laid against Him. He tried to release Jesus and execute the notorious robber named Barabbas. So Pilate ordered Jesus to be scourged. Scourging was gruesome and brutal punishment. It was designed to reach below the surface of the skin when blows were inflicted. This kind of whipping resulted in fainting and death.

Can you imagine the pain? Have you ever had a very bad toothache, bellyache or headache when you desperately searched for a painkiller but there was none? You needed the pain to go away, so you went to see the doctor for him to prescribe something for you. Have you ever been there? Jesus did not have any painkiller; the lacerations were deep-rooted. Severe and excruciating was His pain. His back was turned to the tormentors and they scourged Him without compassion, but the Word of the Lord says in Hebrews 12:2, "Let us fix our eyes on Jesus, the author and perfecter of our faith, who for the joy set before him endured the cross, scorning its shame, and sat down at the right hand of the throne of God." So at such a time as this, we are on the road to our destiny and you need not be despondent because of struggles. Let this truth, and nothing but this truth, remain in your mouth, so help me God, for we have not yet come to the point of shedding our blood in our struggles, but this man Jesus did.

I believe His veins, arteries and capillaries were ruptured and blood gushed from His bared back. I believe He was weary and fainting because of a severe loss of blood, but Jesus struggled to the finish line to declare openly that it is finished. Soldiers shoved Him, spat on Him, and slapped Him in the face. They made Him carry His cross, which was the evidence or symbol of a curse, for the Word of God declares that cursed is anyone who hangs on a tree or cross (Galatians 3:13). Jesus became a curse for us that we might become the sons of God, the righteousness of God in Christ Jesus.

Furthermore, they mocked the King of Glory. They plaited a crown of thorns and put it on His head. The prickly thorns penetrated His skin and caused His blood to seep down the sin-stained road of humanity. Christ reached out to ransom and redeem us. We are redeemed! We are bought with a price. Jesus has changed our whole life. Go tell it on the mountain and everywhere that you are redeemed by the blood of the Lamb. I am also impressed by the words of the apostle Peter as a reminder and an answer to us: "For you know that it was not with perishable things such as silver or gold that you were redeemed from the empty way of life handed down to you from your forefathers, but with the precious blood of Christ, a lamb without blemish or defect" (1 Peter 1:18-19).

Moreover, Jesus was led as a Lamb to the slaughter. Try to picture the sacrificial system in the Old Testament. The animals could be heard crying for their dear lives, but His blood was needed for the atonement of mans' sins. These animals had to die; Jesus had to die. His blood had to be shed. For the Word of the Lord says that without the shedding of blood there is no forgiveness of sins (Hebrews 9:22). Jesus struggled to the place called Golgotha, and the soldiers nailed His hands and feet to the cross. Breathing was difficult, but later Jesus opened His mouth and said, "It is finished," even at the time when His Father had turned His back to Him. God turned His back on Jesus so that we can turn away from our wicked ways to Jesus, the Author and Perfecter of our faith.

It is finished; the salvation plan of man's redemption is completed. It is finished; Jesus, who is greater than His servant Moses, has finished it for us. He is the Son over God's house, and we are His house if we hold fast to the confidence and rejoice in the hope we have in Him to the end. It is finished; Jesus the High Priest has given His life for us once and for all. Because He suffered and was tempted, He can help us in our sufferings and temptations. Be reminded that the blood-bought Church of God does not have a High Priest which cannot be touched with the feeling of our infirmities. He was in all points tempted as we are, yet without sin.

It is finished; Jesus is still superior to all the angels, for the name He inherited is superior to theirs. It is finished; the new covenant is better. It is finished; Jesus' body was broken for our healing. Jesus bore in His body our sins when He was nailed to the tree, so that you, being dead to sin, would live in righteousness. By His stripes we are healed. It is finished; the battle is over. It is finished; the war is over. It is finished; He is the Prince of Peace.

It is finished, and Jesus is Lord! He has risen from the dead and He is majestic and exalted. Every knee shall bow before the King of Glory and give Him the highest praise. Just thinking and writing about this makes me feel like I am wearing the garment of praise. I feel like shouting, "Praise to His matchless name!" One day soon you and I will join the heavenly choir, and what a time of praise and worship that will be! Are you in great anticipation? Turn your eyes upon Him and be steadfast and unmovable.

Prayer: Lord of Lords, because of the sacrifice of the perfect Lamb of God, we have access to the throne of grace. Lord, when we are weary and pressed out of measure to the point of great despair, You bid us to boldly come to You. You promise us that You will be with us to the end of the journey. Amen.

> Can you imagine the pain? Have you ever had a very bad toothache, bellyache or headache when you desperately searched for a painkiller but there was none? You needed the pain to go away, so you went to see the doctor for him to prescribe something for you. Have you ever been there? Jesus did not have any painkiller; the lacerations were deep-rooted. Severe and excruciating was His pain. His back was turned to the tormentors and they scourged Him without compassion.

CHAPTER 27

YOUNG MEN, I CALL UPON YOU FOR YOU ARE STRONG

From the beginning of time God's calling has been evident in the lives of many youthful characters in the Bible. Some were despised in the eyes of men, but God chose them to perform a certain task. These Bible characters, when they understood the plan of God in their lives, were used in extraordinary ways. May the youth of our generation emulate the life demonstrated by the youth of biblical times. John said, "I write to you, young men, because you are strong, and the word of God lives in you, and you have overcome the evil one" (1 John 2:14). Be therefore encouraged, youth, to do exploits for God.

In these last days the devil's cunning and attractive devices have successfully deprived and ravaged the youth of their gifting, blessings and mapped-out destinies. Many are trapped in a world of turmoil by gun violence, prostitution, and addiction of all sorts, but it is only a righteous turn to God that will perform the transformation of young people. The call of God was on some of you even before you were born, and that is a fact. Some of the Bible characters were called even in their mother's womb. Can you believe that?

The Bible makes it quite vivid that God called Jeremiah before he was formed in his mother's womb. Jeremiah 1:5 says, "Before I formed you in the womb I knew you, before you were born I set you apart; I appointed you as a prophet to the nations." Verse 10 reads, "See, I have this day set thee over the nations and over the kingdoms, to root out, and to pull down, and to destroy, and to throw down, to build, and to plant" (KJV). The same testimony could be said of Moses, of whom we discover from the Scriptures that God had a perfect plan for him even before he was a seed in his mother's womb.

Young people, do you not know that God knew what gender you would be before the spermatozoon from your dad united with the ovum from your mom? The God whom you and I serve is one of insight and foresight. He has led me to put a few thoughts in this chapter for you. Besides, this chapter will once again offer you the story of Moses, together with other exemplary youthful characters, to portray how God uses young vessels to accomplish His plans on the earth.

This special boy Moses was born, rescued, educated and trained to deliver God's chosen people from Egyptian bondage. Like Christ, Moses was a deliverer, and his ministry was pointing to the work of Jesus Christ of Nazareth, who was born to deliver us from our "Egypt," our life of sin, a condition which led us into bondage. Moses had many struggles, but because he listened to God he turned out to be an outstanding leader and prophet of God.

Samuel is another youth whom God used mightily. His name means "asked of God." He was also a vessel whom God called when he was but a boy. He ministered in the Temple before the Lord at Shiloh, and he turned out to be a seer and a prophet of God. God has always been interested in the lives of young people.

What about King David, who was chosen by God to be Israel's king when King Saul disobeyed God? He too was called when he was but a young man. He was a man after God's own heart. Even though God called and instructed Samuel to anoint David to be Israel's king, he was not enthroned immediately. He was sent back to tend those stubborn and silly sheep. This was a place of separation for him; let me inform you that the task of tending the flock was not an easy one. But the Omniscient Father of mercy and grace knows how to separate and place us into a place of preparation or training. God was preparing David to be Israel's greatest military leader, warrior, and mighty giant-slayer.

As a shepherd, one is expected to be watchful and skillful, paying attention to predators, ready to defend the sheep. It so happened that one day, according to God's Word, a bear and a lion attacked one of David's sheep, but he rescued the sheep from the paws of these ferocious animals.

Because of his rescue effort, the animals turned on him to tear him to pieces, but David, empowered by the Spirit of God, tore them into pieces with his bare hands. There is absolutely no way that he could kill a lion, the strongest beast of the field, with his bare hands. This was the power of the hand of the Almighty at work. It was the time that God orchestrated so that David could be prepared to assume the promotion divinity intended to place on him when it was time for him to leave the place of separation.

One should have a testimony of things that God has done in his or her life for such a one to have enough faith or confidence to kill the "Goliath" of his or her time. Thus, David killed his Goliath before moving into his destiny. He was destined to be the man after God's own heart, and he certainly was. He was obedient to God and inquired of Him in all matters that needed much concern or attention.

Youth, let no man despise you because you are young, for the time has come for you to fulfill the plan of God in your lives to be an example to all believers in word, in conversation, in charity, in spirit, in faith and in purity. You are called! There is an anointing on your lives! The apostle Paul wrote, "Brothers, think of what you were when you were called. Not many of you were wise by human standards; not many were influential; not many were of noble birth. But God chose the foolish things of the world to shame the wise; God chose the weak things of the world to shame the strong. He chose the lowly things of this world and the despised things—and the things that are not—to nullify the things that are" (1 Corinthians 1:26-28). Nevertheless, you might be asking the question, "Am I anointed?" Yes! You are! The anointing of God is upon your life. First John 2:20 says, "But you have an anointing from the Holy One, and all of you know the truth." Verse 27 says, "As for you, the anointing you received from him remains in you, and you do not need anyone to teach you. But as his anointing teaches you about all things and as that anointing is real, not counterfeit—just as it has taught you, remain in him."

Youth, do not think it strange concerning the things that you are wrestling with. These things could be rejection, dejection, hatred, humiliation, misunderstanding, opposition and other adverse situations. The war is on, and the battle is in the mind and the flesh. It is not strange; do not give up! Do not retreat and die. You have to go forward! You have to persevere! You have to resist the devil! Finally, you have to fight the good fight of faith.

You are under construction! You are on the Potter's wheel and the Potter has His hands on the pottery (the clay), that is you. God is capable of using His hands to cut you and fashion you until He makes you that vessel of honor suitable for the Master's use. You may be in the furnace, but the fire will purify you. I know it is hot, but you will not escape the fire until the dross of sin or the impurities are burnt out of your life. Therefore, to live a life of holiness should be your chief business! Sanctification is important for your life, for the things you used to do or say you cannot do or say anymore. You are a new creation, you are a brand-new man; old things are passed away, and behold, all things are new. Paul wrote to young Timothy to flee youthful lusts, namely a strong desire for the wrong things.

He says, "But follow righteousness, faith, charity, peace, with them that call on the Lord out of a pure heart" (2 Timothy 2:22 KJV). The temptation is real! The distraction is imminent. Also, you have to flee fornication, according to the Word of the Lord in 1 Corinthians 6:18-20: "Flee from sexual immorality. All other sins a man commits are outside his body, but he who sins sexually sins against his own body. Do you not know that your body is a temple of the Holy Spirit, who is in you, whom you have received from God? You are not your own; you were bought at a price. Therefore honor God with your body."

Your body is the temple of the Holy Ghost. Gird up the loins of your mind, be sober, and hope to the end for the grace that is to be brought unto you at the revelation of Jesus Christ. Meanwhile, man is a tripartite being, meaning he is a spirit, soul and body. A scripture to support this fact is found in 1 Thessalonians 5:23: "May God himself, the God of peace, sanctify you through and through. May your whole spirit, soul and body be kept blameless at the coming of our Lord Jesus Christ."

God dwells in the Spirit, but the self dwells in the soul while the senses are found in the body. Also, man is God's temple; the body is like the outer court, occupying an external position with its life visible to all. Here man ought to obey every commandment of God. Inside man's soul, the part which constitutes the inner life of man, are the emotions, volition and mind of man.

Therefore, prepare your minds for action; be self-controlled; set your hope fully on the grace to be given you when Jesus Christ is revealed. You have a race to run. Your journey must lead you to your finish line. The apostle Paul says you ought to run the race to the finish line to receive the prize. Moreover, you have a great work to do!

The mind is the inner man, where the affections are seated. The mind must be girded up with truth. Truth is the Word of Jesus Christ, and we ought to have His mind, according to the Word of the Lord: "Let this mind be in you, which was also in Christ Jesus" (Philippians 2:5 KJV). Disengage yourselves from all those things that could hinder you, and fix your mind upon God; He will keep you in perfect peace, especially those whose minds are stayed on Him. "Do not be anxious about anything, but in everything, by prayer and petition, with thanksgiving, present your requests to God. And the peace of God, which transcends all understanding, will guard your hearts and your minds in Christ Jesus" (4:6-7).

In verse 8 of the same passage, Paul says, "Finally, brethren, whatsoever things are true, whatsoever things are honest, whatsoever things are just, whatsoever things are pure, whatsoever things are lovely, whatsoever things are of a good report; if there be any virtue, and if there be any praise, think on these things" (KJV). Youth, you will have to put off the garment of the old man or the old way of life, and therefore clothe yourself with the garment of the new man. Look at what Ephesians 4:22-28 says:

> You were taught, with regard to your former way of life, to put off your old self, which is being corrupted by its deceitful desires; to be made new in the attitude of your minds; and to put on the new self, created to be like God in true righteousness and holiness. Therefore

each of you must put off falsehood and speak truthfully to his neighbor, for we are all members of one body. In your anger do not sin: Do not let the sun go down while you are still angry, and do not give the devil a foothold. He who has been stealing must steal no longer, but must work, doing something useful with his own hands, that he may have something to share with those in need.

Be an example in your word and conversation: "Do not let any unwholesome talk come out of your mouths, but only what is helpful for building others up according to their needs, that it may benefit those who listen. And do not grieve the Holy Spirit of God, with whom you were sealed for the day of redemption. Get rid of all bitterness, rage and anger, brawling and slander, along with every form of malice. Be kind and compassionate to one another, forgiving each other, just as in Christ God forgave you" (vv. 29-32). Your life must be healthy, and this can be so only if it feeds on the pure Word of God.

Prayer: God of all creation, we thank You that You have called the youth because they are strong. Despite their age, they are required to live holy lives and to let their affection be on You. Help them, Lord, that they will indeed be examples for believers in their word, conversation, faith and life. May they take their minds off the things of the world and look to You in Jesus' precious name. Amen.

In these last days the devil's cunning and attractive devices have successfully deprived and ravaged the youth of their gifting, and blessings, and mapped-out destinies. Many are trapped in a world of turmoil by gun violence, prostitution, and addiction of all sorts, but it is only a righteous turn to God that will perform the transformation of young people.

CHAPTER 28

SANCTIFY YOURSELVES AND ERADICATE THE ACCURSED THING

To *sanctify* means "to make holy; to set apart as sacred; to consecrate; to purify." But to *eradicate* means "to pull up by the roots or to destroy." What, then, is the meaning of *accursed* things? It means to be under a curse or, as *Webster's Dictionary* defines it, it is "to utter a wish of evil against; to swear at; to utter blasphemous words; the invocation of evil upon a person." The accursed thing can be anything. It can be a city or physical things or spoils that God does not want you to partake of—that thing He commands you and me not to do. The accursed thing is abominable or detestable to God. We as the believers who are called by His name will have to endeavor and purpose in our hearts to turn away from the detestable things that could contaminate us, and look instead to God.

We read in the Bible that the God of our forefathers Abraham, Isaac and Jacob chose a peculiar group of people. They were known as the Israelites or Hebrews. These special chosen generations were sometimes referred to as the apple of God's eye. God called these special people His "peculiar treasure" (Exodus 19:5 KJV). The anointed herald, or the apostle Paul, of the New Testament age wrote about these special called-out people in Romans 9:3-5. God also spoke to Abraham, the leader He called out from Ur, about His people, saying, "I will make you into a great nation and I will bless you; I will make your name great, and you will be a blessing" (Genesis 12:2).

God was and is always interested in blessing His people, so here is a very important question: How do we come under a curse? God said to Abraham, "I will bless them that bless thee, and curse him that curseth thee: and in thee shall all families of the earth be blessed" (v. 3 KJV). God's promised blessings for His people were contingent on them hearkening to His Word. We ought to hearken or listen diligently to His voice, to observe and do all of His commandments. The Word of the Lord tells us that if they had not hearkened or listened unto the voice of the Lord their God to observe and to do all His commandments, numerous curses would have come upon them.

Let this be known to you, that Israel was on a journey from their Egypt or their place of bondage to the Promised Land. They were nomads or wanderers. The people of God under the cloud were a group of roughneck rebels. They were disobedient at times, ready to knock out their leader with stones. They were therefore severely chastened when they became stubborn, a punishment which propelled them to look to Jehovah God and cry out to Him. When they did, they were delivered. This was their way of life: rebellion, punishment and deliverance. We are familiar with the account of their bondage in the land of Egypt. In the Book of Exodus, the word of the Lord tells us that they were oppressed by their taskmasters, so they cried unto the Lord. God heard their groaning and remembered His covenant with Abraham, Isaac and Jacob. Exodus 2:25 says, "God looked upon the children of Israel, and God had respect unto them" (KJV). God had chosen a vessel of honor to lead His people out of the land of Egypt.

Their journey from bondage was a difficult one. It was a hard journey for them and a mighty long way to go. It is not easy for us who have answered the Master's call. It is a hard road to travel and a mighty long way, but the One who is faithful promised that He will never leave us or forsake us. What a great assurance! God's people had adverse and diverse situations, but Jehovah God was faithful to them. Hostile nations fought against them, but God fought for them. God is the King of Glory, strong and mighty in battle.

When there was no food, He sent them manna from heaven and quails for flesh to eat. God will forever be faithful. He provided for His people, and it is no secret what He can do for His chosen people. He was their Jehovah-Jireh, their Provider. He has not changed; He is still providing and He will continue to do so. When God's people did not have any water, He instructed Moses to strike the rock. The water was once upon a time bitter and the people murmured against Moses. He cried unto the Lord, and the Lord showed him a tree, which, when he cast it into the waters, made the waters sweet. God has a solution for every situation.

But the people under the cloud were ungrateful. They experienced God's providential care, but in every mountainous situation they never praised or worshipped and thanked God. They murmured about their hard times. Murmuring is sin. The Word of the Lord tells us to do everything without murmuring and complaining. In the New Testament, the apostle Paul writes that these things were written for our examples. First Corinthians 10:10 says, "And do not grumble, as some of them did—and were killed by the destroying angel." The people of God under the cloud wandered in the wilderness in a circle. It is imperative that the twenty-first-century Church take a keen look at what happened to the Old Testament Church. The Church of today is a replica of the Church of yesteryear.

We are aware that the Church, or Ecclesia, is not a perfect body. We are all members of one body (that is, the body of Christ), and we are people of imperfections. Some are weak and feeble. Some are sick, poor and afflicted, striving and desiring to get well. When God called His people His peculiar treasure, He meant what He said, and He will stand by His word or promise because He cannot be less than what He said He is. He was faithful to Israel, and He will be faithful to us. He kept them through many dangers, toils and snares. When their enemies came against them, He subdued them. The Word of the Lord says in Deuteronomy 28:7 that when the enemies come against us one way, they will flee seven different ways. This is the Lord's doing. The Word of the Lord says in Psalm 60:12, "With God we will gain the victory, and he will trample down our enemies."

When the enemies pursued the Israelites and they faced their Red Sea, God said, "Go forward." God is interested in us going forward, and we can do so in the name of Jesus Christ of Nazareth, but we need to sanctify ourselves and eradicate the accursed thing. This is the only way He is going to move by His Spirit in our midst. Here are some very important questions to ask: What must we do? What must take place, before the fire comes? What must happen for the breakthroughs to take place? Let's take a look at the Word of God since it was written for our learning. According to God's Word in Exodus 17, there was a time when the children of Israel pitched their tent at a place called Rephidim and there was no water, so what did they do?

They murmured against their leader. It was also at Rephidim that the Amalakites fought against the children of Israel, but Joshua defeated them with the edge of the sword. However, we see that they were on the move in chapter 19 when they departed from Rephidim and came to the desert of Sinai in the third month.

They pitched their tents at the foot of the mountain and Moses went up unto God, and God spoke to the chosen leader about His people. God said to Moses, "Tell the people of Israel: 'You yourselves have seen what I did to Egypt, and how I carried you on eagles' wings and brought you to myself. Now, if you obey me fully and keep my covenant then out of all nations you will be my treasured possession. Although the whole earth is mine you will be for me a kingdom of priests and a holy nation'" (vv. 3-6). Peter wrote in the New Testament, "But ye are a chosen generation, a royal priesthood, an holy nation, a peculiar people; that ye should shew forth the praises of him who hath called you out of darkness into his marvelous light" (1 Peter 2:9 KJV).

Moses summoned the elders and rehearsed everything God said in his ears. The people answered in unity, "All that the Lord hath spoken we will do" (Exodus 19:8 KJV), and Moses repeated what they said to God. The Lord spoke to Moses and said to him, "I come unto thee in a thick cloud, that the people may hear when I speak with thee, and believe thee forever" (v. 9 KJV). Moses again repeated these words to the people. The Lord said to Moses, "Go unto the people, and sanctify them today and tomorrow, and let them wash their clothes" (v. 10 KJV). They were told to get ready for the third day, for on the third day the Lord would come down in the sight of all people upon Mount Sinai.

It does not matter what the devil is doing in these last days. We are on the brink of breakthroughs, miracles, healing and favor, and the blessings of the Lord are about to rain on Zion. Before God comes, however, it is imperative that the whole body of Christ is sanctified. It is right for me to expatiate on the word *sanctify* for edification purposes. It means "to set apart as sacred or holy; to consecrate; to purify." We need to be holy to be drawn near to God! If we are not holy, we cannot be drawn close to Him. Without holiness we will not be able to please God. God will not come down in our midst if we do not live a life that is holy and acceptable unto Him. This is our reasonable service.

So one may ask the question, "How is one consecrated?" Being consecrated means being set apart for God's use. It involves oneself and one's clothing, symbolizing the need for purity before God. Moses followed God's instruction; he went down from the mount and sanctified the people and washed their clothes. On the third day, God descended on Mount Sinai in thick cloud with the voice of a trumpet, exceedingly loud, so that all the people in the camp trembled. What I would like you to bear in mind is the fact that when God comes down, every knee shall bow and reverence Him because He is the Most High God. God's presence will cause His people to tremble and fall prostrate before Him saying, "The Lord, He is God, for He is a consuming fire."

When He is in your midst you will know, because He comes with fire, smoke and heat, which you will notice and feel. Heat causes you to respond; it burns you! You cannot stand still under heat or fire. You cannot be calm; you will have to move. You will have to do something. Run, or maybe let it burn you to get the job done in you. To the people under the law, God was in a thick cloud, and they were to sanctify themselves to be prepared for the theophany (the manifestation of God to man). The people under the law were to keep their distance. Boundary was to be set. They were not to go into the mountain or touch the border. Whoever touched the mount would surely be put to death.

Come, I believe it is time for the Church to reason together! We as the body of Christ cannot depend upon ourselves and our own efforts. We need to be reminded that God is a consuming fire, and our ungodliness in His presence will open doors for the Enemy of our soul to smite us. God has not changed; He is the same yesterday, today and forever. Let us not be foolish! The apostle Paul wrote to the Galatians saying, "Who hath bewitched you, that ye should not obey the truth, before whose eyes Jesus Christ hath been evidently set forth, crucified among you?" (3:1 KJV).

Let us not merely go through the motions. God's presence will not be with us. His train will not fill the temple. There will be no signs and wonders, no mighty move of Almighty God, until we consecrate ourselves. Our praise and worship, prayer and fasting, and observation of the Word of the Lord will only be superficial, mechanical and emotional until all on the altar of sacrifice is slain. Is your all on the altar of sacrifice slain? Is the Spirit controlling your all? You cannot be blessed and have peace and sweet rest until you yield in your spirit, body and soul. God is interested for every leader to come up higher in Him so that He may give them instructions for His people. The Word of the Lord says in Jeremiah 33:3, "Come unto me, and I will answer thee, and show thee great and mighty things, which thou knowest not" (KJV).

Sin affects the effectiveness of the whole body of Christ, whether you are guilty or not, whether you are clergy or laity. God is interested to bless us so much more than we can imagine or think, but our blatant sin hinders His work. The people under the law faced the thunders and the lightning of Mount Sinai. Under the law, I would like you to know that people tremble at God's presence. The people begged Moses to speak to God on their behalf.

In the twenty-first century, people do not reverence the Lord as He desires. We have missed the mark. We are again entangled with the yoke of bondage. We have gone back to our vomit (we have gone back to our Egypt). The Body, which is supposed to be the body of Christ, is bound by the spirit of fornication, adultery, witchcraft, malice, envy, jealousy, strife, war, hatred, heresies, falsehood and many other fleshly desires of the old man.

Paul wrote to the Colossian church in 3:5-10: Put to death, therefore, whatever belongs to your earthly nature: sexual immorality, impurity, lust, evil desires and greed, which is idolatry. Because of these, the wrath of God is coming. You used to walk in these ways, in the life you once lived. But now you must rid yourselves of all such things as these: anger, rage, malice, slander, and filthy language from your lips. Do not lie to each other, since you have taken off your old self with its practices and have put on the new self, which is being renewed in knowledge in the image of its Creator.

This same apostle Paul wrote about the desires of the flesh in Ephesians 4:17-32 and in Galatians 5:19-21. In 1 Corinthians 6:18 he wrote, "Flee fornication" (KJV). If you have to run for your life, do so in the name of Jesus Christ of Nazareth. Joseph did because of his allegiance to God! Paul continued: "All other sins a man commits are outside his body, but he who sins sexually sins against his own body. Do you not know that your body is a temple of the Holy Spirit, who is in you, whom you have received from God? You are not your own; you were bought at a price. Therefore honor God with your body" (vv. 18-20).

Our sin has separated us from His presence, and now we are overshadowed by darkness, for sin causes darkness. The mountain flamed and was filled with smoke. The thunder and lightning were evidences that the people needed God's grace and that only through faith in His grace could they live lives that pleased God, to receive the strength and power from Him to live as a people called of God and as a peculiar treasure. We too are His peculiar treasure. We are the church of the living God. We are a called-out group of people. The great herald of the gospel of Jesus Christ put it this way in Romans 8:29-30: "For those God foreknew he also predestined to be conformed to the likeness of his Son, that he might be the firstborn among many brothers. And those he predestined, he also called; those he called, he also justified; those he justified, he also glorified."

In Ephesians 1:4 the apostle Paul wrote, "For he chose us in him before the creation of the world to be holy and blameless in his sight." First Peter 2:9 says, "But you are a chosen people, a royal priesthood, a holy nation, a people belonging to God, that you may declare the praises of him who called you out of darkness into his wonderful light." It seems to me that the church of the living God has fallen asleep; as a matter of fact, some are literally in the sanctuary just warming the pew instead of being sober and alive in the Spirit worshiping the Lord God of Hosts. Hear the Word of the Lord: "Knowing the time, that now it is high time to awake out of sleep: for now is our salvation nearer than when we believed. The night is far spent, the day is at hand: let us therefore cast off the works of darkness, and let us put on the armour of light. Let us walk honestly, as in the day; not in rioting and drunkenness, not in chambering and wantonness, not in strife and envying. But put ye on the Lord Jesus Christ, and make not provision for the flesh, to fulfill the lusts thereof" (Romans 13:11-14 KJV).

If we do not sanctify ourselves and eradicate the accursed thing, we will not be able to stand even before our enemies. We will be defeated! So, dear God, consecrate us for Your service. We must do everything in our power to eradicate or dig out sin. If we do not sanctify ourselves and eradicate the accursed thing, the whole Body is going to be affected. Sin is like cancer! It is infectious and can spread rapidly, destroying the members of the Body. If it takes root, soon and very soon the whole Body is going to shut down. The Bible says that a little sin leavens the whole lump. After Israel's chosen leader died, God raised up Joshua to lead the children of Israel. God gave His people great victory against Jericho through him.

In Joshua 6:17-19, the Word of the Lord says, "The city and all that is in it are to be devoted to the Lord. Only Rahab the prostitute and all who are with her in her house shall be spared, because she hid the spies we sent. But keep away from the devoted things, so that you will not bring about your own destruction by taking any of them. Otherwise you will make the camp of Israel liable to destruction and bring trouble on it. All the silver and gold and the articles of bronze and iron are sacred to the Lord and must go into his treasury." Someone, a member of the church under the cloud, had a covetous eye. He did not fear the curse on Jericho, which is to say, he did not fear God. He saw among the spoils a beautiful Babylonish garment, and two hundred shekels of silver and a wedge of gold weighing fifty shekels. He coveted them and took them, and put them in the earth in the midst of the tent.

Bear this in mind: it was Achan who took the accursed thing. Thus, in Joshua 7:11 God said, "Israel has sinned; they have violated my covenant, which I commanded them to keep. They have taken some of the devoted things; they have stolen, they have lied, they have put them with their own possessions." Joshua was not aware of the root of sin in the camp of Israel. Joshua sent men to spy out Ai, and it appeared that Ai was no threat for the Israelites. This battle to them would be a piece of cake, no perspiration; it was going to be an easy battle. They were confident that they needed only three thousand men to go to war and they would come out as winners.

Oh Lord, have mercy! The root to weaken the people of God was in the camp. The root to cause defeat, shame and destruction was in the camp. So when they thought they were standing and had done all to stand, they had to flee before their enemies, and on top of that, thirty-six of their men were killed. What a shock this was! Trouble was in the camp. The Word of the Lord says that the hearts of the people melted and became as water. Joshua was in shock! The Word of the Lord says that he rent his clothes and fell upon his face before the ark of the Lord until eventide; he and the elders of Israel put ashes upon their heads.

Joshua decided to consult God! He said, "Lord, why did you ever bring this people across the Jordan to deliver us into the hands of the Amorites to destroy us? If only we had been content to stay on the other side of the Jordan! O Lord, what can I say, now that Israel has been routed by its enemies?" (vv. 7-8). Joshua had a great concern; he said, "The Canaanites and the other people of the country will hear about this and they will surround us and wipe out our name from the earth. What then will you do for your own great name?" (v. 9). God answered Joshua and said thus:

Stand up! What are you doing down on your face? Israel has sinned; they have violated my covenant, which I commanded them to keep. They have taken some of the devoted things; they have stolen, they have lied, they have put them with their own possessions. That is why the Israelites cannot stand against their enemies; they turn their backs and run because they have been made liable to destruction. I will not be with you anymore unless you destroy whatever among you is devoted to destruction. Go, consecrate the people. Tell them, "Consecrate yourselves in preparation for tomorrow; for this is what the Lord, the God of Israel, says: that which is devoted is among you, O Israel. You cannot stand against your enemies until you remove it" (vv. 10-13).

So Joshua took the children of Israel tribe by tribe, family by family, household by household, and man by man until Achan, the son of Carmi, the son of Zabdi, the son of Zerah of the tribe of Judah, was taken. In verse 24, Joshua and all Israel with him took Achan, and the silver, the gold, his sons, his daughters, his oxen and asses, his sheep, his tent and all that he had, and they brought them to the Valley of Achor. Verse 25 says, "And Joshua said, why hast thou troubled us? The Lord shall trouble thee this day. And all Israel stoned him with stones, and burned them with fire" (KJV). So the question is asked: Why punish Achan's sons and daughters for his sin? They may have helped conceal the plunder. His attitude would have rubbed off on his family. To cleanse Israel, all that belonged to Achan (including his children) had to be destroyed.

Listen to what the Spirit is saying to the Church: There is a time to seek the face of God regarding the Church's many problems, but there is also a time when radical action has to be taken. The thing that causes us to sin has to be dealt with. The thing that causes us to sin has to be mortified. The thing that causes us to sin has to be eradicated. It has to be taken up by the root. It has to be burnt. It must not be covered up or buried.

Remove Joy Vassal, remove praise and worship leaders and backup singers, choir directors and members, Sunday school superintendents and teachers, evangelism teams, deacon boards and you name it, should sin contaminate their righteousness and holiness. But God forbid! We need God's presence again! We need the fire again! Fire! Fire! Fire! Fire that will burn in your bones! Fire that will burn our soul, may it consume us in Jesus' name. When the soul catches fire, it burns out condemnation. Hallelujah, what a Savior! When the soul catches fire, we will stand. When the soul catches fire, we will accomplish much. When the soul catches fire, we will be blessed.

When the soul catches fire, we will see miracles and healings. When the soul catches fire, the old man will be dead and we will dress ourselves with the garment of the new man to the honor and glory of God the Father, God the Son, and God the Holy Ghost.

Prayer: My God, thank You for being merciful to us. You became our sanctification on the cross when You blurted these three words: "It is finished." Help us to separate ourselves from the things that defile us so that we may live sanctified lives and You will tabernacle with us until our time on earth is ended. Amen.

It does not matter what the devil is doing in these last days. We are on the brink of breakthroughs, miracles, healing and favor, and the blessings of the Lord are about to rain on Zion. Before God comes, however, it is imperative that the whole body of Christ is sanctified. It is necessary for me to expatiate on the word *sanctify* for edification purposes. It means "to set apart as sacred or holy; to consecrate; to purify."

Today is the day of salvation! If you hear His voice, let Him come into your heart. You may be asking, "What must I say to Him at this moment?" Romans 10:9-11 says, "If you confess with your mouth, 'Jesus is Lord,' and believe in your heart that God raised him from the dead, you will be saved. For it is with your heart that you believe and are justified, and it is with your mouth that you confess and are saved. As the Scripture says, 'Anyone who trusts in him will never be put to shame."

Turn around and say this sinner's prayer with all of your being: Heavenly Father, I admit that I am a sinner and that if I do not confess You and believe that in Your name I can be saved, I am on my way to hell. I know there is no other name by which man can be saved, therefore by faith I accept forgiveness, salvation, redemption and sanctification. Today I accept You as my Lord and Savior, and now I rejoice because I have changed my destiny from the broad road to the narrow road. Thank You for grace. Amen.

Joy is available for speaking engagements and can be reached at joyvassal@rogers.com and www.Joyvassalministries.com

Coming soon: Healing is the Children's Bread

ENDORSEMENTS

Once again, the Reverend Joy Vassal has written a masterpiece exposing the fallacy of Christians when they do not fully surrender themselves to God. Her meticulous work approaches modern-day egocentric lifestyles with the parallels to Old and New Testament characters. With a unique comparison of various pagan practices, she shows that even your most impossible situations may simply be God endeavouring to get your attention to Turn Around and See the Lord.

Those who are lacking commitment to God's presence need to turn and have a true reverence and love for the Lord. This book, a prophetic and insightful exposition, is a must-read for all those who are genuine seekers of our Lord.

The Rev. Sarah Jacobs
Senior Pastor
Mezuzah Ministries

This is another inspirational book from a woman of God. Indeed, I would say this book comes as a solution to the questions raised by the author's first book, Demons Are Real. The world needs to turn to God Almighty through the only way, which is Jesus Christ our Lord and Savior. This is a masterpiece, a solution to a confused world, and a powerful statement in a time when even preachers are afraid to speak or declare the Word boldly.

As a writer, I value a good work when I find one, and this book really is a good read that I willingly endorse and recommend to everyone to buy, read and keep for future reference.

The Rev. Don Ifepe
Publisher, Miles Christian Magazine International
Senior Pastor, Believers Full Gospel Vineyard

In light of the fact that the Church today needs a fresh outpouring of the Holy Spirit, Reverend Vassal's book speaks to the heart of the matter. It is our relationship with God that is of utmost importance. Turn Around and See the Lord will help the body of Christ to see the need for repentance, which will point us in the right direction—Jesus Christ, the Author and Finisher of our faith. This masterpiece is for the admonishment and edification of the believer at such a time as this.

Andrew Binda
Administrative Bishop of New York State

The Reverend Joy Vassal has given herself unreservedly to the Lord to be used by Him as an instrument of blessing to the body of Christ. Turn Around and See the Lord is a message from the very heart of God. This book is a must for all those who desire to have a deep spiritual encounter with God.

The Rev. Everton Powell

The Reverend Joy Vassal's first book, Demons Are Real, showed us that demonic forces are always in operation, but God has given us the power to tread upon serpents (Luke 10:19). This book is definitely one of God's many blessings. This phenomenal woman shares her testimony with those who believe that all things work together for good for those who trust in God (Romans 8:28). I endorse this ideal book, Turn Around and See the Lord, with utmost pleasure and recommend it as a must-read for everyone who desires for God's light to marvelously shine upon them in whatever storms of life they hope to overcome.

The Rev. Andrew Akinsuyi
Salvation Church of God Mission, Toronto, Canada

BIBLIOGRAPHY

Brown, Rebecca. He Came to Set the Captives Free. New Kensington: Whitaker House, 1992.

Cerullo, Morris. The New Proof Producers. San Diego: Morris Cerullo World Evangelism, 1998.

Dawson, Joy. Intercession, Thrilling and Fulfilling. Seattle: YWAM Publishing, 1997.

Falwell, Jerry. Liberty Commentary on the New Testament. Lynchburg, VA: Liberty Press, 1978.

Lockyer, Herbert. All the Doctrines of the Bible. Grand Rapids: Zondervan, 1964.

Ness, Alex W. Pattern for Living. Oakland County, MI: Agape Publications, 1979.

Rhea, Homer G. A Journey Through the Old Testament. Cleveland, TN: Church of God school of Ministry, 2001.

Tenney, Merrill C. Zondervan's Pictorial Bible Dictionary. Grand Rapids: Zondervan, 1963.

Whitney, Donald S. Spiritual Disciplines for the Christian Life. Colorado Springs: NavPress, 1991.

Matthew Henry's Commentary on the Whole Bible. Peabody, MA: Hendrickson, 1991.

The Encyclopedia Americana, vol. 2. W.B. Conkey Company, U.S.A. 1918, 1920, 1922, 1924.

Printed in the United States
146715LV00004B/1/P